DIGNITY TO SURVIVE

DIGNITY TO SURVIVE

One Family's Story
of Faith in the Holocaust

Yona Emanuel

מוסד יצחק ברויאר

TARGUM/FELDHEIM

Hebrew edition published under the name *Yesupar LaDor* 1994
English edition first published 1998
Copyright © 1998 by Mosad Yitzchak Breuer
ISBN 1-56871-145-x

Published by:
Targum Press, Inc.
22700 W. Eleven Mile Rd.
Southfield, MI 48034

Distributed by:
Feldheim Publishers
200 Airport Executive Park
Nanuet, NY 10954

Distributed in Israel by:
Targum Press Ltd.
POB 43170
Jerusalem 91430
Printed in Israel

Authors' addresses:
Yonah Emanuel 17 Brand Jerusalem 93878 Israel
Shmuel Emanuel Kibbutz Sha'alavim D.N. Shimshon 99784 Israel

Dedication

This book is dedicated to the memory of

Hechaver Rabbi David van Essen ז״ל
נפטר כ״א שבט תשנ״ב
and
Mrs. Fradge (Femmy) van Essen ז״ל
נפטרה כ״ט טבת תשנ״ז

Who took orphans of the Holocaust
into their home in Veenendaal, Holland
and raised them with warmth and love.
During the last twenty-five years
they lived in Jerusalem.
Their final resting place is on Mount Olives.
תנצב״ה

בירת המוסר

ע"ש ר' חיים מנחם להמן ע"ה
רח' הרב סורוצקין 39 ירושלים
מיסודו של תנועת שוחרי מוסר, ירושלים

Institute for Torah Ethics
IN MEMORY OF R'CHAIM MENACHEM LEHMANN
39 Harav Sorotzkin St., Jerusalem

בס"ד [illegible] ניסן תש[illegible]

לכבוד ידידי הרה"ג ר' [illegible] שליט"א ורעיתו!

הנני מודה לכם מאד עבור שליחת החוברות [illegible] עליהן להביע דעתי.
[illegible] זה ספר מעניין – יש שם קטעים המעוררים דמעות אצל הקורא.
[illegible] החוברת הוא מלאה, על יהדות גרמניה שאיננה עוד, [illegible]
והמרכזי [illegible] ... הרי הנשמה של היהודי [illegible] בעולם [illegible]
[illegible] לקיום מלאות [illegible] כמה יראת שמים תמימה
[illegible] של יהודי גרמניה.

אולי יונן לכם [illegible] ... קוסן [illegible] לאור של שנות [illegible]
[illegible] עם [illegible] – לא [illegible] יוכל לצייר.
[illegible] יהדות [illegible] על [illegible] הלוחמות!

והמרכזי [illegible] [illegible] לא יודעת [illegible]
[illegible] לתת לחוברת [illegible] לפרסם את [illegible]
[illegible] נא [illegible] היא [illegible]!

[illegible]

שלמה וולבה

Translation of Rabbi Shlomo Wolbe's Approbation

13 Nissan 5750

To my dear friend, Reb Yona Emanuel, *shlita,*

Greetings and many blessings.

I am very grateful to you for troubling yourself to bring this manuscript to my home. This memoir is a most moving document — certain sections cause the reader to shed bitter tears. It serves as a monument commemorating German Jewry, that noble tradition which has essentially become extinct. Very little is known about this glorious community of the past, even among the most observant Jews.

The *Yeke* Jew of yesteryear tends to be stereotyped as someone who lived by the doctrine of *"Torah im derech eretz* — Torah together with worldly activity" and who had the title "doctor" appended to his name. However, few people remember his honest and pure fear of Hashem, his tremendous devotion to the fulfillment of *mitzvot,* and his scrupulous observance of *halachah.* Such dedication was found even among the Jews who lived in the rural regions of southern Germany....

In light of our community's widespread ignorance of the true nature of German Jewry, I consider the publishing of this book an extremely important project. It is vital to widely publicize the publication of this memoir so that we — and even more importantly, our offspring — will remember our glorious and noble roots.

With great respects, and a blessing for a *chag kasher v'same'ach.*

Acknowledgments

Thanks for supplying pictures and documents to:

Mr. Theo Goldschmidt, Zurich

Yad Vashem, Jerusalem

Mr. Yissachar (Berry) Asher, Beer Sheva

Mrs. Rachel Leventhal, Haifa

Mr. Eli Goldschmid, Jerusalem

Mrs. Channa Piek, Jerusalem

Kamp Westerbork, Holland

van Witsenstichting, the publisher of *Yizkor*, Rotterdam, by Dr.
David Hausdorff, ז״ל

Mr. Jacob de Wolff, Amsterdam.

Additional thanks to the staff of Targum Press, for their dedicated
work.

Foreword

This work is a unique record of the events experienced by one of the many Jewish families which entered the valley of death in the days of the Holocaust. They are the members of just one of many families that made a supreme effort not only to retain a semblance of human dignity, but also to act in accordance with the will of God while living in subhuman conditions. Risking their lives, they adhered to the Almighty and His Torah. I stress again — they are just one of many families which exhibited such dedication and personal sacrifice for the sake of this goal.

What is unique about the Emanuel family is that they were an embodiment of the doctrine "*Torah im derech eretz* — Torah together with worldly activity." Few accounts of selfless dedication to Torah observance in the face of mortal danger have been published by individuals adhering to this way of life. Perhaps this is due to their relatively small number or to their characteristic humility which would not permit them to call the public's attention to their courageous deeds.

Kiddush Hashem (the sanctification of God's name) — for those of us who were not aware of what this phrase meant to the rank-and-file Jew who was learned but not famous, God-fearing and pure but not renowned as a great *tzaddik*, this book comes to teach us an unforgettable lesson.

Let this work serve as a living testimony to refute the claim that there were few if any acts of *kiddush Hashem* in the Holocaust. This false claim is a gross misrepresentation of history, especially when it is voiced by Jews.

Mordechai Breuer
Yitzchak Breuer Institute

Table of Contents

Preface

This book is a chronicle of my family's experiences before, during and after the Holocaust. It is based upon personal memories and a series of letters written during this dark period of history. My purpose in the publication of this book is to impart to future generations the lessons which may be gleaned from the experiences we endured.

In the year 5696 (1936), my grandfather, Reb Yehoshua Goldschmidt, *zt"l*, who lived in Zurich, Switzerland, initiated a regular correspondence with us in which he would discuss the weekly Torah portion. In the year 5703 (1943) we managed to conceal a sack full of his letters, together with all our *sefarim*, under the floorboards of our house. Our *sefarim* and my grandfather's letters remained hidden there until the end of the war. The excerpts selected from these letters, which appear in this book, serve as faithful testimony to the events which transpired during that horrific era.

My grandparents in Zurich also saved every piece of correspondence that my parents sent to them during this period, including the letters they wrote from the Westerbork transit camp in the Netherlands. Some of those letters bear the inscription of the German censor.

In my translations of the letters, I have tried to remain as faithful to the original text as possible; however, it was sometimes necessary for the sake of clarity to omit or add a few words. Most of those modifications are parenthesized. The letters convey the more subtle aspects of our account: the emotions, the religious sensitivities and the great and numerous efforts of the individuals involved to observe *mitzvot* throughout that cataclysmic period of our history.

The portrayal of the events which my family experienced reveals the enormous efforts they made to continue to live in accordance with the laws of the Torah and to observe the *mitzvot* even under the most difficult of circumstances. Throughout the war years, despite the horrifying reality in which they were forced to live, my parents succeeded to an extraordinary degree to continue to lead their lives based on the principles of Torah study, mitzvah observance and deeds of lovingkindness. Their attributes of courage and dedication, which were crucial in order for them to continue living a Torah-true life, are worthy ideals to be passed on to future generations.

The atmosphere in my parents' home, whether in times of tranquillity or in times of distress, can best be described as a continuous state of readiness to serve Hashem and to perform deeds of lovingkindness at any time and under all circumstances. This attitude stemmed from my parents' faith that such was the will of the Creator, blessed be His Name.

Any events and memories related in this work for which no source is given are derived from my own personal recollections. It is my sincere hope that I have presented them according to the chronological order of the actual events described herein.

My brother, Shmuel, who assisted in the preparation and editing of this book, has added to it his own memories of the war years. His recollections have been presented in separate sections, the headings of which bear his name. His experiences provide an added dimension to this account and offer the reader a more vivid image of some of what we underwent. Given the complexity of the subject dealt with in this book, my brother's assistance has been especially valuable — conditions during the Holocaust were so difficult and unconventional that one person alone cannot possibly begin to describe the enormity of the catastrophe, even when focusing on the experiences of his relatives and those who were close to him.

It is impossible to describe the wickedness of the Germans, may their name and memory be erased, nor the villainous and cruel atrocities they committed against millions of Jews, showing no favoritism to children, the elderly or the sick. Because the Germans' objective was to annihilate the Jewish people, they struck sharply at the very essence of its foundations — Torah study and observance of *mitzvot*.

May the accounts related in this book serve as a memorial light for the tens of thousands of families who remained faithful to their Jewish heritage throughout the years of the Holocaust, but did not merit to leave behind even a single descendant to tell of their steadfast faith in the midst of the dark night that enshrouded European Jewry between the years 5700 and 5705 (1940–1945).

I would like to thank Mrs. Yehudit Levin of the photography department of Yad Vashem Memorial Museum for the invaluable assistance she provided us in the field of her expertise. I am especially grateful to the Yitzchak Breuer Institute for undertaking to publish this book. Special thanks go to Rabbi Moshe Schapiro, the very talented writer, translator and biographer who has rendered this book into English and supervised every stage of its production.

Yona Emanuel
Jerusalem, Sivan 5758 (1998)

Chapter One

Our Family

Our parents, Mordechai Marcus Emanuel and Chana Martha Goldschmidt, lived in Hamburg, Germany. They married in 5681 (1921) and established their home in Hamburg, where they had six children: Elchanan, Shlomo, myself — Yona — Shmuel and the twins, Baruch and Bella. In addition, approximately a year after their marriage, they adopted the orphaned daughter of a relative. The little girl's name was Aenchen Hamburg. My parents brought her up and lovingly cared for her; she called them Uncle and Aunt.

My father managed a leather concern in Hamburg. Every morning before leaving for work, he would learn Torah together with his study partner, a Mr. Weinberg. Father had a beautiful voice. He would often lead the prayer services and inspire those in attendance with his heartfelt prayers. On the High Holidays, he was given the honor of leading the *Musaf* service. There are people still alive today who fondly remember my father's rendition of the passages describing the High Priest's service on Yom Kippur.

Father owned a large *machzor* for the High Holidays, which had been printed in Altona, a former seaport near hamburg, in the year 5564 (1804), written in accordance with *minhag Polin*. This *machzor* was especially designed for *chazzanim*; he used the *machzor* in Hamburg whenever he was asked to be the *ba'al tefillah* during the High Holidays.

The Nazis rose to power in the spring of 5693 (1933). Six months later, in the autumn of that year, my family moved to the Netherlands. We settled at first in the city of Utrecht; then we moved on to Rotterdam. Two more children were born to my parents in Holland: Shalom and Bitya. Father swiftly picked up the local prayer tunes, and he was often asked to lead services at the Lev Yam neighborhood shul in Rotterdam on Shabbat, Festivals and the High Holidays.

Father's machzor

Timetable for Yom Kippur 5692 (1931)

* * *

The Nazis invaded Holland in the year 5700 (1940), in the month of Iyar. My father's widowed sister, Malli Gutman, had arrived at our home a few months earlier. She had been on her way to join her children in Eretz Yisrael, but when the outbreak of World War II left her stranded in Europe, she came to live with us. After the German invasion of Holland we were no longer able to communicate directly with the majority of our relatives in Eretz Yisrael, South Africa or England. Because of Switzerland's neutral status, we were able to maintain communications with my grandparents in Zurich. Through them, my parents managed for a while to keep up tenuous contact with the rest of the family.

Before the war and throughout the Holocaust, we kept in close contact with the Abrahams family from The Hague. Aunt Bea was my mother's sister; her husband, Naftali, was a member of the distinguished Abrahams family, which was well known throughout Holland. In his youth Uncle Naftali had learned in the Frankfurt Yeshivah, and he was an accomplished *talmid chacham* who found favor in the eyes of all.

In 5701 (1941) my parents had the great joy of seeing Aenchen married to Joseph Bloemendal. Both of them died in the Holocaust, may Hashem avenge their blood.

The deportations of Dutch Jews to concentration camps began in 1942. At that time my father was forty-eight years old, my mother was forty-one, Elchanan was nineteen, Shlomo was eighteen, I was sixteen, Shmuel was fifteen, Baruch and Bella were thirteen, Shalom was nine and Bitya was three years old.

Chapter Two
Growing Up

How can a young man purify his path?
By guarding it in accordance with Your word.

(Tehillim 119:9)

A person cannot rectify his ways through [Torah] study alone. Rather, he must also act — that is, he must "guard" and observe [i.e., put into practice] the principles he has learned. This is the intention of the words, "By guarding it in accordance with Your word." For if he will do nothing but learn, and he will neglect to act in accordance with the principles he has learned, his ways will not be pure; on the contrary, they will be offensive. The words "a young man" teach that, just as one is obligated to educate one's son in Torah study, one must also educate one's son from a young age to act in accordance with the principles he has learned.... A man is obligated to educate his young children in *mitzvot*. If he begins at a young age to fulfill the words of God in accordance with the principles he has learned, and he becomes accustomed to doing so, then he will "purify his path."

(Radak)

Together with our grandfather, *Together with our parents*
Yehoshua Goldschmidt

In Hamburg we attended a private Jewish school whose curriculum consisted of Torah study as well as various secular subjects. When we moved to the Netherlands in the year 5694 (November 1933), we were enrolled in a public school where both Jewish and non-Jewish children studied together. The Jewish children were exempted from classes on Shabbat and Festivals and, in the short winter days, were dismissed early on Fridays. The Dutch were for the most part quite tolerant towards Jews, and they respected the special requirements of our religion.

To supplement the public-school curriculum in Utrecht, our parents hired private instructors to teach us Torah after school hours. I remember learning Chumash and Mishnah, and later Gemara, with some of these teachers. One of my first Torah teachers was a young lawyer named Aaron De Haas, *zt"l*; I had the privilege of learning with him prior to the Holocaust, and then again after the war. In addition to being a lawyer, he was an outstanding *talmid chacham*.

When my family moved to Rotterdam in the year 5696 (1936), we continued studying in public school, from the elementary grades through high school. We also attended classes at the "*Joodse* (the Dutch word for 'Jewish') school" and studied Torah-related subjects there. Classes were held on Sunday mornings and Wednesday afternoons, when the public schools were closed. In the *Joodse* school we learned Chumash, Tanach, Hebrew grammar, Jewish laws, prayer and Jewish history. Some of the subjects — such as Hebrew grammar and Jewish history — were completely

A list of our birthdays, inscribed by Father in Mother's prayer book

new to me. I studied there for about two years under Rav Levy Vorst, *zt"l,* and Rav Bromet, may Hashem avenge his blood.

Upon graduating from the *Joodse* school, my classmates and I expressed a desire to continue our Torah studies in a similar format. In response to our request, and much to our satisfaction, the school administrators organized a higher grade for us, where we continued our Torah education.

During this period I began learning with Rav B. J. Stein, may Hashem avenge his blood. He was an accomplished *talmid chacham* who knew almost everything he taught us by heart; he would teach Tanach, for example, without even looking in the text. It was said that he could recite all of *"Akdamot Milin"* (a difficult Aramaic song of praise recited on Shavuot) by heart!

We learned Jewish history from a textbook written in Dutch entitled *Israel Among the Nations.* It analyzed Jewish history from Biblical times up to the modern era. In the course of these Jewish history classes, I became painfully aware of the huge disparity between the classic heroic description of the Crusaders, as taught in non-Jewish schools, and the barbaric tale of wanton murder and anti-Semitic cruelty that emerged from our own historical records. We also learned the history of the Dutch Jewish community, which I found most fascinating.

Over the years, I have come to appreciate the value of the Tanach, Hebrew grammar and knowledge of Jewish history that I acquired at the *Joodse* school. In addition to rounding out my Torah education, these areas of knowledge have proven very useful to me in my study of Mishnah, Gemara and halachah.

Shmuel, Baruch and Bella also studied in the *Joodse* school. Elchanan and Shlomo learned Torah with various rabbis. Elchanan studied Tanach with commentaries, Hebrew grammar and Jewish history all on his own. He would deliver lectures to us in Torah, *Nevi'im* and even Tehillim. Although Elchanan primarily dedicated himself to the study of Gemara and halachah, he knew that it

From right to left above: Yona, Shmuel, Elchanan and Shlomo. Below: Baruch and Bella

would benefit him to acquire a broader knowledge in subjects such as Tanach, grammar and history. He had a fervent desire to learn Torah, and he applied himself to his studies with extraordinary diligence and assiduity.

Since Elchanan was a firstborn, he always made sure to complete a tractate of Talmud or an order of Mishnah on the day before Passover. (It is customary for firstborn males to attend the ceremony of the conclusion of a tractate on the day before Passover, and thereby exempt themselves from the Fast of the Firstborn.) By the time he reached the age of bar mitzvah, he had already completed the Mishnaic orders of *Mo'ed, Nashim* and *Nezikin*. After his bar mitzvah Elchanan completed *masechet Shabbat* on the day before Pesach, and when he became fourteen years old, he completed *masechet Eiruvin*. His diligence was truly extraordinary!

Elchanan learned to write in Hebrew at a very young age. He would scrupulously record the difficulties that came to his mind while learning Mishnah and Gemara, and he kept a written record of all the lectures he ever delivered. Unfortunately, only a few

A song that, at the age of ten, Elchanan composed in honor of his cousin Eliezer Lowenstein, at his bar mitzvah, which was celebrated in Hamburg, on Shabbas Parashat Va'eira, 1934

pages of his records remain. They attest to the extraordinary breadth of his knowledge. Shlomo, who was a year younger, was Elchanan's learning partner. Although Shlomo had no intention of becoming a rabbi, he learned Torah with great devotion. Elchanan and Shlomo's diligence and knowledge far surpassed that of their younger brothers.

Shabbat and Yom Tov were very special occasions in our home. During these times, we were able momentarily to forget that we lived among non-Jews and studied in gentile public schools. On Friday afternoons in winter, when we were dismissed early from school, we would rush home in time to prepare for Shabbat. Father also hurried home from his office, and when he arrived at the house, Mother would serve him a piece of fish she had prepared for Shabbat, in accordance with the principle, "Those who taste [Shabbat] merit life. . . ."

During the Shabbat meal we would sing *zemirot*. As I mentioned earlier, Father had a beautiful voice. Sometimes, especially on Yom Tov and other festive occasions, he would sing selections of cantoral music which he had heard in his youth from Cantor Yossele Rosenblatt of Hamburg. Father would also discuss the weekly Torah portion. I remember to this day some of the insights that Father spoke about during our Shabbat meals.

As the boys grew older, they too began contributing to the discussion at the Shabbat table, citing interesting interpretations on the weekly Torah portion. One particular occasion stands out in my mind — it was the Shabbat when either *Parashat Vayishlach* or *Parashat Vayigash* was read in shul. I remember all of us attentively listening to Elchanan translating a passage from *Sefer Hayashar,* which illustrated the courage and might displayed by the children of Jacob in their battle against the Canaanites, and in their confrontation with Joseph in Egypt.

After the Friday night meal we all read the weekly Torah portion with the traditional cantillation. Sometimes friends from the neighborhood would come and join us. Father would begin by reading the first section, and we would continue on our own until the end of the *parashah.* During the Shabbat morning meal, Father would usually read Grandfather's weekly letter on the Torah portion to us, and during *seudah shelishit* he would often discuss an insight from the *Ketav Sofer* on the Torah.

We had many visitors on Shabbat, whose lengthy visits sometimes made it difficult for us to begin *seudah shelishit* on time. At such times we children would start singing from an adjacent room, "Indeed, you will *go out* with joy, and you will be led back in safety. . ." (Yeshayahu 55:12). Needless to say, our parents were somewhat disconcerted by our "song."

Various *shiurim* were given in our home on Shabbat, including a *shiur* for girls and a *shiur* on *Kitzur Shulchan Aruch* for young boys. Later in the day, a *shiur* on *Sefer Bemidbar* with Rashi's commentary was held in the home of our congregation's chief rabbi, Rav Aharon Yissachar Davids, may Hashem avenge his blood. Afternoon prayer services were held immediately after the *shiur*. Rav Davids instituted a rotation system whereby each of the *shiur*'s participants assumed the responsibility of preparing and reading the Torah passages for a particular week's Shabbat afternoon service. Following the afternoon service, Dr. David Hausdorff, *zt"l,* hosted and taught a *shiur* on the *mishnayot* of *masechet Sanhedrin* with the commentary of Rav Ovadiah MiBartenura.

Shiurim were also held in our home throughout the week. These included a Talmud *shiur* for men and a *shiur* for women on the weekly Torah portion.

During the summer months we sometimes attended the activities of the Agudah Youth Organization, which met in one of the back rooms of the Boompjes Synagogue, an ancient shul which stood near the port. This shul and the entire area surrounding it were completely burned and destroyed during a devastating bombing raid by the *Luftwaffe* on May 14, 1940, on the eve of the German invasion of Holland.

The Agudah Youth Organization consisted of male and female participants ranging in age from twelve to over twenty-five years of age. In the summer of 5699 (1939), my brother Elchanan delivered a series of lectures to the Youth Club on the subject of the deeper significance of the sacrificial offerings. The lecture was based on Talmudic and later commentators. Incredibly, Elchanan was only sixteen years old at the time. It was certainly a novelty to the community for a young boy like Elchanan to deliver organized and well-researched lectures to youths on such a difficult topic. Father would go back to his office on *motza'ei Shabbat* after first having recited *Havdalah,* sung *"Hamavdil"* and *"Eliyahu Hanavi,"* and blessed each child. (My parents would bless us on Friday night as well as on *motza'ei Shabbat.*) On Shabbat and Sundays, Father delivered a *shiur* for youngsters on Rashi's commentaries on Torah and Mishnah. We learned *masechet Shekalim* — Father's favorite — and became familiar with the administrative system of the Beit Hamik-

The ancient and majestic Boompjes Synagogue. The steps leading up to the aron kodesh are visible to the right of the raised bimah.

dash. Twice a month, Father also delivered a *shiur* in our home for all the employees who worked in his office. He taught them *Sefer Igrot Tzafon* by Rav Samson Raphael Hirsch. These employees knew very little about Judaism, and Father did his best to bring them closer to the ways of Torah. The workers were very appreciative of Father's efforts in organizing and delivering these *shiurim*.

Several Jewish families lived on our street in Rotterdam, among them the family of the ritual slaughterer, Rav Gans, may Hashem avenge his blood. The Rotterdam congregation had a long-standing custom of hiring Torah scholars from Eastern Europe to serve as the town's ritual slaughterers. Rav Gans, who came from Rumania, was a man of very noble character and distinguished presence. He would deliver numerous Torah *shiurim*, mostly to youths. Both Elchanan and Shlomo studied under him, as well as under Rav Meir Halevy Landau, may Hashem avenge his blood, who served as one of the *dayanim* in Rotterdam's *beit din*.

Rav Landau was a Torah scholar from the city of Chernov. He

Rav Meir Landau, may Hashem avenge his blood

was well versed in Talmud and halachah and possessed tremendous breadth of knowledge. Elchanan studied with him on a regular basis, with extraordinary diligence. Together they covered much more material than the *shiur* had originally been designed to include. Father was very pleased with the positive effect that Rav Landau was having on Elchanan and Shlomo.

Shmuel and I studied Gemara under Rav Mordechai Cohen, *zt"l*, the *dayan* of Rotterdam. In his youth in Galanta, Rav Cohen had been a senior disciple of Rav Yosef Tzvi Dushinski, *zt"l*. I also studied the *mishnayot* of *masechet Shabbat* under Rav Gans. I remember that he would never omit the more difficult comments of Rav Ovadiah MiBartenura, including, for example, the lengthy passage on *mishnah* 1:4, in which he explains the eighteen rabbinical decrees. On Wednesday nights I used to attend an additional *shiur* delivered by Dr. David Hausdorff, *zt"l*, on Rashi's commentary on the Torah. These *shiurim* were held in the renovated *beit midrash* adjacent to the Central Synagogue building. Both the shul and the *beit midrash* were burned and destroyed during the German bombing raid in the spring of 1940.

The Tongdee Youth Organization

In the year 5697 (1937), Elchanan set up a neighborhood youth organization which he called *Tongdee* (an acronym of the Hebrew term "*Torah im derech eretz* — Torah together with worldly activity"). Because the Dutch Jews pronounce the letter *ayin* as "ng," the club soon became known as the *Tongdee* Club. The purpose of the club was to organize Torah *shiurim*, outings and games for the neighborhood children. It was called *"Torah Im Derech Eretz"* precisely because of its dual objective.

As far as Elchanan was concerned, Torah study was the club's primary objective. He even published a weekly newsletter that was a few pages long. Although Elchanan ended up writing most of the articles, he encouraged others — including the city's rabbis — to contribute essays. Father had the newsletter typed in his office, and about ten copies were produced each week.

I remember the occasion when Elchanan asked me to write an article for the newsletter, in the year 5700 (1939), just before Rosh Hashanah. I was only thirteen years old at the time, and I had absolutely no idea how to go about writing such an article, but Elchanan would not take no for an answer. He gave me a book written in German which contained a story about Rav Amnon, the author of the famous *"Unetaneh Tokef"* passage from the High Holidays prayer service. I read the story a few times and then translated it into Dutch. This is how I came to publish my first article, which described how one of the most pious men of Ashkenazic Jewry sacrificed his life and sanctified the Name of Hashem rather than convert to Christianity. I have no idea whether the article had any effect on the newsletter's readers, but I can certainly attest to the fact that it left an indelible impression on the mind of the contributor. Years later, I found out that the story of Rav Amnon appears in *Sefer Or Zaru'a*, near the end of the section outlining the laws of Rosh Hashanah.

My parents were extremely proud of the newsletter, which was discontinued in the summer of the year 5700 (1940), when the *Luftwaffe* bombed downtown Rotterdam — including Father's office — and transformed the bustling area into a smoking pile of rubble. Unfortunately, not even a single copy of the Tongdee newsletter remains in my possession today.

We children fought with one another quite frequently. If my memory serves me correctly, I did not merit to any particular distinction in the fostering of brotherly love, and it seems to me that I was definitely among the instigators of these "civil wars." Mother sometimes complained about this, explaining that although it made her very happy to hear compliments about our behavior from her friends, she would have preferred to hear fewer compliments from others and have more silence within the home! Father was generally more accepting of our boisterousness; he disliked hearing complaints that we children were too wild. Despite our frequent squabbles, we always presented a united front, especially in the presence of other children who were strangers to us.

The Shul

The shul always played a central role in our lives. I have few memories of the neighborhood shul in Hamburg other than a faint picture of the edifice and some of the congregants, including the *chazzan* and the *shamash*. I was never able to stand beside Father during the *Musaf* service on Rosh Hashanah because he was always asked to lead the prayers at this time. I remember one particular Sukkot night in the Hamburg shul when I was about seven years old. I was feeling rather sorry for myself for not having a special Festival prayer book of my own, when suddenly I came across the words, "Who spreads a shelter [in Hebrew, *sukkah*] of peace upon us . . ." in the standard prayer book. Having found these words cheered me up, and I remained in good spirits for the rest of the evening.

I have fond memories of Simchat Torah in the Hamburg shul; it was always a very beautiful occasion. After morning prayers, we would eat a light meal at home and then walk to the Portuguese Synagogue, where we would continue dancing until noon.

I recall once, on the morning after the gentiles' New Year's

Eve, we were forbidden to walk alone to shul for fear of the drunk-
ards who were still lying in the streets. This was one of the few occasions when all of us walked to shul together with Father.

When our family moved to Holland in the autumn of 5694
(1933), shortly after the Nazis rose to power, we settled in the mid-
Holland town of Utrecht. The members of the very small Jewish
community there were not accustomed to seeing children praying
in shul during the week, so our regular attendance raised a few
eyebrows. Some members of the congregation even lodged a complaint against Father for "forcing" his young children to attend
shul services on weekdays, despite inclement weather and snow!

In our eyes, the most prominent figure in the Utrecht shul was
the *shamash*, Reb Levy Hershel, may Hashem avenge his blood. He
served as *chazzan* on weekdays, led the congregation through *Pesukei D'zimrah* on Shabbat and Yom Tov, and read the Torah. During *Selichot* he prayed with great intensity, especially while reciting
the passages *"Shofet Kol Ha'aretz"* and *"Zechor Brit Avraham,"* which
are recited on the day preceding Rosh Hashanah. His heartfelt
rendition of the prayer, "May it be Your will to do good unto Zion,"
never failed to move us.

On Friday mornings following the prayer services, we would
assist Reb Levy with all the preparations associated with the reading of the weekly Torah portion, such as choosing the *parochet* that
would be hung each week, hanging the *parochet* on the ark and
changing the mantle of the *sefer Torah*. He would also examine the
entire *parashah* in the *sefer Torah* to make sure that all the letters
were intact. These tasks completed, we would rush home and run
to the public school we attended at the time.

When we moved to Rotterdam two years later, in the year
5696 (1935), we settled in the west end of the city, not far from a
neighborhood shul called Lev Yam. When choosing a house, my
parents looked for two things: proximity to a shul, and the appropriate conditions required for the building of a proper *sukkah*. Ini-

tially, on weekdays we attended prayer services at the shul of a nearby old-age home, and on Shabbat we prayed at the Lev Yam Synagogue.

After some time, the leaders of the Lev Yam congregation invited Father to attend weekday services as well; however, Father declined. He explained that he could not pray in a shul which, other than on Mondays and Thursdays, did not have a daily *minyan*. He explained to the congregants of Lev Yam that if they wished him to attend weekday services, they would have to guarantee him that there would be a *minyan* every day of the week. The leaders of the congregation agreed to his terms, and from that day on, there was a full *minyan* in the Lev Yam Synagogue every day of the week, both morning and evening.

All the tasks in the Lev Yam Synagogue were performed on a voluntary basis, including *chazzanut* on Shabbat and Yom Tov, with one exception — the shul did not have a regular *shamash*. We jumped at this golden opportunity with gusto and took over the post. Elchanan, Shlomo, Shmuel and I rotated the honor of serving as the shul's *shamash* on a weekly basis. The *gabbai* would give us a list of the congregants who deserved an honor, and of those who needed to recite the Mourner's *Kaddish*. We would hang the *parochet* over the ark and place the appropriate signs on the wall indicating any changes in the prayer services. Since we were also assigned the duty of opening the doors of the shul in the morning, we made sure to arise early and arrive before the other congregants. The various functions that we performed in the capacity of *shamash* gave us much satisfaction.

I experienced what might be termed a "conflict of interests" while serving as *shamash*, because of the dual relationship I had with two of my "bosses" at the shul. The president of the shul and the senior *gabbai* was Rav Stein, may Hashem avenge his blood, who also happened to be my Hebrew-school teacher. The second *gabbai* was Mr. Spanier, my French teacher in public school. The fact that the shul's two main *gabba'im* were also my teachers occasionally unnerved me; however, the *gabba'im* usually agreed that on Shabbat we should let bygones be bygones, and momentarily forget my school antics of the previous week. . . .

The Lev Yam Synagogue was a private shul that had been established by a group of the congregants, and hence it did not receive any financial support from the Rotterdam Jewish Council. On Simchat Torah afternoon a festive meal would be served in shul in honor of *chatan Torah* and *chatan Bereishit*. Because the meal was sponsored by the shul and not by the *chatanim*, as is generally the custom, it was possible on occasion to give the honor of *chatan Torah* and *chatan Bereishit* to some of the more destitute members of the congregation, who otherwise would not have been able to afford to accept this honor.

Following *Kristallnacht* ("the night of broken glass"), Father's

A view of the Lev Yam Synagogue. The bimah and aron kodesh are decorated in honor of Shavuot.

secretarial staff worked around the clock, filling out hundreds of request forms for family members and acquaintances who were desperately trying to flee from Germany to the Netherlands. All those German Jews who came to the Lev Yam Synagogue were very warmly received. However, there was one particular Dutch congregant who would become incensed every time one of these German refugees was given the honor of opening the ark for the special prayer said on behalf of the Kingdom of Holland and the Dutch Queen. This fervently patriotic congregant felt that it was completely inappropriate for a Jew who was not a Dutch citizen to open the ark in honor of the Queen. Since the other congregants and the *gabba'im* did not share his patriotic zeal, the man felt the time had come for him to take drastic steps. He thus bought up all the honors of opening the ark *for the entire year*! Once these honors were his, he distributed them exclusively to Jews of Dutch citizenship. My father became the only exception to this rule. In recognition of my father's efforts to master the Dutch language and integrate with the local community, the "patriot" gave him the great honor of opening the ark for the special prayer, even though he was not a Dutch citizen.

The front page of a special Order of Service celebrating forty years of Queen Wilhelmina's reign in Elul 1938, just a year before the outbreak of WWII

Although my parents espoused the positive aspects of Dutch-Jewish life, they would in no way compromise on the ideals that were of paramount importance in their eyes, those being scrupulous observance of all the *mitzvot* and a strong foundation of Torah education in the home, sometimes in excess of the accepted standards among most German Jews. Father emphasized two key issues in our

education — mitzvah observance and Torah study. We were aware
of the fact that in these two areas our home was different from
many others, but we had learned not to make an issue of these differences.

While living in Rotterdam we came to know Jews from all
walks of life, with lifestyles very different from our own. For example, down the street from us lived a Chassidic man who prayed on
Shabbat and Yom Tov with a Chassidic *Minyan* downtown. On *Chol
Hamo'ed* he would often invite Father to *Ushpizin* and *Simchat Beit
Hasho'evah* in his *sukkah*. Some of the boys would invariably tag
along. It was on one of these occasions that I drank my very first al-
coholic beverage.

Incidentally, after the Holocaust my teacher, Rav Vorst, *zt"l*,
asked me whether I remembered the tune to which father used to
sing a particular passage of the Sukkot *Hoshanot* when he led the
services in the Rotterdam shul. In view of the horrendous calamity
which befell European Jewry just a few years later, the words of this
passage are haunting: "Nation that declares, 'I am a wall!' / Radiant
as the sun, yet exiled and dispersed. / Likened to a palm tree, yet
murdered for Your sake./ Regarded as a sheep for slaughter. . . ."
Rav Vorst explained that the tune to which my father sang this
song left a lasting impression on him. Unfortunately I disappointed Rav Vorst, for I could not remember this particular tune.

Since the city did not have an *eiruv*, we never carried anything
while walking in the street on Shabbat, even before we reached the
age of bar mitzvah. We were therefore quite shocked the first time
we saw children of religious Jews from Eastern Europe carrying
their fathers' *tallit* and *Chumash* to shul.

On Rosh Hashanah we never ate prior to the blowing of the
shofar, even before we reached the age of bar mitzvah. After hearing *Kedushah* of *Musaf*, we would go out to the corridor of the shul,
recite *Kiddush,* have a bite to eat, and then immediately rejoin the
congregation in prayer. Even as young children we never ate any-

thing inside shul, not even candies on Friday nights.

Although the shul sponsored a separate *minyan* for youths, we did not take advantage of it. Father explained to us that since every father is obligated to teach his children to pray together with the congregation of adults, children should not pray in their own *minyan*, but should rather come to shul with their parents. Father's attitude was that nothing in the world can ever replace a parent's guidance.

Traveling in Kralingen, near Rotterdam, Lag Ba'omer 5698 (1938). From right to left: Elchanan, Shlomo, Yona, Shmuel, Baruch, Bella, and Shalom

At the same time, Father strongly encouraged us to deliver Torah *shiurim* to youngsters, explaining that this time would be well spent, since we would learn much through the process of preparing the *shiurim*.

The ritual slaughterer, Rav Gans, may Hashem avenge his blood, used to deliver a *shiur* on *Kitzur Shulchan Aruch* every Sunday after morning prayers. In one humorous exchange during one of these *shiurim*, Rav Gans was talking about the prohibition of succumbing to anger. He had become quite fluent in Dutch, but this time he used the more familiar Hebrew term for anger, "*ka'as.*"

One of the people attending the *shiur* was visibly shaken by this statement and, in all seriousness, asked why in the world the Torah should prohibit trading in *kaas*, which means "Dutch cheese."

Our parents always taught us that while we must do everything in our power to fulfill *mitzvot*, we must not give others the impression that we are different; on the contrary, it is preferable not to separate oneself from the rest of the congregation, although situations sometimes arise which do not allow for any compromise whatsoever. In this respect we differed from the majority of Jews who came to Holland from Germany and Eastern Europe, who intimated that they had absolutely no desire to integrate with Dutch Jewry. Father followed the approach of influencing others through congeniality and personal example.

I must confess that I sometimes failed to emulate my father's tolerant attitude. One particular incident, which occurred in the beginning of Nissan 5700 (1940) when I was fourteen years of age, comes to mind. I got into an argument with a learned young man of a rather stringent and severe nature, and it ended with his slapping me in the face in plain view of all the congregants. Needless to say, I was mortified. I considered various possibilities for my revenge, and eventually came up with a plan: I waited until the following week, which was *Shabbat Hagadol* (the Shabbat preceding Pesach), when it would be my turn to serve as *shamash*. I then gave my adversary the "honor" of taking a second Torah scroll out of the ark, although a second Torah scroll is not required on *Shabbat Hagadol*. As the poor man approached the ark to take out the Torah scroll, the entire congregation raised their voices in protest. Only many years later did I grasp the enormity of my sin in this instance.

Chanukah and Purim

Many pleasant memories of Chanukah and Purim in our home have remained with me to this day.

After lighting the Chanukah candles, all the children in our family would circle the table while singing *"Ma'oz Tzur."* Mother would give a candy or a pastry to each child who completed a full circle around the table. As we approached the end of the song, we walked faster and faster in an attempt to complete one more circle and win another delicious prize.

Mother would occasionally play *"Ma'oz Tzur"* on the violin. In the evenings, Father and Mother would spend time with us playing dreidel and other traditional games, such as Bell and Hammer, which is similar to Monopoly. We did not play cards. Even though we had to go to school the next day, the special atmosphere of Chanukah was not dispelled.

On Purim, when we all gathered around the table for the festive meal, we sang songs together with Father. He would lead us in an ancient song entitled *"Bichvod Tzaddikim Simchah."* Each of the stanzas consists of a blessing for Mordechai and a curse for Haman beginning with the same letter, with the order of the stanzas forming an acronym of the Hebrew alphabet. Thus the first stanza reads, *"**A**havah l'Mordechai* (love to Mordechai); ***A**rur Haman* (cursed is Haman)." The second stanza is *"**B**aruch Mordechai* (blessed is Mordechai); ***B**izayon l'Haman* (disgrace to Haman)." After completing the conventional version of the song, we would begin improvising new stanzas, such as *"**H**itler l'Haman."*

In the course of the festive meal we would also sing the song *"Kichlot Yeini Tered Einai Palgei Mayim"* (As my wine is run out, my eyes emit streams of water). Father told us that the great sage Rav Shlomo Ibn Gabirol composed this song while sitting at the table of a wealthy miser who had invited him to the Purim meal. Despite the fact that it was Purim, the host served his distinguished guest only one cup of wine, and then nothing but water. By way of this song, Rabbi Shlomo poked a little fun at his stingy host. Father sang this song to a special tune which I remember to this very day even though I was a young boy at the time.

Before the war broke out, we would occasionally go on Sunday afternoon outings, usually on foot. On one of these occasions we passed the garden of a monastery where a procession was taking place. As the smell of the incense that the monks were burning wafted in my direction, Elchanan warned us, "It is forbidden to smell this, for one may not derive pleasure from idol worship." We held our noses and continued walking. Little did I know that in the future I would encounter that smell again and face this halachic problem for several months running. Only years later did I learn that this law is discussed at length in *masechet Pesachim* (25b) in the *sugyah* "A [prohibited] pleasure that comes to a man against his will."

Days of Impending Doom

Excerpts of grandfather's letters on the weekly Torah portion:

The thirty-second day of the omer, 5698 (1938)

Dearest children,

. . .We may not question the ways of Hashem. We possess only one truth, and that is the Torah. Numerous individuals have sacrificed their lives for the sake of the *mitzvot* and the Torah, disdaining honor in this world. They chose to be burned at the stake rather than to violate Hashem's *mitzvot*. We who still live in peace, and who see the Attribute of Judgment from afar, are certainly obligated to observe Hashem's laws. During the days of the *omer*, let us remember all those who sacrificed their lives for the sake of sanctifying Hashem's Name; let us express our gratitude to Hashem for guarding over us, and let us make a powerful effort to be upright Jews and earn the respect of all who observe us. Then better times will follow, speedily and in our days, amen!

Love,
Grandfather

Wednesday, Parashat Behar-Bechukkotai, 5699 (1939)

Dearest children,

. . . At every step of the way, we must remember that our destiny is in Hashem's hands, and that He is more benevolent towards us than we deserve. It is forbidden for us to think that the fact that we are still living in good conditions indicates that we are more righteous than the hundreds of thousands who have already been deported, or who are at this very moment being deported from their homes and communities. Among these poor souls are numerous individuals who are far more righteous than we.

We do not understand the ways of Hashem. Let us express gratitude to Hashem for

Anti-semitic caricature which appeared on the front page of Der Stürmer in May 1934. Entitled "The Jewish Murder Conspiracy!" the article announced that the Jews were conspiring to annihilate every gentile on earth.

every bit of good He grants to us; let us try to observe Hashem's *mitzvot* and perform them meticulously. May Hashem bring to us that era, about which we read in this week's *parashah*, "I will grant peace in the land so that you will sleep without fear . . ." (Vayikra 26:6).

Love,
Grandfather

Kosher Meat

In Germany, a new law was passed stipulating that all animals must be stunned prior to slaughter. This practice raised difficult halachic problems, and many rabbinical authorities expressed grave reservations as to whether an animal slaughtered in this manner could be considered kosher.

In light of this situation, my parents sent parcels of freshly slaughtered and salted meat to our relatives still living in Germany. We had heard reports of our relatives' self-sacrifice in refusing to eat the local meat, whose halachic status was unclear, and we saw with our own eyes the efforts our parents made to alleviate their suffering, despite the prohibitive monetary cost which these efforts entailed. These food packages made a lasting impression on us.

Chapter Three

After Kristallnacht

In the Aftermath of Kristallnacht   *(By Shmuel)*

In the autumn of 1938 the Jewish community of Rotterdam was shocked by news of the atrocities that had been perpetrated in Germany on *Kristallnacht* (so called because of the great amount of broken glass that littered the streets following the ransacking of hundreds of synagogues). The vicious pogrom against the Jews and the wanton burning and destruction of numerous synagogues shattered any illusions that may have remained in people's minds about the future of German Jewry. This dark night will remain forever etched in blood, in the annals of Jewish history.

On the *motza'ei Shabbat* following *Kristallnacht*, my parents learned that seven of our relatives had been interned in a concentration camp, and Father immediately launched efforts to obtain their release. The following morning, my father led the congregation in prayer. When he reached the words, "Protector of Israel, protect the remnant of Israel; do not let Israel be destroyed, those who proclaim, 'Hear, O Israel,' " he broke down and wept before the entire congregation. It was a prayer I will never forget.

The Nazis forbade German Jews to notify anyone outside the country of the arrests and concentration-camp internments that had been carried out during *Kristallnacht*. It had become common knowledge that the telephone lines of Jewish families were tapped, and that every word was now being carefully screened. Nevertheless, my paternal aunt Tziporah, the wife of Rav Baruch Kunstadt, disregarded the prohibition and blurted out to my parents over the phone, "My husband and my son Yona are being held in a concentration camp! Please do everything in your power to secure their release!"

The only way to obtain the release of someone who had been interned in a concentration camp in those days was to procure a visa for him to a foreign country. After approximately one week, Aunt Tziporah received a telegram from the British consulate in The Hague stating that visas to Palestine had been issued for Rav Baruch Kunstadt and his entire family. How was all this arranged so quickly? Father had received the immigration certificate to Palestine from Rotterdam's Jewish Agency representative. He traveled to The Hague, the capital of Holland, found the post office nearest the British consulate, and sent the telegram in the name of the British consulate. Miraculously, on the basis of this ruse, Rav Kunstadt was released from the Buchenwald concentration camp. On the day of his release he telephoned his wife to inform her at what hour he expected to arrive at the train station at Fulda. Aunt Tziporah waited for him, but she failed to recognize her husband, so changed was he from his short internment in Buchenwald, until he approached her and said, "It's me."

After a short time, a genuine entry certificate to Palestine was obtained for the Kunstadt family. Father made the arrangements for their departure from Germany to Holland. Rav Kunstadt, Aunt Tziporah and two of their children stayed with us for about a month in order to regain their strength before embarking upon the arduous trip to Palestine. Rav Kunstadt arrived at our home limping as a result of the blows and cruel torture he had endured at Buchenwald. My parents rented a room for them in a nearby house so that they would be able to rest in some degree of comfort.

When we asked Aunt Tziporah how she had found the courage to defy the ban and disclose to us by phone her son and husband's internment, she responded, "Had the Gestapo (German secret police) accused me of violating the ban, I would have responded, 'Just return my husband and son to me, and I assure you that I will call my relatives abroad and inform them that everything I told them is incorrect!' "

The degree to which the Kunstadts felt indebted and grateful towards my parents is impossible to describe. They would frequently remind us of all the things that Father and Mother had done on thir behalf.

Rescue Work

Following *Kristallnacht*, which took place on the twenty-second of Cheshvan 5699 (1938), my parents worked very hard to

The official notification sent by the British Embassy in The Hague to Rav Baruch Kunstadt, informing him that his request for entry visas into Palestine had been accepted

save various relatives and acquaintances who were still trapped in Germany. Numerous family members passed through our home in

Rav Baruch Kunstadt in Rotterdam with his wife and two sons in the garden of the Emanuel family, Tevet 5699 (January 1939)

Rotterdam on their way from Germany to England or Palestine, and many refugees found shelter in our home, sometimes staying for months at a time. My brothers and I frequently shared beds in order to make room for all the guests. Sometimes I would go to sleep at night in my own bed, then wake up to find myself sharing a bed with one of my brothers.

Our home became a makeshift office in which hundreds of requests for German exit permits were prepared. Relatives in Germany were constantly sending Father more lists containing personal details of friends and neighbors who also required assistance. Father spared no effort to ensure that all the forms be prepared as swiftly as possible. These were very difficult times for Father. I remember his profound disappointment when he learned that all of our cousins' neighbors had received exit permits, but that our own cousins' request had been rejected. Eventually, however, our cousins did manage to leave Germany. As children, we never realized how many people our parents knew who were still living in Germany.

I became a bar mitzvah on the Shabbat of *Parashat Vayei-shev* in the year 5699 (1938), one month prior to *Kristallnacht*. I had hoped that my uncle Baruch Kunstadt and his family would arrive in time for the celebration, but they did not arrive in Holland until two weeks later. On the evening of Shabbat *Parashat Vayechi*, Uncle Baruch learned with us the blessings of Ya'akov Avinu with the commentary of Rashi.

Rav Baruch Kunstadt in Eretz Yisrael. From left to right: Rav Shlomo Zalman Auerbach, Rav Kunstadt, and Rav Elchanan Kunstadt

Chapter Four

Germany Invades
the Netherlands

World War II Begins

Western Europe had adopted a policy of tolerance and re-
straint vis-á-vis Hitler, in an attempt to avoid armed conflict.
Czechoslovakia, cowering before Nazi Germany's rapidly expand-
ing and war-hungry army, was finally intimidated into signing the
Munich Treaty, which stipulated that large portions of her territory
be annexed by Germany. This territorial withdrawal effectively
sealed Czechoslovakia's fate, for it exposed the soft underbelly of
her heartland to the vastly superior German army, effacing all
hopes of halting the anticipated invasion through military resis-
tance. The Germans delivered the death blow in March 1939, cap-
turing most of Czechoslovakia in a matter of days.

In keeping with their laissez-faire policy, Western European nations blithely ignored their mutual-defense treaties with Czechoslovakia and overlooked Nazi Germany's flagrant breach of international agreements, naively hoping that this territorial gain and "minor" military skirmish would satisfy Nazi Germany's expansionist
yearnings. However, in August of that same year, the U.S.S.R. astounded the world by signing a mutual non-belligerence treaty with

Germany. With Russia immobilized, Hitler saw a golden opportunity to lunge forward and capture additional territory in Central and Eastern Europe.

Germany did not allow this chance to slip away. She took advantage of the favorable political situation and, on the first of September 1939, launched her next military campaign against Poland. This time, however, England and France responded by declaring war against Germany. World War II — the conflagration which would bring about the Holocaust that was to consume most of European Jewry — had begun.

The inscription "Jews" emblazoned in bold across a window display in Magdeburg, Germany, on Kristallnacht

A letter from Rav Joseph Carlebach, the last rabbi of Hamburg, may Hashem avenge his blood, to my parents:

Hamburg, October 17, 1939

My dear relatives,

As we have been unable to communicate with one another for quite a long time, I take this opportunity to inform you that we are still alive and, *baruch Hashem*, well. We have heard news of Felix and Grete [Goldschmidt] by way of Zurich. I often reminisce about my last visit with you in your home. Your sons are adults by now who bear upon their shoulders the religious lifestyle of Rotterdam.

The woman who is delivering this letter, Mrs. Possenheimer, is my former secretary. She is on her way to America via Rotterdam and must remain in Rotterdam over Shabbat. I ask you to help her and her two daughters to find suitable accommodation during her short stay in your city. She will tell you all about Hamburg and the congregation here. I am indebted to you from the bottom of my heart for your generous assistance.

Blessings from an old friend.

Yours,

Josef Carlebach

A letter from Grandfather to Shmuel on the occasion of his donning tefillin for the first time:

Zurich, the eighth day of Kislev 5700 (1939)

My dear Shmuel,

This week's Torah portion — *Parashat Vayishlach* — describes Ya'akov Avinu's difficult struggle. Finally he was returning to his land and to the home of his dear father after having endured so many years of hard labor, exhaustion and anguish. His heart was filled with profound love for his wives and children, and he yearned to reach his aged and blind father and his beloved mother, whom he had not seen in so many years.

He wondered if he would in fact merit to see his parents again, to be with them and to receive their blessing. He wondered if he would have the joyous opportunity of presenting to them his wives and children, who were his pride and joy. How Ya'akov's heart trembled as he journeyed back to his home, his thoughts focused on the many dangers threatening his family's safety. What would happen to

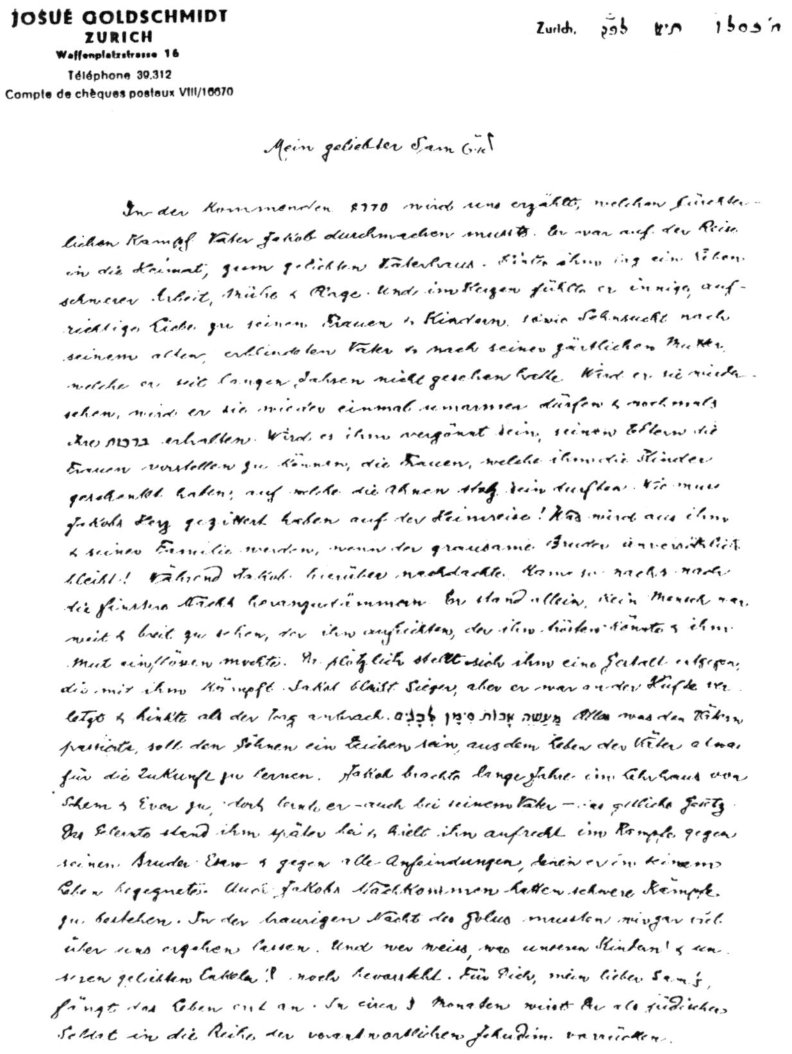

JOSUÉ GOLDSCHMIDT
ZURICH
Waffenplatzstrasse 16
Téléphone 39.312
Compte de chèques postaux VIII/16670

Zürich, בס"ד ט"ו ‏בסב‏ ‏ח‏

Mein geliebter Sam Gn̄ʾ

[handwritten German letter]

A copy of grandfather's letter to Shmuel on the occasion of his starting to put on tefillin

Und nächsten Sonntag wirst Du zum ersten Male die תפילין anlegen,
wenn Du Dich mit dem Siddur, dem Schmuck, bekleidest, den die
תפילין darstellen. In früheren Zeiten trug man sie den ganzen
Tag. Jetzt nur morgens beim Gebet. Keinen Tag sind wir ohne ein
göttliches Zeichen. An שבת ist der שבת selbst ein אות, ein Zeichen, sodass wir
an שבת keine תפילין zu tragen brauchen. Wenn wir auch heute nur an
Wochentagen den תפילין של ראש als תפילין als Krone tragen, so sollen wir
doch den ganzen Tag, Tag & Nacht uns die Worte zu eigen machen & in
die Tat umsetzen אנכי ה' אלהיך "jeden Tag will Dich, Ich, segnen".
Die תפילין sollen für uns ein Panzer sein, eine Rüstung als Soldat im Heere
Gottes zu dienen. Und da gibt es keinen Urlaub; als Soldat im Heere
Gottes müssen wir jeden Atemzug unseres Lebens Ihm, dem höchsten König
weihen. Die תפילין am Kopfe stellen unseren Geist, unser ganzes Denken, in
Seinen Dienst. Und die תפילין am Arm verpflichten jede einzelne unserer
Taten in den Dienst Gottes. Den Sinn der 4 Parschiones sollst Du jederzeit
beherzigen. Dein Denken, Wollen sollen ein Gottesdienst sein. Nie sollst
Du die תפילין gedankenlos anlegen. Und wenn Du sie tagsüber nicht
trägst, so wisse, dass Du sie am nächsten Morgen wieder anlegen wirst.
Halte Deinen Körper rein, halte Deine Gedanken rein. Lass' sie immer
ein Gotteszeichen an Deinem Arm sein; lass' sie ein Kopfkranz-Schmuck
sein an Deiner Stirn, damit bleibe Gottes Lehre stets in Deinem
Munde; Gott, der Dich aus Mizrayim geführt hat, Er bleibe Dein Gott.
Er wird Dich auch einst ins Land unserer Väter führen, sobald
Du Deine Pflicht Gott & Menschen gegenüber erfüllt haben wirst.
Und wenn Du bei den Worten ציון כי ה' שפטים ועשיתי מתים את die
Tefillin berührst, so denke, dass das ש an der Stirnseite, das ד, so der
Knoten an der Nackerseite darstellt, sowie das י am Knoten am Arm
den Gottesnamen שדי darstellen, den Namen Gottes, der jedem Wesen
ד sein Genügendes gewährt. שדי wird auch Dir Dein די spenden,
wenn Du in Gotteswegen wandelst, zur Ehre vor ganz כלל, zum
Stolz Deiner Brüder; zur Zufriedenheit Deiner geliebten Eltern! Deren
Leben nur dann von Wert ist, wenn Du m.G.h. in der Dir vorge-
zeichneten Bahnen wandelst & in Liebe zu Deinem Grossvater נרו
dessen Seele an Deine Seele geknüpft ist & zur Ehre des Namens
Deines Urgrossvaters ל"ז, den Du trägst.

וזו נשורה

his loved ones? Would his cruel brother Esav be disposed to forgive him?

As Ya'akov pondered all these matters, night descended, and "Ya'akov remained alone" (Bereishit 32:25). There was no one with him to encourage him, to strengthen his spirit and to inspire him. Then, suddenly, an image arose before him, as it is written, "A man struggled with him until dawn" (ibid.). Ya'akov ultimately prevailed, but as dawn broke, he emerged from the contest limping.

The Sages say that "the events of the lives of the forefathers are a sign of what will happen to the children" (*Midrash Tanchuma, Lech Lecha* 9), meaning that all that our forefathers experienced foretells what will ultimately befall their descendants in the future. We know that Ya'akov studied many years in the study hall of Shem and Ever; he

A family picture taken in our home in the spring of 1940 on the day preceding Shmuel's bar mitzvah. Standing from right to left: Baruch, Yona, Shlomo, Elchanan and Shmuel. Sitting: Mother, Bitya, Shalom, Father and Bella

learned Hashem's Torah from them, as well as from his father, Yitzchak. All the Torah knowledge that he attained supported and strengthened him as he struggled against his brother Esav, and carried him through all the conflicts and hostilities which he endured throughout his life. Likewise Ya'akov's descendants must necessarily endure overwhelmingly difficult struggles and must continue to stand firm. Numerous decrees have been forced upon us throughout the darkness of exile, and who knows what will happen to our children and grandchildren, may they live long?

My dear Shmuel, you stand now at the threshold of your life. In another three months you will report for duty, one more Jewish soldier among the ranks of Jews who proudly bear the responsibility that has been placed upon them. Next Sunday, when you will adorn yourself with that diamond, the precious jewel known as "*tefillin*," you will recite a blessing over this mitzvah for the first time. In the past, people wore *tefillin* throughout the day; today we don them only during the morning prayers.

Not a weekday passes on which we do not don *tefillin*. The reason we do not don them on Shabbat is that Shabbat itself is a "sign" of Hashem's covenant; thus there is no need for the additional sign of *tefillin* then. Although we place the crown of tefillin upon ourselves only in the morning, we must remember the deeper message of *tefillin* throughout the day, both daytime and nighttime, and turn it into a reality.

The *tefillin* serve as our shields in the battle of Hashem's army. There are no furloughs in this army. As Hashem's soldiers, we have an obligation to consecrate our every breath to Hashem, the King of kings. The *tefillin* that we wear upon our heads consecrates our spirit — our every thought — to His service. The *tefillin* that we wear upon our arms obligates us in all our deeds.

You must always ponder the significance of the four Scriptural passages contained within the *tefillin*. Then your thoughts and desires will be directed towards the service of Hashem.

Never don *tefillin* without the required intentions. Keep your body clean, and preserve the purity of your thoughts.

May the *tefillin* always be a sign of Hashem upon your arm and a precious jewel between your eyes, that the Torah of Hashem be upon your lips all the days of your life.

May Hashem, Who took you out of Egypt, be Your God. If you will fulfill your obligations towards God and man, He will bring you to the land of our forefathers.

When you touch the *tefillin*, as you utter the words, "You open Your hand and satisfy the desire of every living thing" (Tehillim 145:16), remember that the letter *shin* upon your forehead and the *dalet* of the knot resting upon the back of your head and the *yod* of the knot on your arm spell the Divine Name *Shadai*, indicating He Who gives *dai* (enough) to every living being. *Shadai* will say *"Dai!"* (enough) to all your troubles when you will walk in the ways of God. In this manner, you will bring honor to all of the congregation of Israel and to your brothers and sisters, and satisfaction to your precious parents, may they live long. Their lives will have meaning only as long as you, with the help of God, walk in the paths which they have laid before you. Do this out of love for me, your grandfather, whose soul is bound to your soul, and out of love for your great-grandfather, *zt"l* [Rav Shmuel Chaim Schuler], whose name you bear.

Love,
Grandfather

In spite of the tense political situation, Grandfather traveled from Switzerland to attend Shmuel's bar mitzvah celebration. Unlike his previous visits, however, this time he came alone, while Grandmother stayed behind in Switzerland. Shmuel reached the age of bar mitzvah on the Shabbat of *Parashat Vayakhel* in the year 5700 (1940). On the preceding Shabbat, Grandfather had attended the bar mitzvah celebration of our cousin, Michel Abrahams, may Hashem avenge his blood.

Germany invaded the Netherlands less than two months later.

The German Invasion

The Netherlands proclaimed itself a neutral state as soon as Germany invaded Poland in Elul of 5699 (1939) and war was declared. Nevertheless, rumors of an impending German invasion of the Netherlands circulated throughout the following year.

My parents deliberated whether the time had come for our family to flee Europe. The opportunity to do so was certainly not lacking, since father was in constant communication with a number of businessmen in various South American countries. The birth of my sister Bitya around this time made my parents' decision very difficult indeed.

One of the options they seriously considered at the time was to leave Holland on board the *Simon Bolivar*, which was about to set sail from Rotterdam to South America. In the end they decided not to board the ship, and a few days later we learned that it had been torpedoed in mid-ocean by German U-boats. The ship sunk, and

German soldiers in The Hague

all its passengers and crew perished in the watery depths.

Fear of an impending invasion intensified following Germany's successful military campaigns against Denmark and Norway in the early spring, just before Passover of the year 5700 (1940). Despite all the danger signals, we were lulled into passivity by the reassuring statements that were being made by the Reich's leaders in Berlin: they pledged that Germany had absolutely no intention of invading the Netherlands, and that the status of neutral nations would continue to be honored. We desperately wanted to believe that their words were true.

We were placated by this deception until Friday, the second day of Iyar 5700 (May 10, 1940), the bitter day when the hobnail-booted German troops stormed through the Netherlands and Belgium on their headlong race to France. We first became aware of the invasion, which had begun sometime in the middle of the night, when the *Luftwaffe* began bombing Rotterdam at dawn. Occasionally the roar of the German planes was accompanied by the blast of anti-aircraft cannons manned by Dutch army troops. Just a few hours later we were shocked by the news that German paratroopers had succeeded in the capture of Rotterdam's civilian and military airports, and that they were rapidly advancing towards the city's main center. The airport was located near the dockyards, which lay approximately three kilometers from the city center.

The German paratroopers advanced towards the strategic Maas River bridge and quickly captured it. A wild rumor circulated to the effect that the Dutch marines had succeeded in repelling the German paratroopers and had retaken the bridge; however, it soon became apparent that this rumor was completely unfounded.

Reeling from the might of the attack, the Dutch authorities grew concerned that citizens of Germany residing in the Netherlands would commit subversive acts to assist the invading forces. An order was therefore issued to arrest all German citizens in the Netherlands. Ironically, the thousands of Jews who not long before had fled Germany in the wake of Hitler's rise to power were now rounded up lest they collaborate with the enemy! The greatest irony lay in the fact that according to the law we did not even qualify as Germans, for the Nazis had annulled the citizenship of all German Jews. Instead, we belonged to the growing number of *Statenloos* — "people without a nationality." The Dutch showed no interest in such picayune legal details; they arrested all German citizens, Jews and gentiles alike. My father was among those arrested.

The policemen who came to our door to arrest my father calmed and reassured my parents. They informed them that loyal citizens such as my father would be asked merely to report to the authorities and register with the police, and would afterwards be freed and allowed to return to their homes. Despite the assurances, Mother prepared a package of food.

Father did his best to calm her, saying, "With Hashem's help, I'll be back shortly." Nevertheless, he did not leave before taking his *tefillin*. He somehow managed to do so without any of us noticing, and so spared us from even greater anxiety. We later learned that Father had been the only prisoner who had had the foresight to bring his *tefillin* along with him when arrested. All the other religious prisoners used Father's *tefillin* throughout their lengthy internment.

The aerial bombardment forced Mother to stay in the cellar together with her eight children for five consecutive days. We recited *tehillim* some of the time, especially psalm 91: "O you who dwell in the shelter of the Most High and abide in the protection of the Lord. . . ." Our aunt Malli stayed in the cellar with us.

On that Shabbat evening Rav Aharon Yissachar Davids, the chief rabbi of Rotterdam, paid us a visit in the cellar and spoke words of encouragement to us. The Davids family had been our neighbors for five years. (Both Rav Davids and his son Eliah, a young, sweet-tempered boy who was my childhood friend, perished in Bergen-Belsen in the year 5705; may Hashem avenge their blood.)

In the midst of the bombardment, as the walls of our home shook and we all crouched in the cellar, trembling with fear, my mother wrote a postcard in French to her parents in Switzerland. She asked all of us to sign the postcard, as though she feared that this would be our last message to our grandparents. She wrote to them as follows:

Tuesday, May 14, 1940

My most dear and beloved parents,

As the hours pass, we hope that the merit of our forefathers will stand by our side. Likewise, we hope that in the merit of all the assistance that Mordechai has extended to so many people, we too will be saved. We are all here except for Mordechai — he was arrested on Friday.

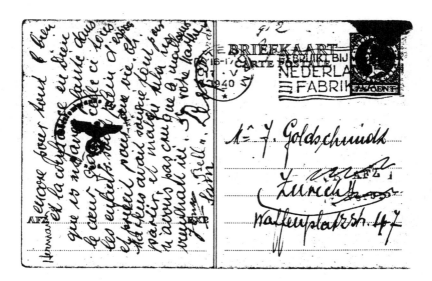

This postcard was written on May 14, 1940, the day the Germans completed the invasion of the Netherlands. It was postmarked only three days later, on May 17, already bearing the stamp of the German censor (near the left margin). The Germans wasted no time in taking over control of the country. The children's signatures are faintly visible to the left of the recipient's address.

I hope that by the time this postcard reaches you, these and other anxieties will be well behind you. I thank you for all the good that you have done for me, and for the faith in God that you have instilled in our hearts. It is surely in this merit that the children continue to pray for their lives and remain full of hope. Mordechai made all the preparations to leave this country, but we did not think that the catastrophe would come so soon.

Yours,

Chana

Several bombs fell on the Cultural Center building in Rotterdam, where the imprisoned German citizens were being held in custody. A number of them died, and some sustained severe injuries. Those who were not injured fled from the burning building and ran for their lives. Among the survivors was Joseph Bamberger, may Hashem avenge his blood. He arrived at our home from the detention center in a state of great agitation, and when he heard that our father had not yet returned, he collapsed in the doorway. He thought that he had seen Father among the wounded.

After a while, Father finally did return home. He explained that he had taken extra precautions and stayed off the streets throughout the bombardment. He had taken refuge in an adjacent building for quite some time, and emerged only when the bombing had clearly come to an end.

Father described to us the miraculous way in which he had been saved: While in the detention center, he had spotted a Jewish soldier and requested of him to try to obtain some kosher food for the religious prisoners. The soldier agreed and asked Father to compile a list of prisoners who wanted kosher food. Father informed the rest of the prisoners that all those wishing to receive kosher food should gather in a particular corner of the building to add their names to the list. Just as the prisoners interested in ko-

Rotterdam in ruins following the ruthless German airstrike that preceded the conquest of the city

sher food began to join Father in the appointed place, the bombardment began.

The section of the building in which they were standing was only one story high, and did not seem very safe. All the other pris-

Rotterdam's Boompjes Synagogue following the heavy bombardment

oners who had been there fled. Only Father and the prisoners interested in receiving kosher food remained in that area of the detention center. However, this ostensibly "unsafe" section turned out to be the only section of the building which was not damaged by the bombing!

On that Tuesday afternoon, the city of Rotterdam shuddered under another vicious bombing raid by the *Luftwaffe*. The city center was completely demolished and engulfed in flames. Hundreds were killed, thousands were wounded and tens of thousands were rendered homeless. Finally the Dutch army surrendered and lay down its arms.

You will therefore serve your enemies when God sends them against you, and it will be in hunger, in thirst, in nakedness and in utter want. He will place an iron yoke upon your neck so as to destroy you. God will bring upon you a nation from afar, from the end of the earth, swooping down like an eagle. It will be a nation whose language you do not understand, a sadistic nation that has no respect for the old and no mercy for the young. . . . Among those nations you will feel no security, and there will be no place for your foot to rest. There God will make you cowardly, destroying your outlook and filling your life with despair. Your life will hang in doubt before you. Day and night, you will be so terrified that you will have no assurance of your life. In the morning you will say, "If only it were night," and in the evening you will say, "If only it were morning." Such will be the inner terror that you will experience and the sights that you will see.

(Devarim 28:48–49, 65–67)

Chapter Five
The First Decrees

Many Jews en route to the United States were trapped in Rotterdam when the Germans invaded the Netherlands. All their possessions were destroyed in the onslaught. The enemy's evil arm managed to snatch them from freedom at the very last moment, just hours before they were to set sail for safe shores. These miserable individuals, who had been so full of hope, were transformed in one moment into destitute refugees who would once again be subjected to the horrors of Nazi cruelty and persecution. Several such individuals came to live with us in our home.

A few months later, approximately two weeks before Rosh Hashanah of the year 5701 (1940), the Germans issued an edict stipulating that all Jews who had previously held German citizenship were to leave the western sector of the Netherlands for the central and eastern regions of the country immediately. We moved back to the city of Utrecht, in which we had lived from 5694 until 5696 (1933–1935). There we renewed old relationships and made new friends.

During our first Shabbat in Utrecht, the chief rabbi, Rav Tzadok Tal, spoke before the congregation and urged its members to accommodate the deportees and make them feel as welcome as circumstances could permit. Rav Tal began his talk by citing a verse from that week's *haftarah*: "Widen the site of your tent and stretch out the curtains of your dwelling . . ." (Yeshayahu 54:2).

Reciting Keriyat Shema at Night

The Germans instituted a two-hour change in the summer clock in Holland, which meant that the prescribed time to recite *Keriyat Shema* at night occurred at approximately 11:00 P.M. Because of the inherent difficulty in gathering a *minyan* at such a late hour, the afternoon and evening services in shul were held approximately two hours earlier. Elchanan asked Father to awaken him at night after *tzeit hakochavim* (the time when three medium-sized stars are visible in the sky, the preferred time to recite *Keriyat Shema*).

When Grandfather learned of Elchanan's insistence on reciting *Keriyat Shema* after *tzeit hakochavim,* he wrote him a letter explaining that this was an unnecessary stringency. Grandfather was of the opinion that the mitzvah of reciting *Keriyat Shema* at night could be fulfilled even before *tzeit hakochavim.* He felt that Elchanan should rely on the *Keriyat Shema* which he recited in shul during the evening services.

Following is an excerpt from Elchanan's response to Grandfather's letter. It is replete with Talmudic and halachic citations. Elchanan wrote the letter in German in order to ensure that it would not be stopped by the Nazi censor. The content of the letter bears witness to young Elchanan's high level of erudition and makes it clearly evident that Torah study was constantly on his lips. He spent much time learning Torah with us and with other young disciples, yet he also graduated from high school with a technical diploma. Elchanan planned to become a rabbi, but he was of the opinion that in our day and age a rabbi must have extensive knowledge of technical subjects, rather than concentrating exclusively on humanities, as was the tendency among Western European rabbinical students in those days.

The tenth day of Menachem Av 5701

Dear Grandfather,

. . . My request to be awakened at nighttime to recite *Keriyat Shema* does not present any difficulty to my mother, may she merit to live a long life. Father awakens some of my younger brothers at night in any case for a completely different — and very physical — reason. Thus it is certainly no great inconvenience for him to awaken me as well, with just a slight movement of his hand, during this "watch." Meanwhile, *tzeit hakochavim* is now occurring at a progressively earlier hour, and since I sometimes rest in the afternoons, there is no longer a need for me to go to bed earlier than that.

. . . I asked myself a basic question: Am I obligated to arrange for someone to wake me in order for me to fulfill the mitzvah of *Keriyat Shema* in a case where I recited the evening prayers before nightfall?

. . . One may rely on the recital of *Keriyat Shema* in shul only if the evening prayer service was conducted no earlier than an hour and a quarter before nightfall. However, here the congregation sometimes conducts services at a time even earlier than that. In reference to this problem, the Chayei Adam (34:4) rules, "It is preferable not to pray with [such a congregation], but rather to pray by oneself at the required time."

. . . Rav Nachman used to ask to be awakened so as to recite the first verse (*Berachot* 13b), and his words are cited as halachah by the Rambam and *Shulchan Aruch*.

. . . I fail to understand how it is possible to fulfill the obligation of remembering the Exodus from Egypt at night if one recites the evening prayers before nightfall. May one

also fulfill the mitzvah of eating matzah on the night of Pesach before nightfall? And what of all the other *mitzvot*
which can be fulfilled only at night? May one also fulfill
them before nightfall? What forces us to say that *Keriyat
Shema* differs from all other *mitzvot*?

. . . Neither the Rambam, the Ramban nor *Sefer Mitzvot
Gadol* consider the mitzvah of remembering the Exodus
from Egypt to be one of the 613 mitzvot. They interpret the
words of Bar Zoma as referring to the mitzvah to remember the Exodus from Egypt specifically on the night of Pesach. However, *masechet Berachot* (21a) clearly states that it is
a mitzvah to remember the Exodus every single day of the
year. *Sefer Mitzvot Katan* rules likewise. The entire matter is
as yet unclear to me.

. . . Surely no one questions that the Torah obligates us
to learn Torah at night. According to Rav Shamshon
Raphael Hirsch, in difficult circumstances this mitzvah may
be fulfilled merely by reciting the passage of *Keriyat Shema*,
which begins with the words, "Teach them diligently to
your children and speak of them . . ." (Devarim 6:7).
Clearly, though, in order to fulfill the mitzvah of learning
Torah at night, this passage must be recited at nighttime!

. . . You cite the opinion of the Rabbeinu Yitzchak and
Rabbeinu Tam (*Berachot* 2a) that one may fulfill the mitzvah
by reciting *Keriyat Shema* during evening prayers when they
are conducted within an hour and a quarter of nightfall.
However, Rashi is of the opinion that at least the first passage of *Keriyat Shema* must be recited at nighttime. To me, it
seems that this difference of opinion constitutes a doubt
concerning a Torah-ordained mitzvah, with all its halachic
ramifications. Indeed, this is the ruling of *Shulchan Aruch*

(235:1) and Rambam (*Hilchot Tefillah* 3:7), and I have found similar rulings in other halachic works.

. . . It seems to me that permitting us to recite the Evening Service immediately after the Afternoon Service constitutes a very great leniency, and I would not want to extend this leniency any further.

"Were not your teachings my delight, I would have perished under my affliction." *(Tehillim 119:92)*

Although life gradually began to change following the invasion, we made every attempt to carry on the established routines of our lives as much as possible.

Our family had been accustomed to going on an outing on the Sunday after Lag Ba'omer and on the Sunday after *Shabbat*

A sign announcing that "Jews are not welcome" hangs on a restaurant door. A Dutch Nazi stands in the entrance.

Nachamu (the Shabbat following Tishah B'Av). All of us cherished these family outings. Following the invasion, we went on outings at more frequent intervals, often on bicycles. Eventually the authorities posted signs in all public places bearing the message, "*Voor honden en Joden verboden*! — Entry is forbidden to dogs and Jews!"

In Elul of 5700 (1940), after we returned to Utrecht, having been forced to leave Rotterdam, we began to attend high school once again. Elchanan began delivering *shiurim* on *Parashat Vayikra* with the commentaries of Rashi, Ramban and Rav Hirsch. Occasionally other commentaries were discussed, such as those of Malbim and Rav David Tzvi Hoffman. Learning *Chumash* in depth, especially such a difficult *parashah* as *Vayikra*, was a new experience for me. Although we progressed slowly, all of us thoroughly enjoyed the *shiur*. Elchanan also delivered *shiurim* on Gemara and on an in-depth analysis of the Book of Tehillim.

The *shiurim* on *Parashat Vayikra* were attended by boys and girls aged fifteen to eighteen. Generally they were held in our home, and on occasion in the Jewish Community Center or the Jewish Orphanage building. A number of youngsters who came to the Netherlands as refugees attended these *shiurim*. One of the most dedicated students was Nora Rothschild, today Mrs. Nora Aharon of Kibbutz Be'erot Yitzchak in Israel. Over fifty years later, she still fondly reminisces about her great thirst for Torah knowledge during that fearful period. She recalls how we would sometimes learn for hours on end without respite. All of us felt a burning desire to study Torah. The learning gave us the necessary strength to withstand the stress and tension that we all felt in those difficult times.

Once, Elchanan charged me with the responsibility of delivering the *shiur* on Tehillim. I agreed only that one time, but refused to deliver the *shiur* regularly, since it required a very thorough understanding of many commentaries.

When the Festivals approached we would study some of the pertinent laws in *Shulchan Aruch*. These *shiurim*, also delivered by

Elchanan, were most rewarding and inspiring. Elchanan was endowed with the skills of a great educator; he was able to capture the attention of his students and to teach any subject with a fascinating approach. Some time before the Shabbat when *Parashat Terumah* is read, Elchanan requested that I review the entire *parashah* with the commentary of Rashi. "Afterwards we'll learn it together," he told me. True to his word, we later looked up the section in *masechet Shabbat* (98b) which discusses the measurements of the beams and coverings of the Tabernacle and methodically analyzed the entire subject.

The Nazis prohibited Jewish boys of Elchanan's age from attending high school, so Elchanan prepared for his upcoming exams independently at home. Even during this pre-exam period, Elchanan's main interest remained the study and teaching of Torah. After he passed his exams, Elchanan began devoting himself exclusively to Torah learning, studying part of the day and teaching others in the hours that remained. Years later, after the Holocaust, I found a slip of paper upon which Elchanan had outlined his daily schedule — every single moment, from morning to night, was accounted for. Hourly and half-hourly slots were carefully allotted to a variety of scholastic endeavors.

At the end of the summer of 5701 (1941), the Nazi regime forbade all Jewish children from attending public school. Since we could not continue our education, Shlomo, Shmuel and I found jobs and began working. The Torah *shiurim* continued without interruption despite our new schedules.

The Nazi authorities ordered that the two-hour change which had been applied to the summer clock be maintained throughout the year. Consequently, the sun rose at a very late hour in the winter. We thus made it our habit to rise at approximately 5 A.M. every winter morning, eat breakfast before the first rays of light appeared on the horizon, and then study *masechet Bava Kama* together with Elchanan. Afterwards we would go to shul, and from there, to our places of employment.

That winter was unusually cold. Because we did not have the means to heat the entire house, we heated only one room. The temperature was so low in the rest of the house that water would often freeze in the rooms. The shul was also unheated.

I would set out for work immediately after the morning prayer service. I was employed in a workshop where I was being trained to operate light machinery. Initially, I traveled there by streetcar, but then the Nazis passed an edict forbidding Jews to use public transportation. I had no choice but to walk to work every morning. The workshop was located on the outskirts of the city, about an hour's walk from the shul where I prayed. At least the work was interesting — I learned to operate a lathe, as well as other metal-shop machinery. On Fridays I left work earlier than usual.

That year, I worked on *Chol Hamo'ed Sukkot*. In view of the great distance that I had to travel every day in order to get to my place of employment, I asked Rav Tzadok Tal, *zt"l*, whether it would be permissible for me to eat bread while at work. Torah law stipulates that bread must be eaten inside a *sukkah* throughout the Festival, but individuals who travel a great distance from home are exempt from this obligation. To my surprise, his response was that the exemption did not apply to my situation. He explained that although a traveler is permitted to eat bread outside a *sukkah*, I did not fit into that category, since the machine shop was my regular place of employment. I therefore did not eat bread at work throughout *Chol Hamo'ed*. Instead, I made do with a jar of potato salad which I brought to work from home.

Torah Study in Utrecht

The Jewish community of Utrecht was originally quite small. However, during the years 5701–5702 (1941–1942), when German Jews who had been forced to leave the cities of the coastal region began pouring into the city, the Jewish population swelled to many times its original size.

A wide variety of s*hiurim* were held every evening in the *beit midrash* next to the shul: there was a Talmud *shiur* on *masechet Sukkah*, a *Chumash shiur* on Bereishit with the commentary of Ramban, a Tanach *shiur* on the Book of Yeshayahu with the commentary of Rashi, and a *shiur* on *Avot D'Rabbi Natan*. On Thursdays, Rav Yosef Weinberg, may Hashem avenge his blood, who also served as the congregation's *chazzan*, delivered a *shiur* on *Chumash* with the commentary of Rashi. Few people attended this *shiur*, presumably because of the teacher's young age. Father expressed his displeasure over the *shiur*'s low attendance — he felt that it detracted from the honor of Rashi's memory. So from that time on Father and I began attending the *shiur* regularly. Rav Yosef Weinberg would first read each verse with Onkelos' Aramaic translation, and only then would he begin to analyze Rashi's comments.

Simchat Torah in Utrecht

Simchat Torah in Utrecht was a very beautiful occasion. The chazzan would first sing an age-old song called *"Asher Biglal Avot Banim Gidel,"* and then the entire congregation would join in and sing the traditional songs together. Dutch Jews did not dance in shul on Simchat Torah. Even Rav Tzadok Tal, *zt"l*, had not been very enthused when Father — shortly after our arrival in Utrecht, in the year 5695 (1934) — roused the young children to dance in shul during Simchat Torah. I remember Rav Tal running after us as we danced and lifting the *tzitzit* of our *taleisim* off the floor.

Acts of Lovingkindness and Torah Study

Around this time, two relatives of Rav Tal's wife — Max Lange and his sister, Roza, both of whom had been living in The Hague — joined the Tal household. Like us, they had been banished from

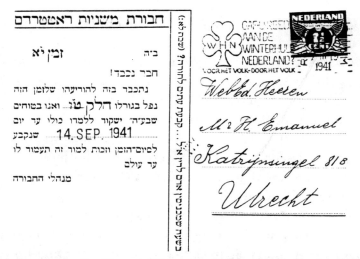

A notice sent by the Chevrat Mishnayot of Rotterdam informing Father and Elchanan which section of Mishnah they were to complete by September 14, 1941.

their homes and ordered to relocate further east. Max and Roza were both around twenty-five years of age. Both of them were hearing-impaired from birth, and they were painfully conscious of their limitations, although they were able to communicate with each other with great speed and dexterity through sign language. Both Max and Roza observed *mitzvot* scrupulously, and Max regularly attended prayer services in shul. My parents frequently invited them to join us at the Shabbat table.

Max noticed the extraordinary diligence with which Elchanan studied and taught Torah. One day, Max gestured to Elchanan that he too would like to learn Torah. Elchanan was willing to teach Max, but at first it seemed that it would not be possible for him to do so, since Max was profoundly deaf and dumb, and could understand nothing but sign language. However, Elchanan would not be deterred. He asked Max to lend him a handbook on sign language. A few days later, to Max's absolute delight, Elchanan delivered his first sign-language Torah *shiur.* Elchanan taught Max *Chumash*, and if my memory serves me correctly, Roza also occasionally joined

A recent picture of the beit midrash in Utrecht

them. The joy that Max derived from these *shiurim* is indescribable.

Through this extraordinary act of kindness, Elchanan taught us a priceless lesson in the true meaning of the words we utter every day in *Shemoneh Esrey*: "The Torah of life and a love of kindness, righteousness, blessing, compassion, life and peace."

Max and Roza perished in the gas chambers. May Hashem avenge their blood.

A letter written by my mother a few days after Rosh Hashanah of the year 5702 (1941), to her parents in Zurich:

. . . It was very beautiful in shul. Tuvia [Rav Tal's only son, may Hashem avenge his blood] blew the *shofar* wonderfully. We had good seats, and from our place in the women's section we were able to hear the boys' voices as they prayed. On Rosh Hashanah, Yona requested that the weekday *minyan* during the Ten Days of Repentance begin at six-thirty in the morning. On Tzom Gedaliah (a public

*The yellow star had to be worn at all times, even on one's wedding day,
as did Mr. Morris Kleerekooper and Ms. Berta Levy on their way to the
chuppah in The Hague. No one knows what became of them.*

fast day beginning on the morning after Rosh Hashanah) a
minyan was formed at six o'clock in the morning in order to
make it possible for Yona to attend. Because of a power out-
age, the men prayed by candle light. Yona went straight to
work after the *minyan*. When I met him at the streetcar stop
in the evening he told me that he did not feel weak from the
fast. He went directly to shul and remained in high spirits
for the rest of the evening.

We broke the fast with tomato soup, potatoes with gravy
made from real butter, apple compote and, of course, bread
and tea. The tailor who employs Shmuel commented to him,
"Moses did not make your lives easy." Shlomo is working,
but he is still not satisfied — he must perform numerous
tasks which are unrelated to his profession [electrician]. Nevertheless, he does not want to seek a different position so
long as the war continues. Elchanan's *shiurim* began on the
fast day. Only Baruch and Bella — and especially Shalom —

have no work with which to occupy themselves. Yesterday Shalom wanted to go with Yona to work. He said, "I want to work like a grownup!" Bitya is getting a little chubbier. She gets a dish of oatmeal cereal every morning. . . .

Sukkot 5702 (1941)

As Sukkot of 5702 approached, members of the congregation began deliberating whether it would be advisable to build a *sukkah* that year. They feared that such an act would incite attacks by the German authorities and local Nazi sympathizers.

Rav Tal was aware of these concerns. He addressed the issue in the course of his *Shabbat Shuvah* sermon and urged the members of the congregation not to neglect the mitzvah of living in a *sukkah*. He said, "King David uttered the prayer, 'Who can perceive inadvertent sins? Absolve me of hidden transgressions! Save Your servant also from deliberate sins; let them not dominate me. Then I shall be upright, and I shall remain clear of much transgression' (Tehillim 19:13–14). It stands to reason that King David's intent was not to pray that he be prevented from deliberately transgressing one of Hashem's *mitzvot*. Rather, his prayer was that he should never feel the need to allow difficult circumstances to influence him to consider himself exempt from the performance of any particular mitzvah." Rav Tal continued, "Know that even this year it is forbidden to eat outside of a *sukkah*! Build *sukkot* for yourselves, and no harm will come to you!"

Rav Tal's sermon proved effective, largely because of its urgent tone, which was completely out of character for him. He was an eloquent speaker, usually conveying his message with the utmost subtlety. His simple and straightforward words on this occasion hit their mark, as a number of families which had already determined not to build a *sukkah* changed their minds and decided to fulfill the mitzvah despite the possible danger.

In the end of the year 5702 (1942), in the month of Elul, Rav Tal was given an eviction notice and ordered to move to Amsterdam. He delivered his last sermon in shul on Shabbat *Parashat Ki Teitzei,* quoting a verse from the *haftarah:* "For a brief moment I abandoned you, but I will bring you back with great compassion" (Yeshayahu 54:7).

Ritual Slaughter Is Outlawed

Several months after the German invasion of the Netherlands, a law was passed stipulating that livestock must be stunned prior to being slaughtered. This law had been introduced in Germany a number of years earlier and had raised difficult halachic problems. When that law was extended to the Netherlands as well, local rabbinical authorities ruled that the meat of animals which had been stunned prior to being slaughtered was kosher.

We did not eat such meat. This halachic ruling greatly distressed Father, because he felt that it would make it even more difficult to reinstate proper ritual slaughter after the war. This was the first time we ever heard Father utter a word of criticism against the rabbinate of the Netherlands. He forbade us to reveal to anyone that we did not eat meat which had been slaughtered by the new method. At first we managed to obtain a chicken which had been slaughtered without having first been stunned, but after that we simply stopped eating meat.

A letter written by my father in Shevat of the year 5702 (1942) to my grandfather:

Dear Father,

Your explanations concerning the current *kashrut* situation are most interesting. I think it was a mistake on the part of the local rabbis to permit ritual slaughter according to the new method without first consulting other opinions. Furthermore, in the future it will be very difficult to reverse this lenient ruling. I am certain that this would never have happened had Rav Tuvia Lewenstein [rabbi of the Adat Yeshurun Congregation of Zurich] been consulted.

A letter written by my mother to the Samson Family of Copenhagen during that same year:

... The package arrived, and we are indeed very grateful to you. I would like to know whether the meat is kosher under the supervision of Rav Yakobson [i.e., that the animal was slaughtered without first having been stunned], that is to say, whether it is kosher according to all opinions. We await your response. The meat looks very appetizing. The boys are very happy, and they have already devoured half of it with their eyes.

Another letter concerning ritual slaughter, written by my mother:

January 1, 1942

... Dear Father, we must consider your suggestion that the older boys learn to slaughter chickens. Meanwhile, they lack not only the time and the opportunity, but also the chickens!

Kosher Milk

In addition to the lack of kosher meat, we began experiencing a severe shortage in the supply of kosher milk (*chalav Yisrael*, which requires that the milking procedure be supervised by a Jew). Although the rabbinate of the Netherlands permitted the consumption of the milk that was available, my parents decided that only the children under the age of bar mitzvah would be permitted to drink such milk. As a result, frequently there were foods of varying levels of *kashrut* upon our table.

For a while we managed to obtain kosher milk through one of the few Jewish families living in the small village of Tienhoven, which lay approximately ten kilometers from Utrecht. Father contacted one of the Jewish residents of the village, who in turn made arrangements for us to procure milk directly from a dairy farm owned by a gentile. They would inform us when the milking was scheduled to begin, and sometimes Shmuel and I would ride there by bicycle in order to observe the milking and transport the kosher milk home.

We always made sure to take a book of *mishnayot* with us on our trips to the farm, for we often had to wait quite some time until the gentile farmer would start to milk the cows. At such times, we would take out our *mishnayot* and learn while we waited. Shmuel and I thoroughly enjoyed our job of bringing the kosher milk home. We concealed the jugs of milk under our coats in order to avoid arousing the suspicion of the police. Milk occasionally splashed onto our coats and wet the cover of the book of *mishnayot* we carried with us, leaving white stains upon it. We managed to retrieve these books of *mishnayot* after the war. We brought them with us to Eretz Yisrael, and they remain in my possession to this day. The milk stains are still clearly visible.

Our milk runs came to a sudden end when the authorities forbade Jews to leave the city limits. Very little bread was rationed to us, so breakfast consisted of barley and oatmeal cereal, served with neither milk nor sugar. Our meager supplies were supplemented by a kindhearted, elderly Jewish gentleman named Mr. Alexander, may Hashem avenge his blood. He owned a noodle factory, and, because of his high regard for my father, he supplied us with more noodles than our ration card allowed. I went to his small factory many times to pick up the noodles. He always received me warmly and gave me a generous helping of his precious merchandise.

Father also arranged with a gentile store owner to exchange

our meat ration — for which we had no use — for extra portions of flour and noodles.

Aunt Malli

Aunt Malli, Father's sister, spent much of her time laboring in the kitchen in an attempt to prepare sufficient food for all the hungry members of our household. Considering the limited supplies at her disposal, she was blessed with a great measure of success. Aunt Malli had attended public school in her youth, as was the custom in those times, yet she was a profoundly God-fearing and righteous woman — a true *"Yiddishe mama,"* comparable to those of earlier generations. She would rise early every morning to pray, recite *tehillim* and utter heartfelt supplications. She would take every opportunity to encourage us to learn more Torah.

Aunt Malli used to visit the city hospital regularly in order to see to the needs of the Jewish patients. She never really mastered the Dutch language, but somehow she managed to surmise the patients' needs. Aunt Malli also took part in the ritual purification of the deceased. People in our community referred to her simply as "Aunt Malli."

Aunt Malli was still in Germany in Cheshvan of 5699 (1938) and witnessed the atrocities of *Kristallnacht*. Following this harrowing experience, Aunt Malli developed a profound fear of the Nazis. Whenever we would say something derogatory about the Germans, such as, "May their name be erased," she would immediately warn us to keep our voices low, saying, "Careful! The walls have ears!"

A letter from Grandfather on the occasion of Baruch's bar mitzvah, Parashat Naso, 5702 (1942):

May 5, 1942

Dear children,

As you know, I had very much wanted to be with you on the day of Baruch's bar mitzvah in order to share with all of you the celebration of this joyous occasion. However, as it appears that the peace for which we all yearn will not have become a reality by that date, I have no choice but to postpone my planned trip. I am with you in spirit, and I give my paternal blessing to each and every one of you.

To you, my precious Baruch, I send a special blessing. Your name itself symbolizes the blessing of peace [in Hebrew, "*baruch*" means "blessed"]. May the spirit of the person after whom you have been named [Rav Baruch Emanuel, *zt"l*, of Hamburg, my father's uncle, in whose home my father was raised from the time of his father's passing, when Father was only five years old] be always with you in all the paths of your life, and may it guard and protect you from all evil. May your family name — Emanuel [which in Hebrew means "God is with us"] — serve also as a shield to all of you. To the extent that you walk in the ways of God, so shall He be with you. "No weapon manufactured against you will succeed" (Yeshayahu 54:17), and all the forces that oppose you shall truly be defeated, for "God is with us" [*imanu-el*].

The priestly blessing appears in the weekly Torah portion that corresponds with the Shabbat of your bar mitzvah. I am sure that its meaning and significance will be discussed during the course of the Shabbat. In my mind's eye, my hands rest upon your head; may they bring Hashem's abundant blessings upon you.

It is written in the *parashah*, "May God show special consideration to you and establish peace for you" (Bemidbar 6:26). In *masechet Berachot* (20b) it is related that the Sages said in reference to this verse, "The ministering angels said before the Holy One, Blessed is He: 'It is written in

Your Torah, "God your Lord . . . gives no special consideration, nor does he take bribes" (Devarim 10:17), yet You give
special consideration to Israel, for it is written, "May God
show special consideration to you. . . ." ' God responded by
saying, 'Shall I not show Israel special consideration? I
wrote to them in the Torah, "When you eat and are satisfied, you must bless God your Lord . . ." (ibid. 8:10), yet
they are even more stringent upon themselves and [recite a
blessing] even [after eating a portion of bread] no more
than the volume of an olive or the volume of an egg.' "

In reference to this statement of the Sages, one of our
generation's greatest scholars asked the following question:
Why did the Sages say, "yet they are even more stringent
upon themselves"? Ostensibly, the word "themselves"
would seem to be superfluous.

This great Torah scholar answered his own question by
explaining that although it is certainly commendable to accept stringencies upon oneself, it is important to realize
that stringencies are liable to have negative repercussions if
they are applied to other situations as leniencies. For example, a leniency could theoretically be deduced from the
stringency of reciting a blessing after eating an olive's volume of bread — one could erroneously conclude that since
an olive's worth of bread qualifies as a meal, one is not obligated to give the poor any more than an olive's worth of
food. For this reason the Sages emphasize that "they are
stringent upon themselves" — indicating that this stringency may be applied only to oneself and may not be extended to other situations in which it may serve as the basis
for a lenient ruling.

In other words, a person may act stringently only towards himself, but never towards others. Be exacting with yourself, but towards others be very generous.

Adopt these principles as you progress through life, and then all three sections of the priestly blessing will be fulfilled for you. May Hashem bless you and protect you, and may earthly possessions bring you joy. May Hashem bless you in every place, and may you always remain blessed to God. May Hashem show special consideration to you, and "then may you find grace and good understanding in the eyes of God and man" (Mishlei 3:4).

And may Hashem bless you with the third portion of the blessing — "May God direct His providence toward you and grant you peace" (Bemidbar 6:26). May you have a life of peace, the life of a servant of God who bears the name "Baruch" with honor. May Hashem bless you in every place, wherever you will find yourself: "Wherever I allow My name to be mentioned, I will come to you and bless you" (Shemot 20:21).

Today you join the ranks of those who are obligated to observe God's Torah and to learn it. *Mazal tov!* Thus shall you bring joy to your precious parents, may they live long.

In spirit, I am very near to you indeed.

Kisses from one who loves you,
Grandfather

A letter from my father to my grandfather and grandmother, written after the bar mitzvah:

And so, the Shabbat of Baruch's bar mitzvah has passed. With a profound sense of gratitude, I can say that it was a most joyous day, permeated with a festive atmosphere. On Friday we went to the railroad station and welcomed the guests who came from Amsterdam and The Hague, and brought them home.

. . . After davening on Friday night, we sat down to partake of a meal together with all the guests. Even though we postponed the speeches until the morning meal because of the late hour, we still did not conclude the meal until around midnight. Dear father, the only item on the menu that would interest you is the lemon ice cream. We bentched with a *minyan*.

The Shabbat morning prayers began at eight-fifteen and concluded at approximately eleven o'clock; the chazzan sang a selection of special cantorial passages in honor of the occasion. Even the choir, which usually performs only on Festivals, gave a surprise presentation.

Baruch read the fifth *aliyah* wonderfully, thereby announcing before the entire congregation his willingness to accept upon himself the yoke of *mitzvot*. After the conclusion of the Torah reading, Rav Tal delivered a beautiful *derashah* in Baruch's honor. In the course of his sermon he mentioned that the inauguration of the Tabernacle was merely a preparation for the Holy Temple which would be constructed at a future date. In the same way, the day of a boy's bar mitzvah is to be looked upon as a preparation for the holiness that he will bring upon himself in ever-increasing measure with the passage of time.

A few of the guests and two of Baruch's friends were present at the morning meal. Baruch delivered a very beautiful *derashah* that Elchanan had prepared for him. One of Baruch's friends sang a rhyming song describing some of Baruch's antics. Afterwards we sang, and then Baruch led bentching.

Following the afternoon service, we held a reception in the Congregation building, which was attended by approximately a hundred and fifty invited guests. The children served the guests light refreshments, such as ersatz lemonade and cookies, on small tables. The reception continued until five o'clock in the afternoon, and at six o'clock we sat down to eat *seuda shelishit*. Some additional guests joined us for this meal: Rav and Mrs. Tal, Mr. and Mrs. De Haas and Mr. and Mrs. Yitzchak Lange. Numerous speeches were delivered during *seuda shelishit*.

After delivering my own speech, I read aloud your letter, dear Father. We could feel your participation in our hour of joy, and everyone listened attentively to the words of inspiration that you addressed to Baruch. We drank a *"l'chayim"* to you, our dear parents. Rav Tal then delivered his speech.

At the end of the meal Baruch made a *siyum* [the ceremony conducted upon finishing a tractate of Talmud or an order of Mishnah]. His teacher, Yitzchak Lange, interjected with a number of questions, which Baruch answered satisfactorily. Bella then read a delightful rhyme composed by Elchanan in honor of the occasion. It humorously described all of Baruch's many pranks in the course of a single day.

... The celebration concluded with the children's presentation of a play written jointly by Elchanan and Shlomo entitled, "Baruch: Twenty Years from Now." It featured a scene in which Baruch reprimands his children and, in all seriousness, informs them that when he was young, he was much more well behaved and calm than they are. At that very moment Elchanan arrives at Baruch's home for a visit and begins reminiscing over the beautiful bar mitzvah celebration which was held in Baruch's honor so many years earlier, which took place on the very last Shabbat before the end of the Second World War (as you can see, the children are hopeful that the war will end soon).

Rav Tal led bentching, and Baruch, *Ma'ariv*. This most enjoyable celebration came to a close with the recitation of *Havdalah*. The guests left in uplifted spirits, hoping that they would be able to retain their warm memories of this special occasion during the coming days, and that we would soon meet again to celebrate other joyous occasions.

A letter from my mother to my grandparents following the bar mitzvah:

June 22, 1942

Dear Parents,

Dear Mother, your postcard confirming receipt of our letter in which we described the bar mitzvah arrived after only six days! I understand that the letter Mordechai sent you likewise arrived quickly, after only seven days. This proves that letters written in only one language [German] arrive more quickly than those which have to be checked by a German-speaking censor, followed by a French-speaking censor, and then perhaps requiring the inspection of a Jew. In short, it is preferable to write in only one language.

. . . I took little Bitya for a walk today. On the way, a German soldier looked at her and commented on her beautiful blue eyes. Bitya does not yet need to wear the yellow star, since she is not yet six. Shalom is excitedly waiting for the day when he will begin wearing it.

Chapter Six
The Deportations Begin

The Germans initiated the large-scale deportation of Dutch Jews to concentration camps in the spring of 5702 (1942). At first the Jews were transported to camps in the Netherlands, but later on they were taken to points further east, in Poland. I began to study the Book of Yirmeyahu during this period; its content resonated very well with the events unfolding before us.

After the deportations began, just before Tishah B'Av of 5702 (1942), Shmuel and I went into hiding in the home of a gentile who lived in the suburbs of Utrecht. We worked in a vegetable garden in the mornings, and at night we would occasionally listen to the Free Holland radio news broadcast. We cooked our own kosher meals, which consisted of almost nothing but vegetables, in two pots which we had brought with us from home. We also had with us a *siddur, tallit, tefillin* and a *Chumash* from home.

Although we had attended public school and worked in a factory, and so were accustomed to being in the company of gentiles, this was the first time we had ever lived among them around the clock. We were therefore very glad to receive a message from Elchanan on the week of *Parashat Devarim*. Typically, it was a quiz on the *parashah*. One of the more subtle questions he asked was "A specific comment of Rashi on this *parashah* indicates that the *sefer Torah* from which he read was different from our own. Find the comment that I

The "Jewish Quarter" in German-occupied Amsterdam

am referring to." We were surprised by the nature of the question, but in the end we found the answer. In our editions the Hebrew word for "I will appoint them" (Devarim 1:13) — *"va'asimem"* — is spelled with a *yod*, yet in Rashi's commentary, the *yod* is omitted.

Approximately two weeks later, the arrests and deportations were temporarily discontinued, so we returned home and I resumed my work at the machine shop. The plant manager was a very decent man who was sympathetic to the plight of the Jews. During one of our conversations, I casually mentioned to him that because of my religion, I was no longer permitted to attend evening classes at the technical college where I had enrolled. He responded by giving me private lessons in mechanics, physics and technical drafting during work hours. These lessons came to an abrupt halt when one of the workers, who was affiliated with the Dutch Nazi Party, informed the authorities of the plant manager's behavior. Although he could no longer risk teaching me, the manager's sympathy did not wane. Some time later, when the deportations to Poland were reinstituted, he provided temporary shelter to my sister Bella. He also lent my father a large sum of money at a very crucial point in our lives.

On especially dangerous nights, Father — and sometimes even Elchanan and Shlomo — went into hiding in the home of the Bosch family. These devout Christians helped us at considerable personal risk. Mr. Bosch held my father in great regard; he most respected him for his piety and faith in God. Father would often knock on their door at a late hour, so he and Mr. Bosch devised a password between them: "My God is your God" (see Ruth 1:15). As soon as either Mr. Bosch or one of his older sons would hear these words, he would swing open the door and swiftly lead my father to his hiding place.

The Bosch family also assisted us when the Nazis forbade Jews to purchase provisions in food stores. They generously supplied us with a variety of goods, including eggs, which were a very valuable food staple in those days. We must never forget the courageous and noble acts of the righteous gentiles of that time.

Eventually we lost touch with the Bosch family and did not hear from them again until many years later. Thanks to the efforts

For most victims, this is how the excruciating journey began.

of one of Mr. Bosch's sons, Henk Bosch, we have today renewed contact with each other. Despite the decades that have passed since the war, Henk still corresponds with us, and often in his letters reflects on those difficult years.

A letter from my mother to my grandparents:

August 8, 1942

Dear Parents,

Today Yona told Shalom about Ya'akov and Esav. Shalom asked Yona whether Ya'akov also wore a yellow star. When Yona answered in the negative, Shalom exclaimed, "Oh no! That means Ya'akov wasn't Jewish!" As you can see, the yellow star has made a big impression on him.

Margarit Lebreicht [Mother's cousin from England; a

code name for the Allied planes that flew bombing raids over Germany] is once again acting very listlessly [the bombing raids have tapered off]. She was feeling better for a while. We would very much like to see her at our home [i.e., in the air on their way to Germany] more often.

Love,
Chana

A letter from my mother to her sister Susanne in Zurich:

August 12, 1942

A girl wearing her yellow star, born in Munich, later murdered in Riga, may Hashem avenge her blood

Dear Susanne,

A letter from Father and Mother arrived this evening, posted on the day before they were to leave on their vacation. I hope they will enjoy themselves. They will be able to do so only if they can somehow manage not to think about us. I hope that you and the girls will make the most of the vacation and go on some nice outings. Do the girls know how to swim? Do you allow them to swim by themselves? I would love to climb Mount Utli with my children sometime, but they are not sportsmen at heart; they would much rather sit and learn.

Elchanan learns every night with Shlomo and Yona. It is very good for them to learn together after their long day at work. Baruch has a *shiur* every day with Yochi Lange, and in the afternoons he attends a children's activity group supervised by one of the teachers from the orphanage.

. . . You cannot imagine what is happening here. Three days ago I. G. Lange recited the blessing, "Who bestows good things upon the guilty . . . ." [the blessing recited by one who has survived a dangerous situation]. I hope that they are still in good health today. There is no difference between night and day. . . . Yesterday, Uncle Gottfried [Grandfather's brother; he and his wife were later killed in Bergen-Belsen] and his family were fine. We have still not heard from them today. . . .

. . . Otherwise, we are in good health, and Mordechai even remains optimistic. The children are in good spirits; that is to say, Yona leaves home at a quarter to seven every morning and is happy when he returns at six in the evening and finds us all still here.
Kisses to the children.

Love,
Chana

A letter from my mother to her sister Susanne in Zurich:

August 13, 1942

Dear Susanne,

I sent a letter to you yesterday; since then, nothing unusual has occurred. I hope that everything is well with you and that our dear parents are enjoying their vacation. Today we attended a wedding — imagine that! From there we traveled into town (we are permitted to enter the city between three and five o'clock in the afternoon), and we even

returned home carrying a load of vegetables. Our neighbors are having a bar mitzvah this Shabbat, and they have
somehow managed to prepare an apple cake for the bar
mitzvah boy.

Each of the children manages to bring something
home before Shabbat. Shmuel, with his extraordinary
charm, brought home a red cabbage and green beans.
[Aunt] Malli and I derive much satisfaction when everyone
rises from the table satiated. Mordechai expends a great
deal of energy to achieve this, but he does it with much enthusiasm — no effort is too great for him.

. . . We wrote over ten days ago, and perhaps we will
now receive the thing that we have requested. If not, you
may inherit my wigs, for they shave everyone's head in that
place. All religious articles must be left behind. Can you
imagine Elchanan, Shlomo, Yona, Shmuel and Baruch
without their *tefillin*?

. . . Another transport is due to leave tonight.

(Author's note: This letter was written in code. "The thing that
we have requested" is an allusion to my parents' urgent plea to our
Swiss relatives to obtain a passport for our entire family from any
neutral South American country. By presenting such a document,
one could postpone the deportation of one's family for an indefi-
nite period of time. My parents had sent our Swiss relatives the required documents with a complete set of photos, and we anxiously
awaited the moment when the life-saving passport would reach us.
After immense efforts, our relatives in Switzerland managed to obtain the passport and send it to us in time.

In her letter my mother refers to the passport as "the family
picture." All of my parents' letters allude to our condition. The Nazis strictly prohibited sending correspondence containing reports

of the inhumane treatment to which we were subjected.

In this letter, my mother expressed her concern that her sons would not be able to don *tefillin* in the camps. Her prayer was an-

Chalked up on the closed cattle-car doors: "74 people." May Hashem avenge their blood.

swered, for their *tefillin* were the *only* objects which her surviving sons were able to safeguard and bring back with them from the camps. My mother also mentions her wigs — she was extremely meticulous about keeping her head covered throughout her stay in the camps, despite the fact that all of the prisoners were infested with lice, which forced the large majority of women to remove their head coverings.)

A postcard from my mother to Uncle Theo in Zurich:

October 28, 1942

Dear Theo,

Theo, even little Bitya recognizes your name when I tell her about our relatives living in Zurich. Shalom was very moved when I read him your letter, in which you mention that all of you are awaiting our arrival. He is anxious to make the trip, but it seems that he will have to learn to be patient a while longer. With the help of God, he will not be forced to travel to a different place. Elizabeth [Aenchen's sister] writes that 1,900 individuals have traveled from the camp eastward. In the course of the transport from Rotterdam to the camp, a three-hour journey by railway, three infants were born. Oh, the poor mothers!

In her letter to me, Mother asks whether Mrs. Slagter's father will also be sent to the camps, being that he is eighty-six years of age. I ask, "And why not?"

A letter from my father to my grandparents:

February 14, 1943

The enclosed letter from Elchanan was written on Friday. Since then, a pleasant Shabbat has elapsed. Davening began at eight-fifteen and concluded around ten-thirty. We invited Mr. and Mrs. Onderwijzer to our home for the morning meal, since they have a long distance to walk home from shul. Elchanan and Shlomo attended the Gemara *shiur* in the home of Mr. De Haas, which began at twelve-fifteen. (Yona and Shmuel were involved in learning something else at the time.) We recited *Minchah* at one-fifteen, and then there was a joint *shiur* on *Orach Chaim* from quarter-to-two until quarter-to-three. From quarter-to-three until quarter-to-four I delivered a *shiur* on *Chumash* with *Rashi* to a few boys, among them Baruch. We ate from four o'clock until four-thirty, and then the boys went off to an *oneg Shabbat* until six-thirty at night.

The *oneg Shabbat* activity stimulates the boys, but also

irritates them, for they often hear viewpoints there which are incongruous with their own set of values. This gives them an opportunity to contend with different attitudes towards life, and to strive for a deeper understanding of our traditional sources. To their great fortune they manage to forget completely the difficulties we are experiencing, and in general, they adjust to all the difficulties much more quickly than do their elders. They are very fortunate indeed.

A letter from my mother concerning the same Shabbat:

All the *shiurim* are continuing, and the boys often carry on lively discussions concerning values and principles of faith. The *oneg Shabbat* group met yesterday, and Elchanan and Shlomo were forced to "crack a few hard nuts" to ensure that the activities were carried out in a manner which would be satisfactory to all of the participants. Most of the youths who participated were from non-religious Zionist backgrounds, but they did have a lot in common — the youngsters were all Elchanan's age, and they all shared an interest in Judaism.

In the end they transferred the leadership of the *oneg Shabbat* group to Elchanan. As you might have expected, he delivered a *derashah* before the sixteen or so participants. Apparently, Elchanan's lecture was very good — although he himself was not satisfied with it, his brothers were, and, as you know, they can be rather critical.

. . . In his *derashah* Elchanan called on everyone to observe Shabbat, and he ended with the statement, "If not now, when?"

When the house is heated well, our thoughts turn to

the suffering and tortured souls who are forced to perform
back-breaking labor in the cold and the rain; we also think
of you, who enjoy the good fortune of living in tranquility
and lending a helping hand to those in need.

A letter from my mother to my grandparents in Zurich:

Shevat 5703 (1943)

Dear Parents,

It is now Tuesday night, and already eight days have
passed since our dear ones — Naftali [Abrahams], his wife
and their seven children — were driven out of their home.
Efforts have been made [to have them released], but so far, to
no avail. The mistake was made by the one [in the Jewish
committee] in charge of Naftali, who told the authorities that
Naftali is dispensable. Now we are hoping that Aunt Para [an
allusion to the Paraguayan passport that our Swiss relatives
were arranging for us] will help. If you should happen to see
any members of the family, please inform them that they can
also be of assistance. A telegram will not be of any help.

Mordechai manifests his concern in a most commendable manner, and everyone is amazed at how he manages to
obtain so much. As long as it is possible to continue sending
packages, you can be certain that our precious ones lack
nothing.

. . . Today is your birthday, dear father. Rest assured that
you have done everything in your power on behalf of your
children. With the help of Hashem, everything will continue
to be well.

Kisses to all,
Chana

The situation became so perilous that I stopped going to work, for I feared that one day I would return home and find a bolted door and an empty house.

We devoted part of each day to Torah learning, but the tension became so great that we found it difficult to concentrate. New rumors were circulating every few minutes.

Father succeeded in obtaining food for all of us, as well as for those members of the Abrahams family who were still being held in the Westerbork camp. He sent them a package of food every single day, without fail. In order to obtain food, Father would sometimes hold a parcel such that it would cover his yellow star, and would daringly enter the wholesale market, where he gave the impression that he was a store owner shopping for merchandise. I sometimes accompanied Father on these buying excursions. Immediately upon our return, both my parents would prepare and send the daily food package to the Abrahams family.

In the morning you will say, "If only it were night,"

and in the evening you will say, "If only it were morning."

(Devarim 28:67)

The Makeshift Storage Room

Our house contained an unusually large collection of *sifrei kodesh*. All five older boys had received *sefarim* for bar mitzvah presents, and Father had an extensive collection of his own, which included numerous sets of full-sized tomes: a *Vilna Shas*, Mishnah, *Malbim* on the Torah and *Nach*, Rav Hirsch's commentary on the Torah, Rav David Tzvi Hoffman's commentary on Vayikra and Devarim (Rav Hoffman was Father's uncle), *Shulchan Aruch "Maginei Eretz,"* and a variety of *Chumashim* and *machzorim*.

At some point during the winter of 5703 (1943), we came to terms with the fact that our chances of evading deportation to the camps were very slim. Once this idea sank in, we began desperately thinking of ways to somehow save our precious *sefarim*. We lived at the time in an apartment on the top floor of a multi-storied building, so our choices were limited. The floor in one of the bedrooms showed the most promise — under the linoleum covering and floorboards, we discovered a hollow about forty centimeters high that ran along the entire length and width of the room. We decided that our best option would be to conceal all of our books in this hollow. It seemed highly unlikely that the Nazis would tear out the floorboards in their search for hidden valuables.

There were other alternatives which we did not even consider, such as sneaking the books out of the apartment under cover of darkness. A few months earlier we had volunteered to move hundreds of *sefarim* from the home of the chief rabbi, Rav Tzadok Tal, *zt"l*, to the house of a gentile who offered to store his books until the end of the war. We performed this operation in the middle of the night, transporting the books to their destination on our snow sled at great personal risk. The intense fear that gripped our hearts throughout this operation was still fresh in our minds, and we had no desire to endanger our lives in such a manner again.

And so, after a good few hours of back-breaking labor, we succeeded in hiding all of the *sefarim* that we had in the house under the floorboards. Not wanting to be left without any *sefarim* whatsoever, we kept out a few for our own use — tractates *Pesachim* and *Bava Kama*, which we were studying at the time, and a few *Chumashim* and High Holiday *machzorim* and books of *Selichot*.

It was a difficult occasion for all of us. What would happen to the *sefarim*? More importantly, what would become of us? Would we ever again merit to study from these books, which we had received as bar mitzvah gifts just a few years earlier? We did not dare give expression to the somber thoughts that passed through our minds. However, there was an unspoken agreement between all of us: any family member who would survive the war had an obliga-

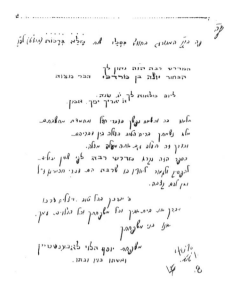

One of the books I got for my bar mitzvah, with good wishes from my uncle Josef Lowenstein

tion to return to this apartment and retrieve our precious *sefarim*.

It was my brother Shmuel who finally performed this task. Following his release from Bergen-Belsen, after convalescing in a hospital in the city of Nymegen, Shmuel returned to Utrecht and went directly to our old apartment. He knocked on the door and matter-of-factly explained to the tenants living there at the time that he had come to retrieve his family's treasure hidden under the floorboards. Single-handedly — and to the tenants' utter dismay — Shmuel tore up the wooden floor and began carrying the heavy loads of *sefarim* down the three flights of stairs. Alas, despite Shmuel's enthusiasm, this formidable task proved too much for him — he suffered a regression and was bedridden for several more months; but the honor of retrieving the *sefarim* remained his!

A letter from my mother to my grandparents in Zurich:

March 14, 1943

Dear Parents,

Elchanan is writing letters to the children who were in the local orphanage, and who are by now in the camp. He writes exclusively about Jewish topics.

This week, a young rabbi who lived here moved away to Amsterdam. The congregation approached Elchanan and requested of him to deliver Torah *shiurim* to the children in the rabbi's place.

Elchanan is now delivering the *shiurim*, but he refuses to accept payment in exchange for Torah study. He would not hear of it. I suggested to him that he accept the money and that we use it to send half a kilo of butter every month to the Abrahams family in Westerbork.

Love,
Chana

A letter from my mother to my grandparents in Zurich:

Purim 5703 (1943)

Dear Father and Mother:

. . . Mordechai is now rearranging the chairs around the large table. Aunt Malli is going upstairs to rest for a while, and I, after finding the bedrooms in such a state that they require at least an hour of steady work to put them in order, have decided to leave the mess for tomorrow. As I see it, it cannot get any worse, and I would prefer to converse with you now for a little while. We extended the table to twice its length in the guest room for the fourteen of us, in-

cluding Mrs. Seckbach and Miss Heineman, who joined us
for the meal.

It is now eight o'clock. "Man makes plans but Hashem
decides." Instead of the short respite we were hoping to enjoy, Shalom and Bitya have returned from their outing after only five minutes, with another four children in tow.

We sat together eating the meal from five until seven-
fifteen. The table was set resplendently, and the menu consisted of a can of salmon (the last of those which we brought
from Rotterdam) divided into fourteen servings, accompanied by vegetables, potatoes, mayonnaise (thanks to the pow-
dered eggs we received from you), soup with dumplings, a
plate of black carrots, and to top it all off — cold cuts with potato salad. . . . We had cake for dessert, a contribution from
Mrs. Seckbach. The boys even managed to procure four bot-
tles of beer. Of course, there was much singing throughout
the meal. Bitya was acting very sweetly, but Shalom was a
little tired.

It is now eight-thirty in the evening, and Elchanan is
sitting together with his two students, Shlomo and Yona.
They were so busy with their celebrating of Purim throughout the day that they did not manage to meet their daily
study quota, so they are working to make up for it now. Elchanan must be very tired, for he read the entire *Megillah*
for me, and then afterwards he read four chapters in a very
comical way before the younger children, and then spoke
before the entire group at length.

In the morning I obviously did not attend my first-aid
course in the Congregation building, but Shmuel dressed
up as a woman and Bella as a nurse. "Mrs." Shmuel decided
to put on a good show. "She" swooned and was rushed into

the room where the first-aid course was taking place for "emergency treatment." It seems that Shmuel played his part very well, for his performance caused all those attending the course to become genuinely agitated and concerned. They concluded that "the young lady" must have arrived straight from the Westerbork camp, and that "she" must be very hungry, so they collected thirty-five gulden from the participants and transferred the sum to the Jewish Committee. The "show" was very successful, and the members of the Jewish Committee remarked that the Emanuel family were not such failures after all, despite their "black" outlook on life!

In short, despite everything, it was a very pleasant Purim. If Pesach will also pass peacefully, as did this Purim, we will have another reason to thank the Creator.

Love,
Chana

A letter from my father to my grandparents describing the same Purim:

The week has ended, and my first activity is to write to you. After Alex [De Haas] delivered a *shiur* in our home this afternoon, we recited *Ma'ariv* with a *minyan*. Elchanan read the *Megillah* most impressively, bringing tears to Chana's eyes. Tomorrow morning we will begin davening at seven-thirty. Elchanan will read the *Megillah* to Chana at home and, thereafter, to Mr. Eisenberger, who is bedridden and unable to leave his home.

. . . As I close this letter, Purim has passed and Chana has already written to you all the news. It was a most pleasant day, and the children truly enjoyed themselves.

Yona, Shlomo, Shmuel, Baruch, Shalom and Bitya, wearing traditional Dutch clogs in Utrecht, winter 1941

Even though 5703 (1943) was a leap year (when an additional month is added before Pesach), Pesach was fast approaching. Due to the tense situation, it was almost impossible to prepare for the Festival. The Germans intensified the rate of deportations to such an extent that Dutch Jewry stood on the brink of almost complete annihilation. Although our family's deportation was deferred, thanks to the Paraguayan passport that had finally arrived from our relatives in Switzerland, we knew we could not rely on this temporary deferral indefinitely.

In the following letter to her parents in Zurich, my mother hints at the increasing rate of deportations and alludes to the fact that we had made plans to escape and go into hiding.

April 12, 1943

Dear Parents,

It is now one-thirty in the morning, and everyone in the house is awake, with the exception of Shalom and Bitya, who are sleeping soundly, *baruch Hashem*. Mordechai experienced another attack today. It began in the afternoon; that is to say, we saw it coming, but the "ambulance" [the vehicles in which the Germans transported the detained Jews] passed. We have made all the preparations necessary for a long stay in "the hospital" [concentration camp].

It seems that, for the moment, the attack has passed, but we do not have sufficient peace of mind to allow us to sleep. Mordechai was calm as always; his wife, less so, but the children were wonderful. The general feeling is that it will happen again. The doctor suggests that we move to a different location. If everything works out, we will be moving four days before Pesach. It seems that Alex [De Haas] is also moving. He is also suffering greatly from asthma. [He is in danger as well.]

Thank you very much for your constant concern for our welfare. We have just enjoyed a good cup of coffee. I hope they will transfer our mail to our new address.

. . . Enjoy the holidays. I hope we will as well.

Love,
Chana

The Saving of Two Lives

Miss Heineman lived near us on a street adjacent to our house. She was an unmarried middle-aged woman who had arrived in the Netherlands from Frankfurt on the eve of the German invasion. She, along with her younger sister, had booked passage on a ship due to set sail for the United States the very next morning. However, the German bombardment brought their plans to an abrupt halt. Like many refugees from various countries who thought they had succeeded in evading the Nazis, Miss Heineman and her sister found themselves trapped after almost having savored the sweet taste of freedom. In Holland, Miss Heineman's sister married a widowed man named Reb Mordechai Seckbach. The two sisters frequently came to visit us.

The day finally came when Miss Heineman and her sister re-

On the way to the death camps — children with blankets . . . and toys

ceived the dreaded deportation notice, which meant that they were headed for the camps. They came to us in tears and told our parents that they would have to appear at the train station at seven o'clock the next morning. The parting was emotionally wrenching and very painful.

My mother lay awake all through the night trying to think of a way to save the two poor women. Then, just before dawn, Mother rose suddenly, in a state of great agitation. Ignoring the curfew which prohibited Jews from stepping outside their homes from eight o'clock at night until six o'clock in the morning, she ran to Miss Heineman's apartment and began wildly pounding on the door. She burst into the apartment screaming at the top of her lungs. Miss Heineman and her sister were wide awake, two impassive figures sitting among their packs, waiting to embark upon their journey. They, too, had not slept the entire night.

Screaming hysterically the entire time, Mother headed for the kitchen and opened the gas valve, and then ordered the two bewildered women to scream and cry as loud as they could. Failing to understand my mother, they became frightened and hysterical themselves. Meanwhile, a strong smell of gas had spread throughout the apartment. The loud sounds of the three crying women awoke the neighbors. At this point my mother picked up the telephone and alerted the first-aid station that a tenant in the building had attempted to commit suicide, and that assistance was urgently required. Mother neglected to mention that the "victims" were two Jewish women who were due to be deported that very morning. When she hung up the phone, Mother made the sisters scream even louder. By the time the ambulance arrived, they were in a state of complete hysteria, screaming and crying at the same time.

My mother pointed to the two disheveled women and explained to the ambulance team that they had attempted to commit suicide. The sisters' hysterical condition, coupled with the strong stench of gas in the house, convinced the medics that this was indeed a suicide attempt, and so they transported Miss Heineman and her sister to the nearest hospital. During the few days they lay recuperating in the hospital, my parents found the sisters a hiding place, where they remained for more than two years, until the end of the war.

Following the war, Shmuel lived in the Heineman sisters' home in Utrecht from the time of his release from the camps until he left for Eretz Yisrael. We stayed in touch even after the sisters emigrated to the United States. A few years later they came to visit us in Eretz Yisrael despite their advanced age, and they were our guests for the Seder night and throughout the Pesach holidays. They were very happy to see us and were moved to see that we had merited to establish our own families.

A postcard from my father to a friend in Switzerland:

Utrecht, April 15, 1943

Dear Friend,

I intended to write to you earlier, but I had much work to do. On Monday we received a permit to move to Amsterdam, and we were given only until today to move. We even found a comfortable apartment to rent, but yesterday we received a notice stating that the permit has been revoked. Now, like everyone else, we have been given until the twenty-third of April to report to the Fucht concentration camp.

Mordechai and his family send their warm regards. They will be traveling and will no longer be able to write. [By this, Father meant that we would all be going into hiding.]

In the same postcard my mother added the following message:

Yes, our fate is the same as that of many others. We hope to see you again in better times. Excuse our [unsteady] handwriting. In these times, it is not possible to do better. [Their handwriting was unsteady due to the intense fear that gripped their hearts.]

My parents were faced with a critical decision: whether to obey the German order and report to the camp, or to attempt to flee and go into hiding. Both alternatives were equally dangerous, but the large size of our family made matters even more difficult. Was it at all feasible for a family of eleven to escape? Where would we go?

Chapter Seven
Going into Hiding

The sound of a rustling leaf will pursue them.

(Vayikra 26:36)

(By Shmuel)

When the mass arrests and deportations to unknown destinations in Eastern Europe began, many Dutch Jews began exploring the possibility of going into hiding in the homes of gentiles. This option was colloquially dubbed "diving." It became the principal objective in the lives of Dutch Jewry. Those Jews fortunate enough to find shelter with non-Jews were referred to as "divers."

Diving was frought with danger, both for the Jewish fugitives and for their gentile hosts. The most ideal environment for "safe diving" was the Dutch countryside — the Gestapo was much too busy with its demonic work in the major population centers to spare the time and manpower necessary to patrol the sparsely populated hamlets and villages of the Netherlands. However, with a family the size of ours (our parents, eight children and Aunt Malli), our chances of finding a secure communal hiding place seemed slim indeed. Nevertheless, despite the logistical difficulties, Father and Mother seriously began to consider the offer of a non-Jewish acquaintance named Rijkse. In the winter of 1943 he informed my parents that he was willing to hide our entire family.

Mr. Rijkse was a carpenter whom we had come to know when we contracted him to build our *sukkah* the previous year. Mr. Rijkse seemed like an honest and reliable man, who also happened to have contacts in the Dutch underground. Father used to hide in Mr. Rijkse's house from as early as 1942. Whenever rumors spread that the Germans were planning another wave of mass arrests (in Dutch, "*razia*") of Jewish males, Father would flee to Mr. Rijkse's home and wait there for the storm to pass. Elchanan and Shlomo evaded the mass arrests by hiding in the homes of some non-Jewish school friends.

In the spring of 5703 (1943), it became evident that the Germans were on the verge of launching a massive campaign to annihilate the last vestiges of Dutch Jewry. My parents decided that the time had come to go into hiding, despite the danger this entailed, and despite their awareness of the fact that this would force the family to split up.

We fled under cover of darkness a few days before Pesach of 5703 (1943) and met up with Mr. Rijkse, who swiftly led us to the various hiding places he had prepared for us. Both my parents and Shalom stayed with the Rijkse family, while little Bitya was taken in by a childless couple living in Aalfen Aan De Rijn, a tiny village located approximately ten kilometers from Utrecht. The rest of us — Aunt Malli and the six older children — were taken to the attic of the school in which Mr. Rijkse worked as a janitor. We brought along a few cooking utensils which Aunt Malli used to prepare food for us. We also brought along a few pots that were kosher for Pesach and a package of matzah left over from the year before. Mr. Rijkse brought us a steady supply of food; during Pesach he brought us vegetables and potatoes. It was a very difficult and complicated campaign that he had undertaken!

Living conditions in the attic were extremely difficult. We had to remain prone on mattresses throughout the day and speak only in whispers in order to prevent the students in the classrooms beneath us from becoming aware of our presence. We managed to learn a great deal of Torah during this period. Each of us learned independently during the day; then, as soon as the students left the school for the day, we reviewed the material together. We studied *masechet Bava Kama* (*Perek Merubah*) and *Chumash* with *Rashi*. We also whiled away the long hours of the day with another quiet activity — playing chess.

Once, shortly after we had moved in, we were nearly para-

The attic in which we hid, 94 Nieuwe Gracht, Utrecht

lyzed with fear when we heard the sound of some students' footsteps running up the wooden ladder which led up to our attic. Thanks to Shlomo's physical strength, we managed to block the door with a heavy crate and narrowly avoided being discovered.

Another time we awoke in the middle of the night to the terrifying sound of someone yelling and banging next to the school's main door. We had no doubt in our minds that it was the Germans; somehow, we were sure, they must have found out about our hiding place. Carefully, we looked through the window and when we understood what was happening, we breathed a sigh of relief. Apparently someone had left a light on in one of the classrooms which faced the street in front of the school, in violation of the strict blackout imposed upon the town by the military authorities. Members of a civil-defense patrol had discovered the infraction and were attempting to enter the building.

We were in a quandary over what to do. If the light remained lit, the police would almost certainly be summoned, and they would break into the school building and possibly carry out a search in order to apprehend the culprit who had violated the blackout. On the other hand, if we would turn off the light, the police would realize that someone was living in the school, which might prompt them to return in the morning to question the principal and launch a full-scale investigation.

Once again, Shlomo saved the day. He ventured out of the attic, located the school's main electric panel and shorted the wires, plunging the street into absolute darkness. He reasoned that if the police would return in the morning to investigate, the janitor — Mr. Rijkse — could prove to them that an electrical short had occurred in the school's main circuit and could thereby dispel their suspicions.

The most dangerous aspect of our hideaway was its location. To the left of the school building where we were living was the Jewish Orphanage, which now housed a German army unit, and to our right was the building which now served as the regional headquarters of the Gestapo.

One warm spring day we were shocked to learn that German soldiers were sunbathing on the school's roof, directly above our heads. As they casually passed by the attic windows on their way to and from the roof, it became evident to us that it was just a matter of time until our hideaway would be discovered. We were in grave danger.

The simple meaning of the curse, "The sound of a rustling leaf will pursue them" (Vayikra 26:36), is that the Jews will be pursued, and they will live in constant fear of their enemies. Hence, even the sound of a rustling leaf will fill their hearts with dread, for it may be a signal that their pursuers are near. Yet the tension and fear that we experienced in those days was much worse — we lived in constant fear that we might be the source of "the sound of a rustling leaf," thereby giving ourselves away to our enemies, who were located no more than a few inches away.

It is difficult to describe the horrors experienced by the Jews in the concentration camps, but it is no easier to convey the burden of constant dread and fear experienced by the Jews who concealed themselves in a large variety of hideouts in an attempt to save their own lives. Some individuals cowered in perpetual fear for an entire year or two in a sealed room, without stepping out even once. Many fled from one hiding place to another; some poor souls hid in ten or more hiding places, only to be caught and sent to the ovens in the end.

Even after reading some of the works, such as *The Diary of Anne Frank*, which describe the horrors experienced by the Jews who went into hiding, one cannot fully understand the overwhelming terror of the curse, "The sound of a rustling leaf will pursue them." As Rashi comments on this verse, "Fear will grip their hearts, and at all times they will have the impression that someone is pursuing them." Numerous Jews were not able to endure the tension — many broke down, left their hiding places and turned themselves over to the police. Others simply lost their minds.

Despite the perpetual tension we experienced, we made a concerted effort to carry on some sort of "normal" routine, and to make the most of the situation. On Seder night of the Pesach of 5703 (1943), we sat next to the window and read the Haggadah by moonlight. Elchanan led the Seder on the first night of Pesach, and

Shlomo led it on the second night. The main course of the night was potatoes, which we ate along with last year's leftover matzah.

Tziporah Gutman, one of Aunt Malli's daughters, joined us in the attic for that Pesach. She was a member of Agudath Yisrael Youth Group's *hachsharah* program in the city of Enschede, which prepared youths to contend with the rigors of traveling to and settling in Eretz Yisrael. Aunt Malli was extremely happy over Tziporah's unexpected visit. After Pesach, Tziporah returned to her hideaway somewhere in the north of the country. She was later caught by the Germans and sent to one of the concentration camps, where she was killed. May Hashem avenge her blood.

In spite of the terrible conditions in which we lived, we tried to fulfill as many *mitzvot* as possible. Elchanan decided, for example, that if he could not fulfill the mitzvah of honoring the Festival with fine food and drink, then at least he would honor it by wearing a fresh set of clothes.

Following the conclusion of Pesach, I suggested that we save our leftover matzah for next year, for who knew how long the war would continue? Elchanan, however, was of the opinion that this was not necessary. We followed his opinion, and we ate the remainder of the matzah.

After spending approximately a month in the attic, Mr. Rijkse informed us that we would be moving to a different hideaway. He felt that the Germans were bound to discover us, and that it was a greater risk to stay where we were than to move to another location. The new hideaway was too small to accommodate all of us, so it was decided that I would join my parents and Shalom in the Rijkses' home. Aunt Malli, Bella and my brothers would stay in the new shelter, which was located a short distance away.

We lived in a room in the second story of the Rijkses' house. Fortunately, my mother had the facilities necessary to cook kosher meals. Obviously, we did not eat our meals downstairs with our hosts, but remained upstairs in our room at all times. A few days after I joined my parents and Shalom, Mr. Rijkse surprised me with the announcement that I would thenceforth be going to work every day in a tailor's large sewing shop situated nearby. A part of me welcomed this decision — I looked forward to working in the shop and operating the kind of machinery which I had been trained to use in the two-year period since I had been barred from the public-school system along with all the other Jewish students. Yet I could not comprehend what had driven Mr. Rijkse to take such a risk. By leaving our hiding place on a daily basis, I would be endangering not only myself, but also my entire family, as well as the Rijkses. I also expressed my concern regarding the queries that the other workers at the plant would surely make regarding my background and place of residence. However, Mr. Rijkse would not relent — I was to go to work every day, and that was that!

Once I began working in the shop, I encountered another problem: how would I manage to cover my head and *bentch* after eating my lunch? The slightest deviation from the accepted norms of non-Jewish society would alert my co-workers to my true identity. The solution came to me after I became more familiar with the plant. On one of my rounds, I found an out-of-the-way nook where I would be able to cover my head and recite the blessing without anyone seeing me. Until this day, I cannot understand why Mr. Rijkse insisted that I go to work, despite the incredible risk this posed to all of our lives, including his own.

About a week after I moved in with my parents and Shalom, Mr. Rijkse informed us that there was reason to suspect that the Germans had learned of our hideaway, and that we would have to move to the home of his neighbors, the Van Der Vlist family. I have nothing but pleasant memories of our stay at the home of Mr. and Mrs. Van Der Vlist. The head of the household was a barber by profession; his spacious barber shop stood directly below their second-story apartment, at street level. They were very comfortable financially, and their children were likeable and friendly, and

The Van Der Vlist family, who endangered their lives to save us

owned a great many toys, much to Shalom's delight.

The apartment in which we stayed did not have a separate entrance, so we essentially lived together with the Van Der Vlist family — we even ate with them. Immediately upon our arrival, the issue of kosher food was brought up. Although we were undeniably in a situation of *piku'ach nefesh* (mortal danger), and were thus permitted to eat nonkosher food, we wished to make every effort to avoid eating food which the Torah explicitly prohibits. It was my mother who found a solution to this problem: she asked our hostess if she would mind letting her do all the cooking, with kosher ingredients, then separate our share and place it in a different pot, and only at that stage add the nonkosher meat or other prohibited foods to the pot. Mrs. Van Der Vlist graciously agreed to this arrangement without a moment's hesitation. My mother explained to me that we must appreciate the extent of Mrs. Van Der Vlist's hospitality — it is no simple matter for a woman to relinquish control of her kitchen and entrust it to a complete stranger. My mother herself even admitted, "If I were in her place, I am not sure whether I would be capable of agreeing to such an arrangement."

The town's wholesale fruit and vegetable market stood directly behind the Van Der Vlists' home. On the first Sunday after our arrival, a large gathering of Nazis took place on the market

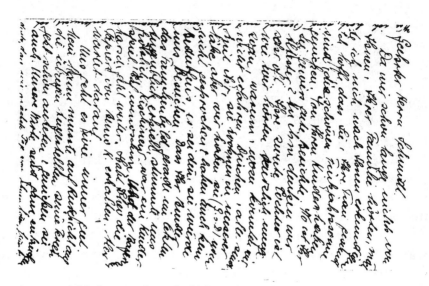

A postcard Mother sent from the hiding place to her family in Switzerland. She addressed it to Family Schmidt (instead of Goldschmidt) and signed it, "M. Ploni, Almonistr. 18."

grounds. The German governor of Holland — the wicked Seys Inquart, who was later to be sentenced to death in Nuremberg for his crimes against humanity — spoke before the large crowd of Nazi sympathizers. I remember well the feeling of satisfaction I experienced at being able to look upon the man whom the Fuehrer, may his name and memory be erased, had appointed to annihilate the Jews of the Netherlands without his being able to see me.

Mr. Van Der Vlist was active in the Dutch anti-Nazi underground, and we never had reason to doubt his loyalty. Upon my return to the Netherlands after the war, I learned that he died in a German prison. May his memory be blessed, along with the memory of all the other righteous gentiles.

After living with the Van Der Vlist family for about a week, at the end of Iyar of 5703 (1943) Mr. Rijkse informed us that the danger had passed and that we were to return to his home.

Just a few days after our return to the Rijkse household, as we were eating our meal on the night of the Shabbat of *Parashat Bemidbar*, we heard unfamiliar steps on the stairs leading up to our room. The door opened before we managed to hide, and in walked Jan Smorenburg, a Dutch Nazi who served as Head of Detectives in the Utrecht police department. He ordered my parents to present their documents.

This was not the first time that I had had the distinct displeasure of setting my eyes on Smorenburg. I had seen him a few months earlier standing in Utrecht's Jewish cemetery during the funeral of a Jewish man who had been shot and killed by the police. The deceased did not have any next of kin, and so we had been asked to fulfill the obligations associated with a *met mitzvah* and help lay him to rest. We were all surprised to see Smorenburg attending the funeral; this behavior was so incongruous for this avid anti-Semitic member of the Dutch Nazi Party. When someone asked him what he was doing there, he explained that he had heard that Jews perform some very "strange" rituals during their funerals. He had mentioned this to the head of the *Judenrat* (the Jewish committee), who had suggested that he attend the next Jewish funeral and see for himself that no unusual rituals were practiced. Smorenburg had come to verify this in person.

Smorenburg inspected our documents and perfunctorily announced that we were under arrest. His decision did not surprise us, since, unlike other divers, we carried identity cards which clearly identified us as Jews. We were not the only ones who were escorted to jail; Mr. Rijkse was also taken in for questioning. He kept his mouth sealed throughout the entire episode and behaved most strangely towards us.

We spent a sleepless, tormented night in jail worrying about Elchanan and the others. If our arrest had been instigated by an informant from Mr. Rijkse's underground group, we reasoned, then Elchanan, Shlomo, Yona, Baruch, Bella and Aunt Malli — who were hiding in an apartment down the street from Mr. Rijke's house — were also in imminent danger.

One of the leaders of the *Judenrat* — a Mr. Fritz Elzas — happened to be on very good terms with Smorenburg. As soon as he learned of our arrest, Mr. Elzas pointed out to Smorenburg that since our family had been carrying a Paraguayan passport, the decrees issued by the Germans against the Jews did not apply to us; hence he had no legal right to arrest us. Smorenburg miraculously agreed to try to have us freed, but only on condition that he first receive a thousand gulden for his "kind" gesture. His offer was relayed to us, and the deal was arranged.

Smorenburg was to telephone Aus Der Funten, whom Heinrich Himmler and Adolf Eichmann had appointed to oversee the mass deportation of Dutch Jewry, and discuss with him a number of administrative issues. Then, at the end of the conversation, Smorenburg would casually mention that a family of Jews carrying Paraguayan identification had been apprehended, and that as far as he understood, they could be released and granted legal-resident status.

Amazingly, the ruse worked. Following that conversation — and Father's assurance to pay Smorenburg the thousand gulden — we were released from jail and issued a permit allowing us to reside in Utrecht, "in keeping with the recommendations of Mr. Aus Der Funten of Amsterdam."

Father now had to pay Smorenburg the promised thousand gulden, a sum far in excess of what he had in hand at the time. He decided to pay a visit to a Mr. Wim Van Dranen, the owner of a local workshop who had once hired Yona. Father went to the man's house together with Yona and asked him for an emergency loan, explaining that the fate of the entire family hung in the balance. Mr. Van Dranen handed him the money without the slightest hesitation. He was astonished when my father repaid the loan in less than a week.

Mr. Fritz Elzas saved many Jews through elaborate and ingenious schemes. He was eventually arrested and did not merit to survive the war. May Hashem avenge his blood.

Armed with this permit, all of us except Bitya (who remained with the family that fostered her, for security's sake) returned to our own home a few days before Shavuot. We were not surprised when we found the house completely empty, for before going into hiding, we had asked Mr. Rijkse to arrange for his people to move our furniture and store it in a different location in order to prevent it from falling into the hands of the Nazis. However, when Father asked Mr. Rijkse to arrange for our furniture to be returned, he made up all sorts of empty excuses. We never saw our possessions again.

After the war I learned that all the Jews who had gone into hiding with Mr. Rijkse's assistance had been caught by the Germans. Not a single one emerged from the war unscathed.

When I returned from the camps, I dropped by to pay Mr. Rijkse a visit. He gave me a very chilly reception and behaved in the strangest way throughout my visit. Most shocking of all was his absolute lack of interest in what had occurred to the rest of my family.

My suspicions are aroused when I consider all these facts. Who was Mr. Rijkse? Friend or foe? The question remains unanswered in my mind to this day. Perhaps significantly — or perhaps not — he died at a young age, soon after the end of the war. His sister was a member of the Dutch Nazi Party; she lived in close proximity to her brother. Did he share her viewpoints? Were his rescue efforts sincere, or were they motivated purely by a desire to extort money and possessions from the persecuted souls who came to him for help? We have no way of knowing the truth, for he has taken his secret with him to the grave.

Smorenburg was apprehended by the Dutch police a few months after the Netherlands was liberated by the Allies. When I learned of this, I contacted the police, reported Smorenburg's act of extortion and demanded that he return to me the ransom money that my father had paid him. I also asked to testify against him when the war-crimes tribunal would review his case.

I appeared before the tribunal on February 24, 1949. My testimony proved vital in repudiating Smorenburg's claim that while serving as the chief of detectives, he had "made continuous attempts to help the poor Jews, for purely altruistic reasons and not for personal gain." After hearing my testimony, he brazenly declared before the court that he had never demanded a thousand gulden from the Emanuel family, and that apparently the money had fallen into the pockets of Fritz Elzas. Smorenburg was sentenced to a number of years in jail, but the ransom money was never returned to us.

The Summer of 5703 (1943)   *(By Shmuel)*

Upon returning to our home in the beginning of Sivan of the year 5703 (1943), we managed to assemble no more than a quorum of men for the Shabbat prayer services and the weekday Torah readings. We, the men of the Emanuel family, were six, and together with Mr. De Haas, Rabbi Van Gelder and another two Jews whose names I do not recall, we were exactly ten. The members of this *minyan* were the only Jews in the entire city of Utrecht who were legally permitted to live there. All the others were either in hiding or had long since been deported.

I returned to work at the tailor shop where I had worked before our family had gone into hiding. Shlomo and Yona, however, decided not to return to their previous places of employment. We participated in a number of *shiurim*. In addition, Yona and I began studying Rambam's Introduction to *Mishneh Torah* and *Hilchot Yesodei HaTorah* with Rabbi Joseph Van Gelder. Although we subsisted on sparse food rations, my parents made an effort to eat sparingly in order to continue sending provisions to our relatives interned in the Westerbork transit camp in northern Holland.

Aunt Malli remained an illegal resident in Utrecht, for her name did not appear in the Paraguayan passport through which we had obtained our release. She somehow managed to evade the attention of the police and returned home along with us, but due to her illegal status, she could not risk stepping outside of the house.

At some point around this time a young Jewish couple appeared at our door. They had been forced to leave their hideout just when the woman reached the last stages of her pregnancy. Not knowing where else to turn, they had come to us. My parents accommodated them until they found a new hiding place. After the Holocaust we learned that they, along with their newborn son, survived the war.

It was a strange feeling we were experiencing then — while hundreds of thousands of tortured souls suffered in the camps, we had been allowed to return to our home. We strongly identified with the words of the prayer service, "We shall thank You . . . for Your miracles that are with us every day, and for Your wonders and favors in every season — evening, morning and afternoon."

Bitya Returns Home

We had been miraculously released, but one member of our family was still absent — little Bitya. My parents had placed her with a Mr. and Mrs. Kersbergen, a childless non-Jewish couple living in the western part of the country. My parents left a number of family pictures with the Kersbergens in order to ensure that Bitya would not forget us. They also gave them our grandparents' address in Zurich, in the event that the worst scenario would manifest itself.

My parents decided to postpone Bitya's homecoming, even though we had been granted legal status and had been allowed to return home. The situation remained very tense and extremely dangerous, with the scent of disaster hovering all around us. It would have been foolish of us to rely upon the tenuous conditions of our release. We were thankful for our freedom in the meantime, but no one knew what tomorrow would bring.

One day our parents informed us that we were in for a surprise — Bitya and her surrogate mother would be coming to visit us! We were overjoyed to see Bitya, and our pleasure increased when we sensed that she felt comfortable with us and at home. After eating lunch together, we recited the Grace After Meals. Mrs. Kersbergen followed suit by whispering some prayers while clasping her hands on the table and crossing herself repeatedly, but we were completely unprepared for what happened next. To our utter astonishment, Bitya followed Mrs. Kersbergen's example. We were apalled — our sweet little Bitya praying like a Christian!

My parents rose and left the room. A short while later they returned and explained to Mrs. Kersbergen that although they had originally intended for Bitya to stay with her, they now felt that the situation was not as dangerous, and they had decided that Bitya would return to us. Mrs. Kersbergen was clearly surprised at this sudden turn of events, but she took it all in stride and left in a friendly and cheerful mood.

Father and Mother were visibly shaken. All they said to us was "We received you children as a deposit from Hashem. We do not know when we will be obligated to return our deposits, but one thing is certain — we will return you as Jews!"

Bitya returned her pure soul to her Creator on Wednesday, the eighth day of Adar of the year 5705 (1945), in the Bergen-

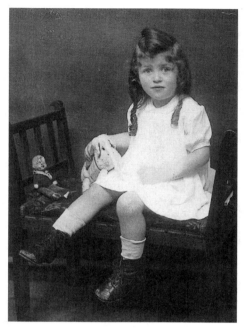

Bitya, Tamuz 5702 (July 1942)

Belsen concentration camp. She was five years and four months old. She returned her soul as a Jewish girl, as our parents had vowed. Little Bitya died of malnutrition. My mother and Bella, my sister, did everything they could to save her, but without medication, food or minimal sanitary conditions, it was an impossible task. Hashem has given, and Hashem has taken away.

On that bitter day they brought Bitya's tiny body to the camp gate, from where it was transported to the crematorium. We recited *Kaddish* by the gate. In the crematorium the bodies of the deceased were burned together. There, the blood of fathers and mothers mingled with the blood of children; the blood of young boys joined the blood of young girls; the blood of erudite men mixed with the blood of wise women; the blood of the righteous, the blood of youths, the blood of elders — the blood of the entire Jewish people was spilled and formed one great pool.

Chapter Eight
Westerbork Transit Camp

Our Arrest

We did not enjoy our freedom for long. Approximately one week before the fast of the seventeenth day of Tamuz, little more than a month after we had returned to our home, two plainclothes Gestapo agents showed up at our door holding an arrest warrant. Mother reacted quickly and helped Aunt Malli crawl out through a back window, without arousing the Germans' attention. Thanks to her quick reaction, Mother saved not only Aunt Malli's life, but our lives as well, for had the Germans discovered an illegal resident in our house, they would have sent us all to the death camps without further delay.

Each of us took along a large backpack containing clothes, blankets, food, a *siddur* and a *Chumash*. Everything had been prepared beforehand for such an eventuality. Those of us over bar-mitzvah age quickly snuck a *tallit* and *tefillin* into each of our packs, while Father carried his *kittel* (a white garment worn during the Yom Kippur prayers) in his pack. Mother managed to write the word *"Moerder"* (murderers!) in block letters on the backside of one of the pictures hung on the wall. This was meant for the eyes of the Germans who would surely come the next day to seize our furnishings and whatever other valuable objects they could find. At least my mother let them know what we thought of them! It was a small

Jews on their way to the transport depots, from which they were eventually sent to the camps

act of defiance that gave us a sense of satisfaction.

Our arrest marked a new stage in our odyssey. For the first time, we would experience the bitter taste of the camps.

A few days before our arrest, Elchanan had written a letter to the Keiser family, in which he outlined a unique interpretation of Tehillim 126. He had been teaching Tehillim, as understood by the major commentators, to the boys and girls of the Keiser family before the deportations had begun, and he apparently intended to continue these *shiurim* through correspondence. Elchanan never managed to end this letter. It somehow reached the Keisers, who were in hiding at the time.

Elchanan wrote the following:

It is written, "Those who sow in tears will reap in joyous song" (Tehillim 126:5). One does not sow seeds during the summer months, but rather in the season of rain and storm. Indeed, it is impossible to conceive of a fruitful harvest where there had been no rain and wind. A farmer must venture forth into the fields during the height of the storm season and endure the rain in order to sow his seeds. He knows that he must do so in order to reap a bountiful crop.

So too, our nation's most opportune time to sow its seeds has always been in the midst of dreadful persecution. Let us remember the great sages of Israel who lived in the very generation that saw the destruction of the Second Temple — Torah luminaries such as Rabbi Yochanan ben Zakkai and Rabbi Akiva, who made Judaism blossom by risking their own lives. Let us remember Rashi and his disciples, who succeeded in their most crucial contributions in the dark shadows of the Crusades.

This is the end of the letter. It contains neither a concluding word of farewell nor a signature. Its only message is the unique insight that Elchanan conceived during those difficult days — that generations plagued by persecutions, evil decrees and cruelty also merit to see a blossoming of Torah study.

The Rebbe's Envoy

The Gestapo transported us to Amsterdam. We were taken to S.S. headquarters, and then on to the "Jewish theater" — a central depot where all the Jews caught throughout the country were held. A few days later we were summoned to appear before an S.S. committee that would decide our fate. As we stood tensely in line waiting to enter the committee room, an old acquaintance by the

The enclosed backyard of the central depot, "the Jewish theater"

name of Reb Chaim Ehrenreich, a Belzer chassid, suddenly approached Father. He hurriedly informed my father that he was expecting the imminent arrival of a Honduran passport, but that all he possessed in the meantime was a written statement from the embassy confirming that the passport had been ordered. He was in a quandary as to what to say to the S.S. committee. How could he possibly persuade the Germans not to send him to the camps in Poland?

Father thought for a moment. He then instructed Reb Chaim to tell the Germans that, due to his anxiety and confusion during his arrest, he had taken the wrong documents with him, and that he would need to write home to receive the Honduran passport. My father assured Reb Chaim that by the time the deferral expired, the passport would arrive, and that he and his entire family would be out of danger.

Reb Chaim Ehrenreich was clearly disappointed by my father's suggestion. He was convinced that the ploy would not work — he felt it was just too obvious a lie. Yet Father adamantly insisted that Reb Chaim tell the Germans exactly what he had told him.

The line moved forward, and as Reb Chaim's turn approached, he lost his nerve and returned to my father's side once again, telling him that he was afraid of stating such an obvious lie before the S.S. committee. Father did not mince words with him — he literally *commanded* Reb Chaim to say exactly what he had instructed him and not to change a single word.

The truth is that my father's suggestion did seem rather feeble. However, to our surprise it worked — Reb Chaim was granted a deferral of a week, by which time the Honduran passport arrived. As a consequence, he and his wife and daughter were spared from being sent to the death camps. Instead, they were sent to Bergen-Belsen with us. Reb Chaim continued to seek my father's advice throughout our incarceration in Bergen-Belsen. I remember frequently seeing my father listening to Reb Chaim with utmost patience, and then giving him detailed instructions regarding various problems which they encountered in the camp. Once I saw Father even admonish Reb Chaim for not exercising sufficient caution.

I met Reb Chaim again in The Hague approximately two years after the war ended. I had come to the city to participate in the monthly study convention of Po'alei Agudat Yisrael. When Reb Chaim saw me, he requested that I accompany him to his home, for he said he had something of great importance to tell me.

After we had entered his simple quarters, he took out a photo of the Belzer Rebbe from his pocket and said to me with emotion, "Do you remember the instructions your father gave me in the waiting room before I faced the S.S. committee? At first it seemed like such a strange piece of advice! I was really at a loss over what to do! Your father did not speak to me then in his usual calm way. Rather, he literally *ordered* me to follow his instructions, as though he were relaying someone else's message.

"I want you to know that I held on to this picture of the Belzer Rebbe, Rav Aharon of Belz. The Rebbe could not be everywhere in order to protect his *chassidim*, so he sent faithful envoys to carry out this task. I have no doubt that the Rebbe appointed your father, *zt"l*, as his personal envoy to save me and my family from death. From the moment I received the seven-day deferral, I realized that this was the case. I continued seeking your father's advice throughout my stay in the camps, and I faithfully followed his every word, for I was absolutely positive that your father was the Belzer Rebbe's personal envoy."

The postcard Father sent to the Goldschmidts in Zurich to notify them of the change of address

BERICHT VAN ADRESWIJZIGING	
NAAM MET VOORLETTERS:	*H. Emmanuel*
BEROEP, KWALITEIT:	
OUD ADRES	
STRAAT EN HUISNUMMER:	*Schroder v. d. Kolksstr. 19 bis*
NAAM DER WOONPLAATS:	*Utrecht*
NIEUW ADRES	
STRAAT EN HUISNUMMER: (ZOO NOODIG HUISGEDEELTE)	*Barak 63 Lager Westerbork*
TELEF.- & POSTBUSNR.:	
POSTREKENING NR.:	
NAAM DER WOONPLAATS: (TOEVOEGEN, INDIEN NOODIG: CENTRUM, NOORD, ZUID, OOST, ENZ. OF KANTOOR V. BESTELLING)	*Hooghalen Oost - Dr.*
DATUM VAN INGANG EN HANDTEEKENING:	*2/7 43*

Change of address notice; the new address: Barrack 63, Westerbork

Westerbork Transit Camp

Westerbork transit camp was located in the northeastern sector of the Netherlands. It served as a translocation point for tens of thousands of Jews. The large majority of Westerbork's inmates spent no more than a few days in the camp before being transported in railroad cattle cars to death camps such as Auschwitz and Sobibor. In an effort to prevent disturbances, the Germans deceived the inmates, telling them that they were headed for work camps, when in fact almost all those who left Westerbork were killed immediately upon their arrival at their destination. Approximately ninety percent of Dutch Jewry — about a hundred thousand souls — were murdered in this way.

The inmates in transit to the death camps were kept in a cluster of large barracks. Men and women had separate sleeping quarters, but they were not separated during the day. Westerbork's permanent inmates — who were charged with the camp's maintenance and administration — benefited from slightly better living conditions than those headed to points east.

Our Arrival on Shabbat Evening

It was late Friday afternoon as the train hurtled towards the unknown. We sat immobile in our places, our hearts full of trepidation as we pondered what the future had in store for us. German soldiers stood at our side throughout the journey. No one spoke a word. Then, suddenly, in a clear, confident voice, Father announced, "The time has come to sanctify the Shabbat." Following his lead, we all recited *Ma'ariv*, and then Father uttered *Kiddush* over some bread. We ate a little and then bentched together. Father's *Kiddush* that Friday night on the train served us all as a life-long lesson.

We arrived at our destination some time around midnight, along with another several hundred Jews. The commandant of the camp strolled onto the platform to examine the new shipment of the "spoils of war." After reviewing the list, he ordered that our large family of ten souls be placed aboard the very next transport to the east, which was due to leave on the coming Tuesday. Father courageously walked up to the commandant and requested that he take into consideration our Paraguayan passport and honor our foreign-resident status, especially in light of the fact that we had lived in Paraguay for a number of years.

The commandant screamed back that the passport had absolutely no validity in his eyes. He was well aware that Jews were purchasing such passports on a large scale.

Father tenaciously retorted that he had managed a large leather concern in Paraguay, and that we had all been born there. Father's audacity took the commandant by surprise, but he continued screaming at him. Father reciprocated by firmly maintaining that we were authentic Paraguayan citizens and demanded that the commandant honor the passport. Father knew that this encounter would decide the fate of our entire family — it was a matter of life or death.

Father succeeded in convincing the commandant of our Paraguayan citizenship. We were thus classified as foreign citizens who, for the time being, would not be transported to the Polish death camps. Consequently, we were not included in the transport of the 2,209 souls that left Westerbork on the seventeenth day of Tamuz, headed for the ovens of Sobibor death camp. Three days later, not a single member of that transport was alive. May Hashem avenge their blood.

My cousin, Eliezer Kunstadt, may Hashem avenge his blood, was placed aboard this transport. He was the son of Rav Baruch Kunstadt, *zt"l*, who would later be appointed *rosh yeshivah* of Yeshivat Kol Torah in Jerusalem. Reb Eliezer had been injured while attempting to escape from a different camp and had to be carried onto the train.

The transports generally left on Tuesday mornings. The lists of those who would be on board were read aloud in each of the barracks at about 3:00 A.M. of the same day. The entire day was filled with dreadful, unreal scenes of human anguish and suffering.

Some of the letters written by my parents to our grandparents in Switzerland will appear in a later stage of this narrative. Because every letter sent from the camp was censored by the Germans, my parents could not explicitly mention the weekly transports of thousands of Jews to the death camps in Poland.

The Seventeenth Day of Tamuz 5703 (1943)

(By Shmuel)

A particular scene from Westerbork remains firmly implanted in my mind. It was three o'clock in the morning. The dim lights in our barracks were lit. Everyone's attention was focused on the barrack leader, who stood in the center of the room. He was about to begin calling out the names of those who would board the train that morning and travel to their deaths. The names were read in alphabetical order.

Unbearable tension pervaded the entire room. Those whose names were called were required to respond in acknowledgment. Many times, their responses were followed by heart-rending screams of raw misery and despair simply too awful to describe.

The sides of the barracks were lined with triple-tiered bunks. I was sitting on a bed in the top tier of the bunk. Not far from me, on a bed on the same level as mine, sat Reb Shlomo Loewenberg. My parents had known the Loewenbergs before our imprisonment in Westerbork. They were relatives of the De Haas family, who had been our dear friends in Utrecht. Like us, he, his wife and their two daughters had arrived at Westerbork four days earlier, on the evening of Shabbat *Parashat Balak*. They had been arrested in an *aktion* (raid) in Amsterdam that same Friday morning and had been immediately transported to Westerbork. Reb Shlomo and his family had ridden in a different railway compartment. He — like Father — had defiantly recited *Kiddush* aboard the train. Ignoring the German soldiers who stood on guard, he had taken two *challot* from his pack and recited *Kiddush* loudly enough for all the passengers of that compartment to hear.

When the barrack supervisor began to read the names beginning with the letter *L*, I heard him call out, "Loewenberg." The usual "Yes!" was not heard, nor the usual screams of despair. Instead, a single Hebrew word emerged from Reb Shlomo's lips and echoed loudly in the room: "*Hineini* — Here I am." He responded to his death toll in the same way that Abraham had responded when Hashem called upon him to sacrifice Isaac, his firstborn son. As Rashi explains in reference to the verse in Bereishit (22:1), " '*Hineini*' — such is the response of the pious, which conveys humility and readiness." In this context "humility" refers to a person's complete submission to divine decrees; this requires that he harbor not the slightest trace of skepticism in his heart. What Rashi means by "readiness" is a willingness to fulfill God's every command.

I believe that the "*hineini*" that Reb Shlomo Loewenberg uttered when he was assigned to the transport to Poland contained an even stronger message — it was an expression that emerged from the depths of his soul as it bonded with the souls of the great multitudes of Jews who had sacrificed their lives for the sanctification of God's Name, from the days of Abraham until this very day.

The names of 2,209 Jews were called out in the barracks of Westerbork during the early morning hours of that seventeenth day of Tamuz. Men, women and children of all ages were loaded onto dozens of cattle cars parked in the center of the camp, waiting to carry their human cargo to the Polish death camps. Some of the leading rabbinical figures and community leaders of Dutch Jewry were included in this transport. Many of these individuals had registered for emigration to Palestine, and so their deportation to Poland had been postponed thus far. There were also quite a few members of various *hachsharah* groups (training programs to prepare prospective *olim* to contend with the conditions they would encounter in Eretz Yisrael). My cousin, Eliezer Kunstadt, may Hashem avenge his blood, belonged to Young Agudath Yisrael's *hachsharah* group, which was based in the city of Enschede.

Reb Shlomo Loewenberg's family managed to write a short letter before they were loaded onto the train. It was entitled, "The fourth fast, 5703." (Tamuz is the fourth month of the Jewish calendar; the seventeenth day of that month is a public fast day.) The letter continues, "A new evil decree has been added to the others which took place on this day . . . Hashem's divine providence enables us to look ahead . . . to an uncertain future. . . ."

The Loewenbergs managed to throw five postcards out of the sealed cattle car just before the train crossed the border into Germany. Four of the postcards were found by Dutch farmers who regularly came to the area to collect the numerous letters and jottings that were scattered along the railroad tracks following every transport of Jews to the east. In these postcards the Loewenbergs described the crowded conditions inside the cattle cars: "Fifty-seven individuals are packed into the wagons, which are meant to accommodate beasts, not human beings. The beasts that usually ride in these cars enjoy more space than we do. How many days will we be able to survive this torture? . . ."

On the fifth postcard they wrote the following words: "They say that the train is headed for Riga, but we know nothing. We are about to throw the postcards outside. May God bless all of you! From all of us." Their eldest daughter, age eleven, wrote on the bottom of the letter, "See you in Eretz Yisrael!"

The train arrived at the Sobibor death camp three days later, on the twentieth day of Tamuz, on the Friday of *Parashat Pinchas*. We know today that by sundown of the day of their arrival, not one of the 2,209 souls who boarded that train was alive. May Hashem avenge their blood. The verse "We were regarded as sheep to be slaughtered" (Tehillim 44:23) was fulfilled in those days.

The Loewenbergs had a third daughter who had gone into hiding with a non-Jewish family. Her name was Yocheved; she was four years old at the time. She survived the war and was brought up by her aunt and uncle, Mr. Aaron De Haas and his wife.

About fifteen years after the Holocaust, Yocheved met a Mrs. Klara Asher-Pinkhoff at a wedding celebration in Eretz Yisrael. Mrs. Pinkhoff was a famous educator and writer — the well-known book, *The Children of the Stars*, is just one of her works. After introducing themselves to one another, Mrs. Pinkhoff asked Yocheved whether she knew why her parents had chosen this name for her. Yocheved responded that she did not and admitted that the question had always intrigued her, for she knew that there were no ancestors from either branch of the family who had borne this name.

Mrs. Pinkhoff then surprised her by saying, "I never met your parents, but I can tell you why you were named 'Yocheved.' " Mrs. Pinkhoff related that before the war she had written a regular column in a Jewish newspaper in the Netherlands. In 1939, when war loomed on the horizon, she wrote in one of her articles that the time had come for the Jews of Europe to emulate Amram and Yocheved (Moses' parents).

The Sages interpret the verse, "A member of the house of Levi went and married Levi's daughter" (Shemot 2:1), as referring to Amram's decision to remarry his wife, Yocheved. The Sages explain that following Pharaoh's decree to drown all Israelite male children in the Nile, Amram decided to divorce his wife and so abstain from fulfilling the commandment to be fruitful and multiply. *Why should we labor in vain?* he reasoned to himself. Following the divorce, his daughter Miriam said to him, "Father, your decree is harsher than Pharaoh's. He issued a decree affecting only the male children, while you have made a decree against both male and female children!" Upon hearing his daughter's words of admonishment, Amram decided then and there to remarry Yocheved.

Mrs. Pinkhoff explained to Yocheved that soon after the article was published, she received a letter from a reader who wrote that she had been very moved by the article, explaining that she was in an advanced stage of pregnancy, and that after discussing it with her husband, she had decided that if she would give birth to a boy, she would name him Amram, and if she would have a girl, she would name her Yocheved. That woman was Yocheved's mother.

Yocheved is the only member of the Loewenberg family to have survived the Holocaust.

Jews Rule over Jews

After becoming more familiar with Westerbork camp, I came to a most shocking realization — I almost never saw German soldiers in the camp! Westerbork's entire bureaucratic apparatus was supervised and operated exclusively by Jews. The personal details of new inmates were recorded by Jews; the lists of the poor souls who were sent to the death camps in Poland were prepared by Jews; the names of those who would be sent to their deaths on the next transport were announced every Tuesday morning by the Jewish foremen of the barracks; the damned souls destined for the ovens were even assisted onto the train by Jewish attendants. German soldiers and Dutch policemen could be seen next to the trains, but other than that, the entire operation — from entrance to exit — was operated by our own people.

Westerbork transit camp was built in the year 5699 (1939) by the government of the Netherlands. It was originally intended to serve as a detention camp for the large number of German Jews who illegally entered the Netherlands in their desperate attempt to escape the Nazi dragnet. These refugees obtained the most influential positions in the camp and maintained their special status by administrating the camp with utmost efficiency. Recognizing the usefulness of these Jewish managers, the Germans gave them incentives, such as better living conditions and a temporary reprieve from being sent to the gas chambers. But eventually their turn would also come. . . .

It was an awful feeling to know that the entire organizational structure of the camp was planned, supervised and implemented exclusively by Jews. Even the guards in the camp's prison were Jewish!

Most of the camp's residents were Jews who had been apprehended in the course of an *aktion* (raid). However, a separate section of the camp was reserved for Jews who had been caught "diving" (i.e., who had gone into hiding with the assistance of non-Jewish citizens) within the territorial boundaries of the Netherlands. The large majority of such individuals ended up in Westerbork and were classified as "criminal prisoners." They were held in a separate barrack (number 67), which was surrounded by barbed wire and guarded by a select group of guards, all of whom were Jewish. The male prisoners were abused and tortured on a daily basis — after completing an arduous day of back-breaking labor, they were forced to run back and forth until they collapsed from exhaustion. I saw Jews who still wore the yellow patch with the word *"Jood"* emblazoned upon it, tormenting their own brethren and embittering these poor souls' last days on earth. The scenes that pass through my mind's eye are just too awful to describe.

Indeed, the German extermination machine operated in a most diabolical way, taking full advantage of man's instinctive desire to prolong his own life. Groups of "criminal prisoners" were sent to the east in railway cattle cars within which they endured inhuman conditions. The Germans' aim was not merely to punish these hapless individuals, but also to make an example of them. They wished to convey to the camp's other inmates that if they follow orders and behave correctly, they would be treated humanely in the "work camps" to which they were headed. These carefully planned methods of deception played a critical role in the Nazis' efforts to implement the Final Solution.

It never ceased to amaze me how these "criminal prisoners" kept up their spirits in spite of the anguish and suffering they endured on a regular basis. They even had their own Dutch song that they would sing sometimes. It went, *"Wij zijn de toffe jongengs van de S-compangie . . ."* which, translated loosely, means, "We are the good guys of the 'criminal' bunch. We work like horses, but we have neither despaired nor given up hope. The day will come when we will return home; the day will still come when we will be unfettered from this filth. . . ." This was the song they would sing prior to the arrival of the cattle cars which would transport them to the ovens.

The fact that Jews were the camp's administrators sometimes worked in our favor. Those who were in charge of recording the names of newly arrived inmates occasionally saved lives simply by neglecting to write the words "criminal prisoner" beside someone's name.

The Work Performed in Westerbork

I chose not to try to obtain a position in any of the camp's factories, because I knew this type of work would entail violations of

Working in Westerbork transit camp

Torah-ordained laws on Shabbat. My uncle, Naftali Abrahams, who had already spent a number of months in Westerbork, informed me that he had joined a work detachment assigned to transport materials within the camp. He had opted for this type of work because, although it was physically taxing, it did not involve any serious violations of the laws of Shabbat. Carrying objects around the camp did not constitute a Torah-ordained prohibition, since the camp was completely surrounded by barbed wire, and was thus considered a *reshut hayachid* (private domain). On the basis of this consideration I decided to join my uncle's work crew. I enjoyed working by his side and listening to his words of Torah.

A few weeks later, I was transferred to a different work group that was assigned the job of repairing and paving roads. Certain aspects of this work did involve violating Torah-ordained laws on Shabbat, but for the most part, such jobs were performed by skilled workers. Since I executed non-skilled labor, I was able to avoid committing serious Torah violations.

In the beginning of the winter of the year 5704 (1944), I was again transferred to a different work unit. My new job involved un-

The barracks in Westerbork

loading railway tracks from a ship docked in a canal just outside the camp perimeter. I sustained skin burns as a consequence of handling the ice-covered metal tracks — I'd had no idea that cold metal could cause such severe burns on one's skin. The tracks were used for the construction of a narrow railway which would facilitate the transport of raw materials and merchandise to and from the camp. This railway was not connected with the wider one, which ran through the center of the camp, and which was used exclusively to transport Jews to the death camps in Poland.

I was comforted by the fact that I was once again able to refrain from commiting any Torah-ordained violations of the laws of Shabbat. Because I was the youngest member of the crew, I was not assigned the important task of assembling the tracks. Although my job demanded that I carry objects outside the enclosed compound, the area extending from the camp to the canal did not qualify as *reshut harabim* according to Torah law. One of my duties was to carry a heavy sack of nails on my back and to place four large nails next to each tie and eight nails next to each crosstie. Although my actions constituted a violation of a rabbinically ordained Shabbat prohibition, at least I was spared having to transgress a Torah-ordained law.

Working outside the camp gave rise to another halachic consideration related to the laws of Shabbat: carrying any object beyond the boundaries of the camp constituted a violation of a rabbinical decree; I did not have a legitimate reason for carrying my food to our work area on Shabbat. This was no simple matter. To

Laying railway tracks

work on Shabbat and to carry a heavy sack up and down the tracks all day long was difficult enough; to deprive myself of food because of the rabbinically ordained prohibition of carrying would have been almost too much to bear.

I gave the matter some thought and came up with a solution. I took my food with me to work, but instead of carrying it to our work area, I ate it during the roll call, which always took place at the side of the gate within the boundaries of the camp. I would recite the bentching — including the additional passage recited on Shabbat, "May it please You, Hashem our God, give us rest through Your commandments and through the commandments of the seventh day, this great and holy Sabbath . . ." — while standing, and I always made sure to swallow all the food that remained in my mouth before we walked through the gate. We would return to the camp in the evening, just as Shabbat drew to a close.

My ability to refrain from carrying objects which the Germans did not force me to carry for a number of successive *Shabbatot* gave me a great sense of satisfaction and raised my spirits. It also braced me for what the future held in store. One thing became very evident — the Torah ideals we had been taught by our parents had withstood the harsh tests of reality.

Though I walk in the valley of death's shadow . . .

(Tehillim 23:4)

Some time later, my group was assigned the job of repairing the road leading from the canal to the camp. The road passed alongside the crematorium, where all the corpses were incinerated. The Nazis would not allow the dead to be buried, so this hideous facility had been built to dispose of the bodies. It gave Westerbork the appearance of a death camp, although officially it was a work camp. All the ghastly tasks in the crematorium were performed by Jews.

The bodies were carried into the crematorium in a respectful manner, but the sights were utterly horrifying. Every so often, the Jewish workers would bring in a small package on a kind of tray, containing the corpse of an infant who had died in the camp. Many infants died of disease, or as a result of their premature birth following their mothers' traumatic arrest at the hands of the Germans, may their name be obliterated! At first I didn't know what was in those small packages, but once I realized what they held, I was completely overwhelmed by the scene I saw repeatedly unfolding before me — a group of Jewish men carrying parcels of dead babies to the furnace! Jews were burning the bodies of their own brothers and sisters, their own children and infants! Overwhelmed with emotion, I watched as one Jew carried another to the flames, while smoke and ashes spewed forth from the chimney. Afterwards, their job done, the package-carriers would shuffle back to the camp. Will we ever be able to describe the scope of this tragedy to our fellow Jews living in the free world? I wondered to myself.

One afternoon, as we sat down to rest next to the crematorium, a strange thought struck me: Maybe I will be the only survivor of this camp who will be able to testify that the Nazis burned our men, women and children in this building. The crematorium seemed deserted just then; apparently, for some unknown reason, no corpses had been brought in that morning. Impulsively, I asked my group leader — his name was Mr. Kornblit — for permission to take a quick look inside the crematorium. Mr. Kornblit was taken aback by my bizarre request, but he agreed to let me go in, on condition that I return immediately.

While making my way to the entrance, I was feeling somewhat surprised by my own boldness. Frankly, I was already regretting my decision, and by the time I reached the door, I was hoping that it would be locked. I pushed at the metal door of the main entrance, and to my disappointment, it slid open. Tentatively, I walked a few more steps and entered the facility. It was a low building of strange design, with metal poles reaching from floor to ceiling all along the entranceway. I saw a large cylindrical container in the center of the room. Its purpose first escaped me, but then it dawned on me that I was looking at the "oven" in which the corpses were actually incinerated. I was suddenly overcome with panic. What am I doing here? I thought to myself. Have I come to find out how they burn the dead? Do I want to see what burnt bodies look like? What will happen if they find me here? . . .

A rare picture from Westerbork

I was surrounded by utter silence, an awful, deathly stillness. Then I began to hear voices, a low sound of many voices chanting. . . . I broke out in a cold sweat that drenched my entire body from head to toe. My mouth felt dry, and my tongue clung to my palate. The room began swirling before my eyes, and I felt certain that I would faint. I took a few steps forward, and the sound of the voices became clearer. Were the dead communicating with me? It was then that I recognized a familiar tune — the lilting sound of prayer! Perhaps the souls of those who were burned here were praying to their Creator, I thought. The chanting seemed to be coming from somewhere off to the right. As I headed in that direction, I noticed a door. With trembling hands I slowly pushed it open, and there before me I saw a group of Jews reciting *tehillim* in a mournful tune, a song of lamentation.

These were the very Jews I had seen carrying the corpses the day before. I do not think they saw me intruding upon them, but I certainly recognized them, sitting there forlornly, clothed in the same kinds of rags that I wore, with the same yellow patch sewn on. Although theirs was the gruesome task of bearing their fellow Jews to the furnace, it appeared that they recited *tehillim* between each load, between the delivery of each tiny parcel. I retraced my steps, exited the building and returned to my job of repairing the road. I learned an invaluable lesson from my impulsive excursion: despite their ghastly task, the men who carried the corpses to the furnace were Jews of no lesser worth than I.

The following day, I again saw the Jews working in the crematorium, carrying corpses and small packages to the furnace. This time, I felt great pity for these poor men who had been assigned the awful task of incinerating their brethren.

Years after the Holocaust ended, I learned that the crematorium workers in Westerbork had exerted tremendous effort to ritually purify the corpses before they brought them to be incinerated.

Torah Study and Prayer

Despite all the difficulties we faced, we found some time for Torah study. Reb Yisrael (Julius) Goldschmidt, *zt"l*, delivered a *shiur* almost entirely without the aid of a book on the well-known Talmudic theme *"ho'il"* (Tractate *Pesachim*), as well as on the prohibitions of Yom Tov. To this very day I remember his voice as he repeated the words of the Sages over and over in order to highlight an important point.

The *shiur* was attended by Shmuel, Michel Abrahams, Alexander Dinkel, Jack Finkel and myself. I also studied a little with Uncle Naftali Abrahams and my brother Elchanan. We managed to pray in a *minyan* and hear the reading of the Torah, usually in a tent. On Shabbat mornings we prayed earlier, in order to arrive punctually to the workers' roll call. For the sake of honoring the Shabbat, we changed our underclothing on Friday afternoon. It felt strange to wear our work clothes over a clean set of underclothing, and to set out to work on Shabbat; the dichotomy of simultaneously honoring and desecrating the Shabbat disturbed us to the depths of our souls.

A letter sent by Father to my grandparents in Switzerland, mailed from Westerbork Transit Camp:

Dear Parents,

Since it is doubtful whether we will manage to obtain the Four Species in this place, it would be very kind of you to send us a set. You may do so via Mr. De Haas.

We have a *shofar.*

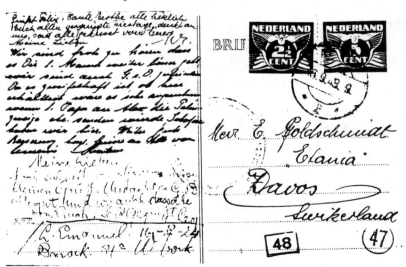

The postcard sent by father to my grandparents from Westerbork

Shlomo Abrahams' Bar Mitzvah

My cousin Shlomo became a bar mitzvah on the Shabbat of *Parashat Shoftim* of the year 5703 (1943). His parents, Uncle Naftali and Aunt Bea, made great efforts to ensure that Shlomo would enjoy a pleasant bar mitzvah celebration. To this day Shlomo fondly remembers every single detail of his bar-mitzvah celebration, including the rhyming song that those in attendance sang to the Dutch tune of *"Shir Hama'alot."*

A letter from Father to Grandmother, addressed to the convalescent home in the Swiss city of Davos:

... Shlomo's bar mitzvah yesterday was very enjoyable, far beyond our highest expectations. He read the Torah twice, very capably. Uncle Gottfried and Aunt Berta were there and, of course, Julius [Goldschmidt]. . . .

The message Mother appended to the same postcard:

Dear Mother,

Yes, you would have enjoyed hearing the delightful rhymes that Susy [Dinkel] composed. . . . The highlights of the entire celebration were Shlomo's suit, the table. . . . Alex Dinkel participated in the celebration last night.

Your postcards have been arriving very quickly. I'm glad that you always have a pleasant visit. With Hashem's help, everything will be fine. . . . Live in good health!

On the morning of Rosh Hashanah I reported for work as usual, but later I snuck away to attend the prayer service and hear the *shofar* together with a *minyan*. I then hurried back to work. I did the same thing on the second day of Rosh Hashanah, as well as on Yom Kippur.

My mother's letter to her parents in Zurich:

11 Tishrei 5704 (1943)

My dear parents and sisters,

We will be able to send this letter only in a week from now, but I already begin to write to you today and acknowledge receipt of approximately ten postcards, plus an additional four letters. We were happy to read that Mother's health is improving.

In spite of our concerns, the great day [Yom Kippur] passed by yesterday uneventfully. During the meal prior to the onset of the fast we had tomato soup with rice, carrots and potatoes . . . enough that we were not even able to finish all the food. Yitzchak Lange led *Ma'ariv* and Mordechai led *Shacharit;* it was very nice. Afterwards it was Uncle Gottfried's turn — very moving. After him came Yitzchak Lange, and in the end, Rabbi Dr. Frankel [from Halberstadt, Amsterdam]. We also had enough to eat on the following night. The boys have gone to make arrangements for a *sukkah*. Can you imagine? All this is taking place in Westerbork!

My dear mother, your worries are superfluous. May all Jewish children be so healthy!

It would be fitting for the entire congregation of Israel to sit in one sukkah.

(Sukkah 27b).

The letter above omits one important fact — the camp authorities permitted the construction of only *one sukkah*. This single structure was to be shared by the several hundred observant prisoners being held in Westerbork.

A large number of inmates showed an interest in fulfilling the Torah-ordained mitzvah of eating a *kezayit* (a measurement equal to the volume of a halachic olive) of bread in the *sukkah* on the first night of the Festival. We stood at the end of the long line which had formed before the *sukkah* and waited quite a while for our turn. We entered and ate quickly in order to make room for all the others waiting in line. During the remaining days of the Festival, however, the *sukkah* was not nearly as crowded. Many people found it difficult to come to the *sukkah* and eat their meal inside it, so there was plenty of space for all of us. We sang festive songs during some of the meals, and we were able to feel the joy of the occasion, in spite of the fact that we had to go out to work. Nevertheless, our celebration of the Festival was not complete, for we had not been successful in our efforts to obtain the Four Species.

On the night of Hoshana Rabbah, Rav Shimon Dasberg, may Hashem avenge his blood — the last chief rabbi of Amsterdam in the pre-Holocaust era — delivered a *shiur* on one of the central issues discussed in *masechet Rosh Hashanah*. With one brilliant insight, Rav Dasberg eloquently solved a host of difficulties which the commentators raise in reference to this issue.

This was the first time that I had seen Rav Dasberg in person. I was very impressed by the breadth of his knowledge and by his imposing presence. In time, my initial positive opinion of him would grow increasingly stronger.

A letter from Mother:

19 Tishrei 5704 (1943)

. . . In the meantime, we ate all our meals in a lovely *sukkah*. On Shabbat night, we ate together with the Abrahams family and with the boys from the pioneer training group. On *motza'ei Shabbat*, we stayed in the *sukkah* from eight until ten o'clock. It was a bit chilly, but the words of

Torah, the speeches and the singing, made us feel warm inside. It is indeed a miracle — the *sukkah* protects us even in the midst of exile, as we strengthen ourselves with the more profound concepts of the Festival.

. . . Bitya is healthy once again, but Elchanan has been sick with hepatitis for five days now. He is staying in his barracks because the hospital is completely full. Shlomo and Helen [Abrahams] were hospitalized two days before Elchanan took ill. Fortunately, Elchanan receives many visitors, which staves off boredom. Bella cooks sweet porridge for him.

The message Father appended to the same letter:

I had a conversation today in the *sukkah* with Uncle Gottfried and his family. They send their warm regards. As of today, Uncle Gottfried will begin learning with Baruch. I have no doubt that Baruch will reap much benefit from this arrangement.

Please make an effort to request papers in the office of Palestine Affairs for Mrs. Lange (née Cohen). . . .

Uncle Gottfried asks me to inform you that he was satisfied with the performance of the individual who led the Morning Service on Yom Kippur. As for me, I was very satisfied with the manner in which Uncle Gottfried led the *Musaf* service!

A portion from Mother's postcard to Grandmother:

October 19, 1943
. . . At this moment, Yona and Shmuel are returning home from learning with Julius [Goldschmidt]. Even Michel has joined them. They are thrilled with their *shiur.*

Postcard dated October 19, 1943, from Westerbork to Grandmother in Davos, Switzerland

A letter from Mother:

October 27, 1943

We will not have the opportunity to send out this letter until this coming Sunday, but I am taking advantage of a calm interlude now in the barracks to thank you for your continuous correspondence and to tell you about the enjoyable time we had during the Festival.

The weather was wonderful throughout Sukkot, and we were able to eat all of our meals inside the *sukkah*. Even though women are not obligated to eat in the *sukkah*, I chose to do so, since the *sukkah* was more pleasant than the barracks. Also, it was nicer to eat the meals with the entire family gathered together.

Simchat Torah passed uneventfully. Mordechai managed to observe the Yom Tov in spite of the restrictions. On Shabbat night, we even ate bread with cold cuts (the Samson family from Copenhagen sent them to us; their package arrived on Yom Kippur). We sat in our corner of the *sukkah* and sang a number of festive songs to the traditional tunes of Hamburg, Zurich and Utrecht. When we were about to finish, all the members of the pioneer training group appeared. Sadly, only six of the group remained and sang with us. We savored the tasty pastries that Alex [De Haas] prepared for the occasion.

Under our current circumstances, it is easier to honor Shabbat and the Festivals at night than during the day. However, with the changing of the season, the days are getting progressively shorter, and Shabbat is beginning at an increasingly earlier hour. It will be more difficult for us, for the men will not be able to return from work before nightfall.

Only Mordechai, Shlomo and Shmuel are working at the moment. Elchanan has been sick with hepatitis for two weeks already. Henry [Abrahams] and other family members are also lying sick in the barracks, and as a result, the evening visiting hour — between seven and eight o'clock — has turned into a family gathering.

Bitya has also taken ill. Only because of her young age have I been permitted to keep her with me. Nevertheless, she is quite lively.

Yona is sick with diphtheria. He is in quarantine and received the vaccine. He has not contracted as severe a case of the disease as Shalom did last year. They are all receiving "good" treatment [in sarcastic terms]. God willing, they will recuperate before the harsh winter sets in.

. . . Our sleeping arrangements are as follows: Shalom

occupies the third level of the bunk, Bitya lies beside me and Bella lies beside Mrs. Gradenwitz. You, dear Mother, wrote that you are incapable of understanding how we can live here. I am doubtful if even the wise King Solomon, in all his wisdom, would have been able to understand such a thing!

Mrs. Dina Eisenman, who perished in Bergen-Belsen

. . . Dina Eisenman [Dr. Yitzchak Breuer's mother-in-law] is still struggling for her life. We hope that the Shabbat will bring her some well-deserved respite. Her daughter, Elisheva Yoshua, somehow managed to obtain half a glass of milk for her, which gave her much pleasure. My heart is filled with deep pain as I remember Mrs. Eisenman's numerous good deeds and the beautiful families that her sons have established since their escape. She was always so energetic and full of vigor!

Elisheva does everything that can be done for her mother, but the conditions in which we live are too powerful for her. What a tragedy!

. . . I received an exemption from work this week, and I hope to relax a little. I have much to do — laundry, mending clothes, many errands to run and many difficult emotions to deal with.

Forgive me, please, for the contents of this letter.

A letter from Mother:

End of Cheshvan 5705 (1944)

. . . With us, everything is progressing more or less as usual. We are kept informed about the condition of our "patients" by the nurses, who live here in our barracks. The sick members of our family are in good company — Mrs. Hugo Kahn and Rebbetzin Auerbach lie in the proximity of Bella, but not close enough for her to be able to speak with them.

Uncle Gottfried and his family are well. Julius [their son] is a man of rare qualities who manages to assist his cousins as well. Everyone loves him. He makes extraordinary efforts on behalf of his parents, including attending to their dietary needs. . . .

Mrs. Eisenman, the mother of Elisheva Yoshua, still clings to life, but Dr. Alfred Klee passed away this week, and his body was incinerated.

I can hear the sounds of Mordechai and the other members of the *minyan* praying now. They pray together early in the morning in a corner of the barracks.

Theo, we are in barracks 63. Many thanks for the small packages. Bea and I would greatly appreciate a slice of soap for our personal use. Bitya is calling to me now. Everyone is beginning to stir. All the boxes must be placed on the beds. Our day has begun. . . .

In just a few more weeks the lights of Chanukah will shine their brilliance upon us, and from there, we will march forward to Pesach!

If He will give me bread to eat and clothing to wear . . .
(*Bereishit 28:20*)

On the Shabbat of *Parashat Vayeitzei* 5704 (1943), I contracted diphtheria and was quarantined in an empty barracks. As I lay there alone with my thoughts, I pondered the prayer uttered by Ya'akov before he left Eretz Yisrael for Aram:

". . . If He will give me bread to eat and clothing to wear, then I will dedicate myself totally to God" (Bereishit 28:20). At first glance, it would seem that Ya'akov was requesting the minimal essentials necessary to sustain life: food and clothing. In truth, however, Ya'akov had to be requesting something more, for his words were "bread *to eat* and clothing *to wear.*" Is it not self-evident that he wanted bread for the purpose of eating and clothes in order to wear them? What do these seemingly superfluous words convey?

The answer came to me as I languished on my sickbed and felt my body drained of all strength. Ya'akov was requesting not only food and clothing, but also sufficient health to be able "to eat" the bread and "to wear" the clothes that God would provide him. To a bedridden sick person, lacking both appetite and the strength to rise from bed, food and clothing have absolutely no value. It is for this reason that Yaakov asked God for "bread *to eat* and clothing *to wear.*"

The food in the camp was not kosher, but neither was it completely *treif*. We did not eat the meat stew that was served twice a week. On Shabbat afternoons we would accept the soup and potatoes, but because the food was cooked by Jewish kitchen workers, we would not eat it until *motza'ei Shabbat*.

Father worked at the tedious, yet not terribly difficult job of inspecting and sorting seeds for planting. During that period Father learned almost every evening with Rabbi Frenkel, may God avenge his blood, the *dayan* (chief rabbinical justice) of the city of Halberstadt. On one occasion, Father asked the *dayan* how he could avoid violating the Shabbat prohibition of *borer* (literally, "sorting"; the removal of undesirable objects from a mixture is one of the thirty-nine types of work prohibited on Shabbat) while carrying out his assigned task of sorting seeds. After devoting some thought to the matter, the *dayan* instructed Father to leave a few bad seeds in the pile.

At the time, I did not fully understand the *dayan*'s ruling. Years later, however, I found a statement in the Jerusalem Talmud (*Shabbat* 7:2) that clearly confirmed his decision. There the Talmud explicitly states that one who separates pebbles from a pile of grain is not regarded as having violated the Torah commandment of *borer*, for this is considered only a rabbinical prohibition. Rav Frenkel had apparently decided that those of us living in the life-threatening environment of Westerbork could rely upon this Talmudic ruling.

This is the true intent of the words we utter in the *Shemoneh Esrey* prayer of Shabbat afternoon, ". . . and through their rest, they will sanctify Your Name."

Songs from the Valley of Tears   *(By Shmuel)*

To this day, I recall several songs and tunes that I learned in the Westerbork transit camp.

Young children used to sing songs in Dutch about the fate that awaited them. They were simple songs that lacked content, but the children sang them with great enthusiasm. The tunes, too, were simple. One song went as follows:

> To Poland we will travel,
> Torn shoe soles upon our feet.
> We will travel together in cattle cars,
> Ahh! It will be so great! . . .

Mr. Hans Krieg organized a choir and taught the boys songs about Eretz Yisrael. I recall one song in particular entitled, "There in the Land that the Patriarchs Cherished." I remember lying in the barracks on the top bunk, burning with fever from a severe case of hepatitis, while below me Hans Krieg patiently taught a group of boys the song:

> There, in the land that the Patriarchs cherished,
> all our hopes will be realized.
> There we will live;
> there we will create a life of freedom, a life of liberty.
> There Hashem's Presence will rest;
> there the language of Torah will flourish.
> "Turn over for yourselves the fallow land" (Hoshea 10:12).

Two tunes that we learned in the children's recreation center have left their indelible impression upon me. The lyrics were familiar, but the tune was new and very moving. The first tune accompanied the words of *Shacharit*, "O Guardian of Israel, protect the remnant of Israel; let not Israel be destroyed — those who proclaim, 'Hear, O Israel.' " The other tune accompanied the words from the

Ninety-three transports left Westerbork.

Book of Eichah, "Bring us back to You, Hashem, and we shall return; renew our days as of old."

Even today, these two tunes — and in particular the tune to ". . . renew our days as of old" — evoke within me a sense of heartfelt prayer. Their somber notes are like the cry of a lonely group of travelers crossing an arid wasteland, like a plea for redemption and deliverance welling up from the depths of the soul.

Some of those designated to be transported to the camps in Eastern Europe faced their fear and anxiety with great courage. As they marched to the cattle cars, they sang in Hebrew:

> We shall meet again in our land,
> after our term of exile has ended,
> Oh, quickly and immediately, quickly and immediately.

> We shall meet again!
> We shall meet again!
> We shall meet again!

Sometimes, those who were to remain behind in the barracks joined those marching to the cattle cars and sang,

> We shall meet again in our land,
> after our term of exile has ended!

They began by raising their voices in song, but before they finished their chorus they were in tears.

Among the many bizarre aspects of camp life were the cabaret-style performances of a certain band of performers. Almost every week, two or three days after the weekly transport to the extermination camps in Poland, these performers — mostly German Jews — would put on a show for the Jewish inmates, the S.S. camp commandant and his senior staff officers. Admission was free.

On the day following the performance, the cabaret's top hits could be heard all over camp. . . . The performers were awarded a temporary deferral from "expulsion to Polish extermination camps" — that is, death in the gas chambers. It is for this reason that

DE DEPORTATIETRANSPORTEN

15 juli	1942-1137 personen naar Auschwitz		10 maart	1943-1105 personen naar Sobibor
16 juli	1942- 586 personen naar Auschwitz		17 maart	1943- 964 personen naar Sobibor
21 juli	1942-1002 personen naar Auschwitz		23 maart	1943-1250 personen naar Sobibor
24 juli	1942-1000 personen naar Auschwitz		30 maart	1943-1255 personen naar Sobibor
27 juli	1942-1010 personen naar Auschwitz		6 april	1943-2020 personen naar Sobibor
31 juli	1942-1007 personen naar Auschwitz		13 april	1943-1204 personen naar Sobibor
3 augustus	1942-1013 personen naar Auschwitz		20 april	1943-1166 personen naar Sobibor
7 augustus	1942- 989 personen naar Auschwitz		27 april	1943-1204 personen naar Sobibor
10 augustus	1942- 547 personen naar Auschwitz			196 personen naar Theresienstadt
14 augustus	1942- 505 personen naar Auschwitz		4 mei	1943-1187 personen naar Sobibor
17 augustus	1942- 510 personen naar Auschwitz		11 mei	1943-1446 personen naar Sobibor
21 augustus	1942-1003 personen naar Auschwitz		18 mei	1943-2511 personen naar Sobibor
24 augustus	1942- 551 personen naar Auschwitz		25 mei	1943-2862 personen naar Sobibor
28 augustus	1942- 608 personen naar Auschwitz		1 juni	1943-3006 personen naar Sobibor
31 augustus	1942- 560 personen naar Auschwitz		8 juni	1943-3017 personen naar Sobibor
4 september	1942- 714 personen naar Auschwitz		29 juni	1943-2397 personen naar Sobibor
7 september	1942- 930 personen naar Auschwitz		6 juli	1943-2417 personen naar Sobibor
11 september	1942- 874 personen naar Auschwitz		13 juli	1943-1988 personen naar Sobibor
14 september	1942- 902 personen naar Auschwitz		20 juli	1943-2209 personen naar Sobibor
18 september	1942-1004 personen naar Auschwitz		24 augustus	1943-1001 personen naar Auschwitz
21 september	1942- 713 personen naar Auschwitz		31 augustus	1943-1004 personen naar Auschwitz
25 september	1942- 928 personen naar Auschwitz		7 september	1943- 987 personen naar Auschwitz
28 september	1942- 610 personen naar Auschwitz		14 september	1943-1005 personen naar Auschwitz
2 oktober	1942-1014 personen naar Auschwitz			1943- 305 personen naar Theresienstadt
5 oktober	1942-2012 personen naar Auschwitz		21 september	1943- 979 personen naar Auschwitz
9 oktober	1942-1703 personen naar Auschwitz		19 oktober	1943-1007 personen naar Auschwitz
12 oktober	1942-1711 personen naar Auschwitz		16 november	1943- 995 personen naar Auschwitz
16 oktober	1942-1710 personen naar Auschwitz			
19 oktober	1942-1327 personen naar Auschwitz		11 januari	1944-1037 personen naar Bergen-Belsen
23 oktober	1942- 988 personen naar Auschwitz		18 januari	1944- 870 personen naar Theresienstadt
26 oktober	1942- 841 personen naar Auschwitz		25 januari	1944- 949 personen naar Auschwitz
30 oktober	1942- 659 personen naar Auschwitz		1 februari	1944- 908 personen naar Bergen-Belsen
2 november	1942- 954 personen naar Auschwitz		8 februari	1944-1015 personen naar Auschwitz
6 november	1942- 465 personen naar Auschwitz		15 februari	1944- 773 personen naar Bergen-Belsen
10 november	1942- 758 personen naar Auschwitz		25 februari	1944- 811 personen naar Theresienstadt
16 november	1942- 761 personen naar Auschwitz		3 maart	1944- 732 personen naar Auschwitz
20 november	1942- 726 personen naar Auschwitz		15 maart	1944- 210 personen naar Bergen-Belsen
24 november	1942- 709 personen naar Auschwitz		23 maart	1944- 599 personen naar Auschwitz
30 november	1942- 826 personen naar Auschwitz		5 april	1944- 289 personen naar Bergen-Belsen
4 december	1942- 812 personen naar Auschwitz			1944- 240 personen naar Auschwitz
8 december	1942- 927 personen naar Auschwitz			1944- 101 personen naar Bergen-Belsen
12 december	1942- 757 personen naar Auschwitz		19 mei	1944- 453 personen naar Auschwitz
				1944- 238 personen naar Bergen-Belsen
11 januari	1943- 750 personen naar Auschwitz		3 juni	1944- 496 personen naar Auschwitz
18 januari	1943- 748 personen naar Auschwitz		31 juli	1944- 213 personen naar Theresienstadt
23 januari	1943- 516 personen naar Auschwitz			1944- 178 personen naar Bergen-Belsen
29 januari	1943- 659 personen naar Auschwitz		3 september	1944-1019 personen naar Auschwitz
2 februari	1943- 890 personen naar Auschwitz		4 september	1944-2087 personen naar Theresienstadt
9 februari	1943-1184 personen naar Auschwitz		13 september	1944- 279 personen naar Bergen-Belsen
16 februari	1943-1108 personen naar Auschwitz			
23 februari	1943-1101 personen naar Auschwitz			
2 maart	1943-1105 personen naar Sobibor			

Detailed list of the transports that left Westerbork for the extermination camps in the east including dates, number of passengers and destination.

they danced and joked so enthusiastically before our tormentors.

Our spiritual exile was truly awesome — imagine having to sing and dance in order to save one's life!

Our attitude was that those who participated in the cabaret performances exhibited a shocking degree of insensitivity and a great lack of sympathy for the unfortunate Jews who had been transported in cattle cars to unknown destinations. Most observant Jews refrained from any involvement in these performances.

A postcard, dated October 31, 1943, to Grandmother in Davos, Switzerland. Mother wrote: "In four weeks will be Chanukah. The lights will burn dimly. . . ."

Chapter Nine
Our Arrival at Bergen-Belsen

From Westerbork to Bergen-Belsen

We arrived at Bergen-Belsen on the seventh day of Shevat 5704 (February 2, 1944).

Thanks to our Paraguayan passports, we were not sent to the extermination camps, but to Bergen-Belsen instead, which according to German terminology was merely an *Aufenthaltslager*, or "detention camp." One should not be fooled by this ostensibly benign classification — the camp regime was brutal and murderous. The only reason Bergen-Belsen did not earn the status of a full-fledged extermination camp is that it lacked the facilities for mass extermination.

An *Appel-Platz* (roll-call square) was located in the center of the camp. Every morning, all working men and women gathered there for roll call. After the Germans counted them, they marched to work in columns, five abreast. We saw a hint to this formation in the verse, "And the Jews left [Egypt] one out of five" (Shemot 13:18).

The *Appel-Platz* was the epicenter of camp life. Several hours after the workers' roll call, a second roll call was held for all those who remained behind in the camp — children, old people over eighty years of age, the sick and all other camp workers. This roll call sometimes took several hours to complete. The long delays resulted from frequent discrepancies between the number of inmates who should have been there according to the Germans' lists and the number of those who were actually present. The discrepancies often resulted from calculating errors that had occurred during the first roll call, or simply from the absence of those who had died since the previous roll call.

The Germans took special delight in prolonging these roll calls. Sometimes we would return to the camp at noon for our half-hour lunch break, only to discover that the children and the aged were still standing in the square, and the demonic roll call far from finished. At such times the Germans would order us to join ranks with the others, which resulted in our missing our lunch, and it robbed us of some much-needed rest. The Germans sometimes went completely insane and made us stand through a second roll call in the evening. As they would say in their inimitable style, "*Ordnung muss sein in der Schweinerei! —* There must be order in this pigsty!" This was the type of insults to which we were subjected day after day — they called us pigs, dogs, subhumans, filthy wretches, idlers and hated outcasts. They constantly reminded us that we had no right to exist. Words cannot adequately describe the demoralizing effects that these words had upon us, and particularly upon the non-observant Jews, who lacked the tools that could have helped them to comprehend why this calamity was befalling them.

The daily roll calls were a nightmare for the camp's thousands of prisoners. Mr. Joseph Weiss, the vice director of the camp, is to be fondly remembered for the great efforts he made in attempting to solve the discrepancies in the roll calls. Beatings were a regular occurrence during the roll calls. Even momentary delays in lining up were punished with beatings, usually in the form of kicks.

The morning roll call began a few minutes after six o'clock in the morning. Those of us who prayed had to rise at around five-fifteen for a half-hour service. Afterwards, we would wash our hands, quickly gulp down two slices of bread, recite *Birkat Hamazon* and run to roll call. This was our daily schedule, seven days a week.

During our first few months in Bergen-Belsen, I worked in *Transport-Kommando* 25, a small work group consisting of about fifteen men. We were assigned the job of moving sand, coal, building materials, cement and other items from one place to another within the confines of the camp, usually to points beyond the fenced-in section where we lived. It was very difficult work that entailed pushing a heavy wagon or wheelbarrow loaded with materials and, on occasion, carrying heavy cement bags on our backs. Part of our work also involved the building of roads.

I worked on the main road, which ran alongside the camp's headquarters. One morning, due to a delay on our way to work, I managed furtively to raise the curtain that separated our camp from the adjacent non-Jewish camp. I wanted to see in what conditions they "lived." I will never forget the scene that I witnessed.

All those prisoners were gathered for morning roll call. The "healthy" ones stood in a slumped position, while the sick and dying lay out in the frigid air. Beside them lay another group, a covered pile of the corpses of those who had died in the course of the previous night. . . .

This was the state of the proud and noble German people in the year 5744! (1944).

Miscellaneous Facts about Bergen-Belsen

Located in North-Central Germany, Bergen-Belsen was divided into several sectors: political prisoners, Russian prisoners-of-war, etc. Our camp was called "The Jewish Camp," or "The Star Camp," because of the shape of the yellow Star-of-David patches that had to be sewn to the clothing of everyone above the age of six. Stitched onto the yellow patch was the word "Jew" — *Jood* in Dutch, *Jude* in German and *Juive* in French.

Numerous books and studies about Bergen-Belsen were published after the war. The following facts and statistics were recorded in the book, *Bergen-Belsen: The Transition from Detention Camp to Concentration Camp, 1943–1945* (Jerusalem 1985), by Professor Everard Kolb. The book, originally written in German, was subsequently abridged and translated into various languages, including Hebrew. The author, a non-Jewish researcher, accurately describes the transformation of Bergen-Belsen from its original designation as a detention camp into a concentration camp in late 1944.

Professor Kolb writes that in the spring of 1943 the German Foreign Ministry issued a recommendation to keep alive a certain number of Jews who were citizens of Allied countries or of any non-European state. These Jews were to be kept as bargaining chips for future prisoner exchanges between Germany and the Allies. Pursuant to this recommendation, the S.S. received orders to send approximately ten thousand "exchange Jews" to a detention camp. Bergen-Belsen was the natural choice — it had originally been built as an important training base for the German army and since 1941 had served as a Russian P.O.W. camp, in which tens of thousands of Russian soldiers had died of starvation and torture. By the fall of 1944, approximately six thousand "exchange Jews" were held in Bergen-Belsen, of whom Dutch Jews comprised the overwhelming majority. The camp population steadily grew as a result of the continuous arrival of prisoners from other camps, who had been classified as "unfit for labor."

Living conditions in Bergen-Belsen began to deteriorate rapidly in the summer of 1944. In response to the encroaching Allied offensives, the Germans began transporting concentration-camp prisoners in ever-increasing numbers, from outlying regions to camps located within the German heartland. Tens of thousands of prisoners perished during this relocation process; they died from exposure to the elements, starvation, exhaustion and German bullets.

Most of the "lucky" ones who survived the relocation were placed in Bergen-Belsen.

A new commandant took charge of the camp in the end of 1944 — Joseph Kramer "the butcher," who previously had presided over the Auschwitz-Birkenau camps. Kramer transformed Bergen-Belsen from a detention camp to a "regular" concentration camp. At that time, the prisoner population of Bergen-Belsen was 15,257.

As the number of new arrivals increased — many of whom were extremely sick and frail — the situation in the camp steadily deteriorated. The size of food portions continually dwindled, and in the last weeks of the war, in the spring of 1945, the German supply system completely collapsed. Food distribution came to a virtual standstill, and it often happened that not even a morsel of food would be handed out for days at a time. Sanitary conditions are beyond description; they simply did not exist. Water shortages were so severe that many prisoners died of thirst or went mad.

The camp was not designed to absorb such an enormous number of people, and this resulted in terribly cramped living conditions. All these factors made Bergen-Belsen fertile ground for rapid and unchecked epidemics, which claimed the lives of thousands. Once someone fell ill in the camp, the chances of recovery were next to nil.

The following statistics of the number of prisoners (both Jewish and non-Jewish) and deaths from February 1945 are presented in Professor Kolb's book on Bergen-Belsen:

Date	No. of Prisoners	No. of Deaths
February 1945	22,000	App. 7,000
March 1945	41,520	18,168

Date	No. of Prisoners	No. of Deaths
April 1, 1945	43,042	App. 9,000
April 15, 1945	60,000	
Post-Liberation		App. 14,000
Sum total of deaths from February to the end of May 1945: nearly 50,000!		

In the second week of April 1945, the remnants of the "exchange Jews" were sent from the camp. Several thousand men, women and children were crammed into three trains for a terror-filled journey through a collapsing Germany. They were eventually liberated by advancing Russian and American troops.

Thus ended the infamous Bergen-Belsen detention camp.

We are counted as sheep led to the slaughter, to be slain and destroyed, to be smitten and shamed.

(From the siddur)

Chapter Ten

Observing Mitzvot
in Bergen-Belsen

Prayer Customs in Bergen-Belsen

In our barracks — 11 E — we recited the Morning Service with a *minyan* each morning before going off to work. We all donned *tallit* and *tefillin*, and on Mondays and Thursdays we read the Torah portion from Uncle Naftali Abrahams' *sefer Torah*. When he was sent to Bergen-Belsen, he had given up his right to bring a bag of clothing and instead brought along a box holding the *sefer Torah*. There were other righteous people who brought concealed Torah scrolls with them as well, and in their merit, several *minyanim* in Bergen-Belsen were able to read from Torah scrolls. Father always insisted that our *minyan* take precautions to avoid disturbing anyone who wanted to remain sleeping until the morning roll call.

We greeted the Shabbat with the recitation of *Kabbalat Shabbat* upon returning from work on Friday evenings. In the first few months following our arrival at Bergen-Belsen, we even changed our clothing in honor of the Shabbat. We entered the Shabbat with the hope that the words of the prayer would be fulfilled: "Too long have you dwelled in the valley of weeping. He will shower compassion upon you. . . . May your oppressor be downtrodden, and may

those who devoured you be cast far off " (*Lecha Dodi*). After everyone finished reciting the *Shemoneh Esrey*, the leader of the services
would read aloud the *Me'ein Sheva* (Seven-Faceted Blessing)
prayer, which is recited in every synagogue in the world.

I mention this last point because I once overheard a conversation between Father and an acquaintance of his who prayed in a
different *minyan*. This *minyan* omitted the *Me'ein Sheva* prayer, in
fulfillment of the law stipulating that this prayer be recited only in
a permanent synagogue (*Shulchan Aruch* 268:10).

Father told the man that he disagreed with their application of
the ruling, for as long as countless numbers of people — including
entire families — were compelled to live in this terrible camp, there
was an obligation incumbent upon all the Jewish men to organize
public prayer services. Since these services were organized and
conducted at set times (as well as in the presence of a *sefer Torah*),
Father felt that the *Me'ein Sheva* prayer should be recited.

Difficult as it may be to believe, differences of opinion regarding halachah existed, even in the morbid darkness of Bergen-
Belsen.

The reading of the Torah portion on Shabbat was the most
problematic aspect of our prayer service. Since, as mentioned earlier, we held the Morning Services before dawn, we had to read the
Torah with the aid of artificial light. On Shabbat, however, since we
could not turn on the lights, it was impossible for us to read the
weekly Torah portion.

Our solution was to read the weekly Torah portion from the
sefer Torah on Friday evening, but obviously without calling seven
people to the Torah and without reciting blessings before and after
the reading. As soon as we finished reading the Torah, we scurried
off to sleep to gather some strength for the back-breaking work
that we would have to perform on the following day.

In the morning we recited the morning and *Musaf* services,
quickly ate our two slices of bread and ran to roll call and then to

our appointed jobs. Although we had no choice but to work on Shabbat, we tried not to become insensitive to the sanctity of the day. Sometimes it seemed to us that of all the days of the week, Shabbat dragged on the longest — it felt as though time were standing still. It was very difficult, if not impossible, to think all day of how to avoid Torah violations of the Shabbat by performing the work in an irregular manner. We worked twelve hours a day on Shabbat — six hours in the morning and six hours in the afternoon. All day long we carried materials, dug ditches, built structures and performed various types of prohibited labor which seemed never to end. How long will this go on? we thought in exasperation. Today is Shabbat, from morning until evening! And yet we were deprived of our Shabbat.

In Bergen-Belsen, we learned a valuable lesson — to appreciate how many precious hours are contained in one Shabbat!

Lovi, the Libyan Teacher *(By Shmuel)*

Shortly after our arrival in Bergen-Belsen, a group of about two hundred Jews from North Africa were brought into the camp. They came from Bengazi and Tripoli, two Libyan cities, and they were British citizens. Their arrival deeply shocked us. Were there no limits to the Germans' hatred of our people?

It seems that the leaders of the Third Reich gave higher priority to the Final Solution than to the war effort, for while the retreating German army was forced to leave behind most of its military equipment in North Africa, the S.S. was busy transporting hundreds of Jewish captives to Europe. Tens of families — including infants and the elderly — were shipped across the Mediterranean, placed in trains and transported to Bergen-Belsen. The Germans sacrificed valuable cargo space in order to bring these Jews to Europe from a distance of over three thousand kilometers!

Mr. A. Hertzberg, in one of his articles on Bergen-Belsen, describes the North African Jews as follows: "Upon their arrival, these families looked as though they had just been exiled from Jerusalem by the wicked Titus."

The central figure among these families was unquestionably Lovi, a young and righteous teacher. His family name appears to have been "Lavi," but everyone called him "Lovi," with the accent on the first syllable. This unique, righteous and courageous man will forever remain engraved in my memory.

Memories of the North African Jews

It is now eleven o'clock in the morning. The second roll call — for those who have not gone to work outside the camp — has just ended. Lovi leads a group of about thirty boys to the square. They are singing Hebrew songs: *"Am Yisrael Chai"* (The Jewish nation lives), *"Ashreinu Ma Tov Chelkeinu U'mah Na'im Goraleinu U'ma Yaffah Yerushateinu"* (We are fortunate — how good is our portion, how pleasant our lot and how beautiful our heritage!) and their favorite, "Go up to Tzion, standard and flag, the flag of the camp of Yehudah. Who by carriage? Who by foot? Together we go; we return to the land of our forefathers, to our beloved land, the cradle of our birth."

I could not turn my eyes away from this holy sight. What great spiritual strength! Even the S.S. officers stood as though hypnotized by what they saw, and, miraculously, they did not dare to harm Lovi.

In spite of the severe prohibition against teaching the children in the camp, Lovi organized a "school" for the Libyan children immediately upon their arrival. Lovi did not recognize the camp laws — he considered himself subject only to Hashem's laws. This gave him the inner strength to brazenly sit the children in the middle of the square and start teaching them *"Yigdal Elokim Chai V'yishtabach"* (Exalted be the Living God and praised).

Young children studying Torah raised their voices in the Valley of Death and cried out to their Father in Heaven: "At the end of days He will send our Messiah to redeem those longing for His final salvation" (end of *Yigdal* prayer).

I learned a great lesson from the self-sacrifice of Lovi, the Libyan teacher who would not submit to the Germans.

Several months later, the Germans transferred the North African Jews, including Lovi, from Bergen-Belsen to an unknown destination.

Their pleas went up before God. *(Shemot 2:23)*

I performed very taxing work in our transport group. Occasionally, an S.S. guard would bring his dog along to accompany us. On one of these occasions I whispered to a co-worker, "Today we are being guarded by two dogs!"

The Germans made us perform construction work, build roads and transport materials from one location to another. Most of the work that we were assigned was unnecessary, for the Germans' primary goal was to break our spirits with continuous back-breaking labor.

I was assigned the most difficult task of all: to wield a heavy hammer and break the huge stones which the Germans intended to use for the foundation of a new road. Using only my two hands, I had to lift the hammer behind my back and swing it down on the stones with full force. This was my job all day long, seven days a week — to work and work without respite. At times, I worked while being beaten by an S.S. soldier. We saw the fulfillment of the verse, "They made the lives of [the Jews] miserable with harsh labor" (Shemot 1:13).

A civilian engineer who arrived daily from his home outside the camp supervised our work and instructed us how to build the road. He explained how to prepare the foundations, lay down the stones, cover them with sand and, finally, spread the tar and level the surface with a heavy roller that had to be pushed by several men. Although he was a tough man, he never beat us.

One day, after we had finished laying down the stones and were about to refill the wagon, this engineer approached the S.S. guard, pointed at me and instructed him to leave me behind. "This boy doesn't know how to work! I'm going to deal with him once and for all!" The S.S. guard happily complied and went off to guard the rest of the men.

I remained behind, alone with this non-Jew. Here I was, a gaunt eighteen-year-old next to a tall, sturdy German. I continued working with all my strength, in a desperate effort to sidestep the evil decree that I felt looming over me. As the non-Jew approached me, I prayed, "Please, Hashem, save me now!" But instead of hitting me, he said in a soft voice, "Don't be afraid. I kept you here in order to give you a little rest. I see how they abuse you. We are being observed from all around by the guards in those watchtowers, so be careful! I will walk in front of you and drop a package for you. Afterwards, go and pick it up discreetly, but be careful!"

The man strolled away and dropped something. I furtively picked it up and quickly placed it in my pocket. Only later did I check its contents — slices of bread! *White* bread, no less, and meat! It had been a very long time since I had last seen such delicacies. The engineer approached me again, as if to yell at me, and I was able to thank him for the bread. The group returned a few minutes later with a wagon full of stones. I did not tell anyone about the incident.

I did not eat the bread immediately. At that time I was still able to observe the halachic requirement of washing the hands prior to eating bread; in addition, I did not want to add nonkosher meat to my diet. Although we did eat the nonkosher food served in the camp, at least it did not contain actual pieces of meat. In the afternoon I brought the bread to Shalom and Bitya, who were in the women's camp. They were overjoyed. Mother was also surprised. I received bread and meat packages once or twice more, in similar incidents.

Then all the curses will come to bear on you.

(Devarim 28:15)

I was once strolling in the *Appel-Platz* after roll call. There was no one there, and all was completely still. I engaged in a silent dialogue with myself:

"You are living in the civilized twentieth century. Perhaps this is all a dream? No, this is no dream!

"You are standing in this camp, where they torment you and all your family for only one reason — because you are Jewish! Is this possible? True, we heard of persecutions in the Middle Ages, but now, in the twentieth century?

"Yes! God is truth and his Torah is truth! I am experiencing the living manifestation of God's admonishment" (see Devarim 28:15–68).

I approached the wall of a barracks and touched it, and I said, "My hands are touching Exile incarnate. If ever I will merit to leave this place, if I refuse to believe that I had been here, these hands will testify to the contrary!"

In spite of the suffering, starvation, illness and degradation, we felt a strong connection to the Jewish nation. In our eyes, we were living an historic chapter in the unique history of the Jewish people. Day after day, the Germans tried to degrade us — they screamed at us, calling us subhumans who did not deserve to be treated as human beings. But the more they tormented us, the more we became convinced that we are the most unique nation on earth.

Most of us had been under the impression that the suffering of the Jewish people had come to an end long ago; that in this new "enlightened" age, we would finally be able to live in peace. But here, once again, we were afflicted by cruel and inhumane masters, bent on exterminating us from the face of the earth.

Could there be any more compelling proof of the timelessness of Torah and the words of the Prophets? Many had thought that the non-Jews of Europe had improved their relationships with Jews, and that the more we would assimilate, the more our image would improve in their eyes.

And yet, here we were in Bergen-Belsen, being treated like subhumans. On our flesh we felt the repercussions of having fallen prey to the false enticements that assimilation had promised.

Passover in Bergen-Belsen, 1944 *(By Shmuel)*

Several days after Purim, the question arose: What would we eat during the eight days of Passover? Should we forgo the bread rations and try to subsist solely on the soup and unpeeled potatoes that were served for lunch?

The rabbis in the camp ruled that in our circumstances the Torah prohibition of eating *chametz* (leaven) on Pesach was overridden by the Torah injunction to "live by them" (Vayikra 18:5). The Torah obligates a Jew to violate all commandments for the sake of preserving a Jewish life, including one's own. Murder, illicit relations and idolatry are the only exceptions to this rule. The Rabbis went so far as to compose a special "*Yehi Ratzon*" (May it be Your will) prayer to be recited by the prisoners prior to eating *chametz* on Passover. It read as follows:

> Father in heaven, it is revealed before You that our will is to do Your will, and to celebrate Passover by eating matzah and by abstaining from eating *chametz*. Alas, our hearts are filled with anguish, for our servitude prevents us [from fulfilling these commandments], and we find ourselves in

mortal danger. We are ready and willing to fulfill Your commandment to "live by them" (Vayikra 18:5) — and not to die by them — and also to obey the warning, "Take heed and watch yourself very carefully" (Devarim 4:9). We therefore beseech You to grant us life, sustain us and speedily redeem us, that we may observe Your commandments, do Your Will and serve You wholeheartedly. Amen.

"אבינו שבשמים הנה גלוי וידוע לפניך שרצוננו לעשות רצונך ולחוג את חג הפסח באכילת מצה ובשמירת איסור חמץ, אך על זאת דאבה לבנו שהשיעבוד מעכב אותנו ואנחנו נמצאים בסכנת נפשות. הננו מוכנים ומזומנים לקיים מצוותך "וחי בהם ולא שימות בהם" וליזהר מאזהרה "השמר לך ושמור נפשך מאד". ועל כן תפילתנו לך שתחיינו ותקיימנו ותגאלנו במהרה לשמור חוקיך ולעשות רצונך לעבדך בלבב שלם, אמן."

Our special "Yehi Ratzon"

Lacking the means to distribute sufficient copies of this prayer, only a few were passed out among the prisoners. My brother Elchanan volunteered to make several handwritten copies of the prayer. He fastidiously performed this tedious task — even including the Hebrew vocalization symbol of each letter — in the evening, after having spent the last twelve hours chopping down trees, and in spite of his own personal intention to forgo eating *chametz* on Passover. The famous original copy of this prayer that appears in many documentary works is a photograph of one of Elchanan's handwritten copies. This scrap of paper bears testimony to his supreme self-sacrifice for the general welfare of the prisoners, and for his observance of Torah commandments throughout the years of the Holocaust.

Without casting any doubts on the validity of the rabbinical ruling permitting the consumption of *chametz* on Passover, our family decided to try to make alternate arrangements and attempt to subsist without it.

Some people who had heard of our plan offered to exchange their cooked potato portions for our bread rations, but Father flatly refused their offer. "It would be unthinkable," he said, "to observe the prohibition against eating *chametz* by passing off our bread to other Jews."

We did manage, however, to come up with an acceptable solution. I performed various forms of maintenance work around the camp and also assisted in bringing the men's food rations, including those of my father and my brothers. Father asked me to try to store away food for Passover from our own rations. I began approximately three weeks before Passover, removing two potatoes from each of our portions, so that by the end of each day, I managed to store away ten potatoes.

Our next problem was to find a way to preserve the food for a period of close to a month. The solution we found was to dry the potatoes on top of the heater in our barracks. Just before Passover, I prepared potato cakes from our stored potatoes.

We ate these potato cakes in the mornings and in the evenings throughout the eight days of Passover. For lunch, we ate the fresh potatoes that were served every day for lunch. Obviously, the food we ate was not kosher for Passover according to the letter of the law, but we did succeed in avoiding eating pure or mixed *chametz*.

Most of the people in our barracks had no idea that the Emanuel family was not eating bread during Passover. When bread rations were distributed on the days of Passover, we requested of the man in charge of the distribution that he place our bread rations in a particular suitcase which we had previously set aside for this purpose. We had declared the suitcase and its contents "ownerless," which meant that the bread that was stored there during Passover was not legally ours. After Passover, we reclaimed ownership of the suitcase and ate the bread.

Our supply of potato cakes was depleted on the last day of *Chol Hamo'ed* (the sixth day) of Passover, and we were at a loss as to what we would eat on the last two days of the festival. Miraculously, a new transport of Dutch Jews arrived at the camp on the *very day* that our rations ran out, and among that group we found our former neighbors from Utrecht, the Hirschmans. When I informed them that we had nothing left to eat for the last two days of Passover, they presented us with a bag of beans, and our problem was solved.

Before Passover, we made arrangements to bake sufficient *matzot* for everyone to fulfill the commandment of eating a *kezayit* (the volume of an olive) of matzah on the night of the Seder. Baruch obtained flour from the group of Libyan Jews who had arrived from the city of Bengazi. Elchanan prepared the *mayim shelanu*. He *kashered* a glass bottle by filling it with water for three consecutive days, and then he refilled it with water which he left in the bottle overnight. Mother readied some utensils for preparing the dough, and we "borrowed" wood from the camp premises to heat the oven. Finally, we inspected the oven in our barracks to determine if it was fit for baking.

Several people joined us in the baking of the *matzot*. A young boy named Yosef Adler, may his blood be avenged, oversaw the baking; my teacher, Rav Davids, supervised my mother while she kneaded the dough. All of us pitched in to ensure the success of the project. We placed a sheet-metal surface into the oven and baked the meticulously prepared dough upon it.

As we baked, people from neighboring barracks brought even more flour for *matzot*, and our supply of *mayim shelanu* was quickly depleted. However, Rav Davids ruled that as long as some of the original contents remained, other water could be added to the bottle and used for baking the matzah.

While we baked, we were secure in the knowledge that my brother Baruch and Ya'akov Yoshua were standing guard outside the barracks, but suddenly, the order *"Achtung!"* rang out in the room, and to everyone's dismay, an S.S. man strutted into the barracks and demanded to know what we were doing.

Meanwhile, Mother had managed to remove some of the utensils, while others who were there explained to the German that we were making birthday cakes! Fortunately for us, this older Nazi soldier readily accepted our explanation. To our intense relief, he turned and left.

Seder night was observed without disturbance. We fulfilled the commandment to drink the Four Cups using four cups of tea as a substitute for wine. We read the Haggadah, and everyone ate a very small amount of matzah.

At the end of the Seder, we fervently recited the prayer, "Pour out Your wrath upon the nations. . . . Pursue them with anger and destroy them from beneath the heavens of God." The following morning, everyone except Yona went to work. He had a purulent wound, on the merit of which he managed to avoid having to work during Passover, both on Yom Tov and on Shabbat.

Chapter Eleven

Summer in Bergen-Belsen

Shabbat Minchah Prayer

One particular event that took place on a Shabbat in the summer of the year 1944 made an especially powerful impression on me. It was six-thirty in the evening as hundreds of broken and starving Jews returned from a day of back-breaking labor. Every day, as they entered the camp gate, the Germans would recount them. Their hatred for us was so intense that they counted us not only when we left for work, but also when we returned.

Father had not returned from work that Shabbat afternoon on time to recite *Minchah* with the rest of us. His work group, called the Benedict Unit, which consisted almost entirely of middle-aged men, had been selected for punishment — they were made to stand at attention beside the camp gate for several hours.

Utter torture! Who knows why? Perhaps they failed to chop down their daily quota of trees; maybe the Germans discovered that they were not working today — on Shabbat — at the same pace as they did on weekdays. Father had devised a system to minimize the amount of Shabbat desecration they would have to commit by putting away a few cut pieces of wood throughout the week, and using them to fulfill the Shabbat quota. Perhaps the Germans had discovered them?

There they stood, exhausted and broken, beside the camp gate. The S.S. guard in the watchtower made a point of having these poor, suffering Jews stand at absolute attention the entire time. After an hour, the S.S. guard came down from the watchtower, and a great fear descended upon the group: perhaps he would beat them! Instead, he passed right by them and continued walking in the direction of the camp's administration buildings. Since each prisoner's name was registered, they could not leave the formation, but they felt an overwhelming sense of relief nevertheless.

Once the guard disappeared at the end of the roadway, the men were able to stand in a more relaxed position, and they even exchanged a word or two with one another. Father then took the entire group by surprise when he began melodiously to recite the Shabbat *Minchah* prayer:

> Praiseworthy are those who dwell in Your house; may they always praise You, *Selah.* . . . A redeemer shall come to Zion. . . . "And as for me, this is My covenant with them," says Hashem. . . . May his great Name be exalted and sanctified. . . . You are One, and Your Name is One; and who is like Your people, Israel? . . . And through their rest, they will sanctify Your Name. . . . May you be pleased with our rest. Sanctify us with Your commandments and grant us our share in Your Torah; satisfy us from Your goodness and gladden us with Your salvation . . . graciousness, kindness and compassion, upon us and upon all of Your people, Israel.

When the S.S. guard reappeared, the men once again snapped to attention and remained standing there until very late at night.

This story was related to me on the following day by Mr. Levi Van Leeuwen, may God avenge his blood, who had been one of the members of the Jewish Burial Society in The Hague. He added, "In my entire life, I have never heard a *Minchah* like that!"

. . . to keep them alive in famine.

(Tehillim 33:19)

Once, while we were paving a road in the camp, a fellow worker bared his soul to me and asked, "Why is all this happening to us? Why are we starving? Can't Hashem provide us with food? Life has become totally unbearable! The hunger is going to drive us all to insanity, God forbid!"

I admitted that these same questions had been troubling me as well, and that I did not know the answers. However, I added, we should consider the meaning of the verse, "To deliver their souls from death, and to keep them alive in famine" (Tehillim 33:19). I pointed out that Hashem never promised to always grant us enough food to feel sated. He promised only that He would always give us enough "to deliver" our souls "from death" and to keep us "alive in famine." Therefore, even in our current miserable conditions, it is incumbent upon us to thank Hashem for fulfilling His promise to us.

Between Hope and Despair

"Bread" was the catchword in Bergen-Belsen. To obtain bread was the ultimate aspiration of each and every prisoner. Even the few individuals who did not succumb to the instinct of scavenging after any edible object — including potato peels — were unable to free themselves from agonizing thoughts of food. Respectable and noble individuals would quarrel over rations, claiming that a fellow inmate had received a thicker portion of soup; or they would heatedly argue that their portion of bread was smaller than that of everyone else.

Another catchword that instigated countless altercations in Bergen-Belsen was "*Austausch*," which literally means "exchange," as in "prisoner exchange." Our section of the camp was comprised exclusively of Jews who possessed either foreign passports or entry visas into Palestine. Rumor had it that we had been brought to Bergen-Belsen in preparation for a massive prisoner exchange — our freedom would secure the freedom of German citizens being held by the Allies. Despite all the hopeless signs and the inhumane treatment to which we were subjected, we sensed that our section enjoyed some sort of privileged status; for example, we were allowed to wear civilian clothing, whereas the rest of the inmates wore convict-style uniforms.

The rumors, however, were incongruous with the harsh reality that continuously sapped our strength. The camp was run by cruel and merciless men, and the crushing burden of the work was simply too much to bear.

A few weeks after Passover of the year 5704 (1944), a list of approximately three hundred names was called during one of the roll calls. Our names did not appear on this list.

This group of three hundred individuals was transferred to a separate sector, situated not far from our own. They were immediately given better living conditions and additional food rations, apparently in preparation for an imminent prisoner exchange. However, a few days later about thirty of them were returned to our sector, and then a month later, fifty more were returned. What a disappointment! A few weeks after that, the entire group was sent back. Poor fellows! They had almost tasted freedom, only to come back to our group.

Nevertheless, the rumors persisted: "An exchange will take place soon; an exchange *will* take place!" Indeed, several weeks later, over two hundred men, women and children were ordered to prepare for a journey. This time they did leave, and according to the prevalent rumors, they were sent to Eretz Yisrael while we remained behind!

From time to time, rumors circulated that an additional group was due to leave the camp. Such rumors never materialized, and in fact our condition deteriorated even further.

The Germans occasionally sent a small number of individuals to unknown destinations, an event that did not bode well. One day, they took the two young men who worked in the crematorium, burning corpses. Apparently the Germans did not want to leave behind witnesses who would describe how they extracted gold teeth from the dead and burned corpses in the crematorium. There were quite a few select individuals who disappeared in this manner.

The Energetic and Personable Baruch

My brother Baruch was fifteen years old when we arrived at Bergen-Belsen. At that point, children his age were not required to work; however, the Germans occasionally recruited youngsters for specific projects. At such times Baruch was also taken and, in spite of his young age, was cruelly beaten as well.

Baruch was energetic, and he knew what it meant to help people in difficult situations. One day in the summer of 1944, my work group was punished — we were ordered to stand in the square adjacent to the front gate into the late hours of the night. We stood there suffering in silence as we shivered with cold; a healthy individual would not have felt cold, but we were suffering from malnutrition, diarrhea and intense physical exhaustion following a twelve-hour work shift.

Suddenly Baruch appeared, wearing an overcoat. As he passed by me, he let the coat slip off his body and innocently continued walking. I was able to put on the coat without the guard in the watchtower taking notice.

I was not the only one who benefited from the coat. An hour later a member of our group — Joseph Freihan, of blessed memory — fainted from exhaustion, and I used the coat to cover him. When the S.S. guard passed by, he ordered one of our men to fetch a pail of water . . . and to spill it on the prone man.

"They will be bloated by famine" and consumed by lice.
(See Devarim 32:24)

The combination of oppressive labor, beatings, starvation and diseases transformed camp life into a living hell. The impossibly substandard hygienic conditions created a breeding ground for fatal diseases, which spread in epidemic proportions throughout the camp. Everyone suffered from chronic diarrhea, and many inmates had contracted typhus. It is impossible to describe the "bathrooms" and the sanitary condition of the barracks.

Malnutrition caused our arms and legs to swell, and festering sores appeared all over our bodies. At one point, in addition to suffering from diarrhea, a giant sore appeared on my left knee. After treating and bandaging the wound, the Jewish doctor assured me that it would heal soon. However, the next day I felt intense irritation in the bandaged area, which grew ever more painful as the hours passed. The doctor assured me that this was a sign that the wound was healing and that I must refrain from removing the bandage. After a day or two I could not tolerate the pain any longer, and in desperation I removed the bandage. I saw an open wound, and inside . . . dozens of lice eating away at my raw flesh. This was the "sign" that the wound was healing!

The "Hospital"

The "hospital" (*Krankenlager* or *Krankenrevier*) was the most bizarre facility in the camp. Paradoxically, the Germans cruelly oppressed us and rejoiced over every Jew who collapsed and died, and yet at the same time, they permitted the existence of a "hospital" staffed by Jewish doctors and nurses.

I was admitted to the hospital twice. The first time was in the summer of 5704 (1944), when Dr. Nussbaum diagnosed signs of swelling in my feet as a result of malnutrition. I was admitted again several months later, when I contracted typhus and was running a very high fever. I am forever grateful to nurse Gerda Kahn (today Mrs. Gerda Hirsch), who did everything she could for the welfare of her patients. Once, after a German doctor ordered her to inject me with a certain medicine, Gerda informed me (after he had gone) that since this medicine was harmful, she would not fulfill his order. She instructed me to answer in the affirmative should the doctor ask me whether I had been given the injection.

Mother came to visit me in the hospital, and she brought me a portion of her food ration. Mother suggested that I attempt to speak with her uncle, Shalom Goldschmidt, may Hashem avenge his blood, who was also bedridden in the hospital. As a young man, Uncle Shalom had traveled to Siberia as an agent for Hirsch, a metalworks facility based in Halberstadt, Germany. Finding kosher food in Siberia had been no simple matter, and Uncle Shalom had many interesting stories to relate about his experiences in those days. Mother thought it would be good for me to hear some of those stories. Unfortunately, Uncle Shalom's bed was too far away from my own, and I was unable to speak with him.

Heresy in the Outer Fringes of the Camp

As has already been noted, my limbs swelled as a consequence of malnutrition and the heavy work that I performed, building roads and transporting materials, and so I was admitted into the "hospital." Following my discharge I was given an easier job, working in the Shoe Tent. Hundreds of Jews worked there disassembling tens of thousands of used shoes that were brought to Bergen-Belsen from all over Germany.

I worked with a group of Zionist pioneers who were very far from any interest in religious observance. Every morning, a member of this group would relate a ten-minute segment of a story. It was a good idea, but the story was extremely sad. It was based on

Franz Warfell's work, which describes the terrible suffering of the Armenians at the hands of the Turks following World War I.

I asked the storyteller why he did not tell a more encouraging story. His answer astounded me: "Many members of our group feel that the Jewish people are unique among all the nations. We must erase such thoughts from their minds, and thereby prevent them from succumbing to religious observance. The story of the Armenians is ideal, since it proves that the Jewish people do not have a special destiny. The Armenians suffered to the same degree that we are suffering now."

Needless to say, I did not feel comfortable with these pioneers. I remembered a particular *shiur* on the first verse of the Book of Tehillim: "Fortunate is the man who has not followed the counsel of the wicked, nor stood in the ways of sinners, nor sat in the company of scoffers." We had studied Malbim's comments regarding the dangers involved in seeking the "counsel of the wicked" and in following "the path of the sinful," as well as Rav Hirsch's words of caution against "sitting in the company of scoffers." I desperately sought a way to leave this group of self-professed apostates.

Thankfully, it was not long before the opportunity arose: one day, a supervisor walked into the Shoe Tent and asked for a volunteer to gather all the scraps of shoes that were strewn throughout our workshop and to dump them onto a large heap of shoe remnants that had formed in front of the tent. The inmates of Bergen-Belsen referred to this heap of shoe scraps as *Schuhberg* (Shoe Mountain). The supervisor mentioned that it would take about a week to complete this job. When everyone remained silent, I volunteered. The pioneers looked at me with pity in their eyes. "The work is too difficult for you," they warned me; but I insisted.

It was horrible work. Boards were placed over the thousands of shoe remnants in order to make it possible for the workers to push a wheelbarrow to the top of the heap, but this did not prevent me from falling countless times as I made my way up. The S.S.

guards prodded us to run all the way up the ramp to the top of the heap, and they often beat us while screaming, "*Das ist die Juedische Klagemauer* — This is the Wailing Wall of the Jews!*"

Although I worked there for no more than a week, the experience left me deeply traumatized. Upon finishing this brief stint, I was to resume my regular work in the Shoe Tent with the pioneer group, but I had absolutely no desire to do so. I had heard that there was a group working in one of the barracks that was comprised of individuals such as Rav Shimon Dasberg and Reb Alexander Zimmer, may Hashem avenge their blood, along with a number of other acquaintances. I knew that there was no point in asking to be transferred to that group, so I simply showed up at their barracks one morning and informed the supervisor that I had been sent to work under him. The work was relatively easy, and I enjoyed the opportunity to be in the company of such worthy men.

Learning about the Holy Temple

King David said, "I have learned from all those who have taught me" (Tehillim 119:99). Even though I had disliked being with the pioneers who worked in the Shoe Tent, I appreciated their idea of setting aside fifteen minutes every morning for storytelling. After I had worked alongside my new companions for a few days, I suggested to them that we incorporate this practice in our daily routine, in a slightly different format — rather than telling over some inane story, one of us would deliver a short presentation on any Torah topic.

To my delight, my suggestion was enthusiastically received by the members of my new work group. Rav Dasberg was given the honor of being our first speaker. He delivered his presentation on the very next morning, the first day of the month of Menachem Av 5704 (1944). In honor of Rosh Chodesh, he spoke about the *tehillim* that appear in *Hallel*. I still remember some of the thoughts that he elucidated in that presentation. He explained that the passage beginning with the words *"min hameitzar"* (from the straits) contains the prayers that were uttered by those who made the pilgrimage to Jerusalem. As they ascended towards the Holy Temple they would say, "Open the gates of righteousness for me, that I may enter them and thank God. This is the gate of God — the righteous shall enter through it. I thank You, for You have answered me and have become my salvation. The stone that the builders despised has become the cornerstone. This is God's doing; it is wondrous in our eyes. This is the day that God has made; let us rejoice and be glad in it" (Tehillim 118:19–24).

As the pilgrims entered the Holy Temple, they prayed with great emotion, "O God, please deliver us! O God, please grant us success!" (ibid., 25).

The Levites greeted the pilgrims by singing, "Blessed is he who comes in the name of God; we bless you from the house of God!" (ibid., 26). Then the Levites would tell them, "Bind the festival offering with cords to the corners of the Altar" (ibid., 27) — in other words, "Prepare the sacrificial offering."

In response the pilgrims declared, "You are my God, and I will thank You; [You are] my God, and I will exalt You" (ibid., 28).

The Levites then called out to them, "Give thanks to God, for He is good!" (ibid., 29).

Reb Alexander Zimmer, a member of the pioneer training group *No'ar Agudati*, spoke on the following morning. He was a diligent Torah scholar of noble character who, in spite of the great difficulties to which he was subjected, made a very deep impression on all those who merited to be in his proximity. A description of him appears in the work *He'emanti Ki Adaber* (p. 322), by Shlomo Samson:

> He was a prodigy, a diligent Torah scholar and a pioneer, whose Talmud never left his hand. [Reb A. Zimmer had a miniature set of Talmud, so he was able to carry around a

Sketches of Bergen-Belsen

No war-time photographs of Bergen-Belsen have ever been found. The British troops who liberated us photographed some of the horrific scenes they encountered, including the macabre sight of thousands of gaunt corpses scattered throughout the camp. But these post-war photographs fail to capture the full extent of our suffering.

Mr. Yehudah A. Asscher, may Hashem avenge his blood, spent much of his time sketching the grim environment of Bergen-Belsen during 1944–1945. It's difficult to imagine the conditions in which he practiced his craft — only a very skilled and determined artist could have worked under such circumstances. Somehow he managed to look at our dismal surroundings with his artist's eye and illustrate the stark scenery with his skilled hands. In his numerous sketches he depicts familiar images: rows of dilapidated barracks, tiered bunks, ominous watchtowers, a slice of the coarse brown bread on which we subsisted, even an ailing inmate in the throes of death. His sketch of Shoe Mountain, which I mention in my memoir, awakens many of the painful memories that are eternally etched in the recesses of my mind.

There is no doubt in my mind that Mr. Asscher's collection of sketches has a similar impact on other concentration-camp survivors. Anyone who was in Bergen-Belsen during the Holocaust must be moved to the core of his being by these sketches.

I would like to thank the artist's son, Mr. Yissachar (Berry) Asscher, and his sister Mrs. Rachel Leventhal, for granting me permission to include a number of these works in my memoir. Mr. Yissachar Asscher provided the following biographical details of the artist.

Yehudah Aryeh (Louis) Asscher, zt"l

My father was born in Amsterdam on September 3, 1885. He perished on April 19,1945 aboard the last train to leave Bergen-Belsen — "The Lost Transport" — near the village of Shipkow in East Germany. He was buried there in a mass grave alongside the hundreds of other passengers who died in the course of this ill-fated journey.

From an early age my father expressed a desire to attend art school, but being one of twelve children, he worked as a diamond polisher to help his father sustain the household. He continued sketching on his own, honing his craft to perfection.

My father raised us in the spirit of Torah. He earned a good reputation among Dutch Jews, and a constant stream of rabbis and members of Chovevei Tzion visited him in our home.

My parents and siblings were sent to the camps soon after the German invasion of the Netherlands. Before he was taken away, my father managed to stuff paper and other drawing implements into his knapsack. During the two years he spent in Bergen-Belsen, he managed to complete thirty-five sketches of the camp. The S.S. guards strictly forbade taking photographs or drawing sketches of our surroundings, so my father was taking a considerable risk. If he were discovered, he would likely be shot to death, but a deep urge to draw prompted him to continue his work despite the dangers.

His son Eliezer, who died two months after liberation, brought my father's sketches to the Netherlands. Upon Eliezer's death, my sister Rachel took possession of the collection and brought them with her to Eretz Yisrael. Part of the collection has been on display for a number of years in the Yad Vashem Holocaust Museum in Jerusalem.

The artist's father, a Sofer Stam in Amsterdam, Rabbi Eliezer Asscher, zt"l

Yehudah Aryeh (Louis) Asscher's self-portrait completed in 1938

One of the many watchtowers in Bergen-Belsen

A second watchtower

A row of barracks

More barracks

Barrack 27, the artist's living quarters

The sign warns that anyone who crosses this point places his life in mortal danger.

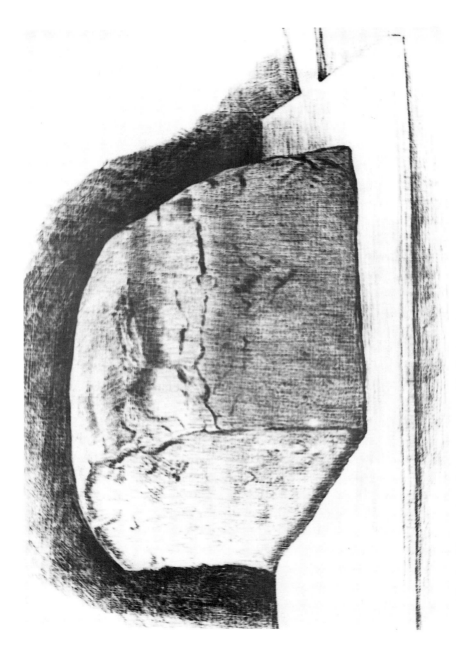

The hard brown bread that was served to the inmates

The triple-tiered bunks that lined the barracks

Three inmates sharing the top layer of a bunk.

The hut in which two young members of the crematorium staff lived, completely isolated from the rest of the camp

Shoe Mountain

A Jew from Salonika lies dying on the artist's bed.

volume wherever he went.] He would study and teach Talmud in every spare moment, even during the short afternoon breaks. He strove to study at all times, regardless of the late hour or the inclement weather. Eventually, illness and malnutrition claimed his life — only then did he stop learning. He was an extraordinary man. . . .

On the second morning of our "lecture series," Reb Alexander discussed *Perek Eizehu Mekoman shel Zevachim*, the chapter from *masechet Zevachim* that we recite every morning in the *Korbanot* section of the prayer service. I was greatly impressed with the quality of the *shiur*. During the next several mornings, he explained to us the manner in which each type of sacrificial offering was brought to the Altar, and he included the commentary of Rav Shimshon Raphael Hirsch.

In addition to his extensive knowledge of the laws relating to the sacrificial offerings mentioned in *Perek Eizehu Mekoman*, Reb Alexander was also extremely well versed in Rav Hirsch's commentary on *Parashat Vayikra*, which explains the deeper significance of these laws. He explained to us, for example, why a sacrifice may be ritually slaughtered by a non-priest, why the individual offering the sacrifice must lean upon it with all his weight while confessing his sins, why the blood of the animal sacrificed must be sprinkled upon the Altar, why a portion of the sacrificial offering must be consumed by the priest, why the bullock and goat offered on Yom Kippur must be entirely burned. These were just some of the many topics he taught us in the course of this series of lectures. To this day, Reb Zimmer's *shiurim* stand out in my mind as a paradigm of how the abstract laws governing sacrificial offerings may be understood through an analytical approach, woven together with the dazzling ideas of Rav Hirsch.

All the members of the work group, including the person who was delivering the *shiur* at the time, would continue working without respite. The lecture would come to an abrupt pause whenever an S.S. guard would come within earshot. It was truly an uplifting experience for me to manage to learn such lofty words of Torah in such a makeshift manner and under such difficult circumstances. I must say that I took special pride in having initiated these *shiurim*.

I do not recall how long it was that I spent working with this group, but eventually I was transferred back to the unit to which I had belonged before my bout of illness and my subsequent hospitalization. It seems that someone finally noticed that I was not registered as a member of this group; so there I was, back where I had started — paving roads and transporting materials from one end of the camp to the other.

I learned very little Torah during the years of hiding and internment, but on occasion I was able to savor the sweet taste of Torah study, despite the horrific conditions under which we lived. In Westerbork and in Bergen-Belsen I hardly managed to learn at all. We worked from sunrise to sunset on Shabbat and holidays, so it was impossible to learn at these times. During our first few months in Bergen-Belsen we did not work on Sunday afternoons because the S.S. guards were off duty then. I utilized some of those rest hours to learn, even though it was very difficult to concentrate. In light of the terrible conditions in which we subsisted, I regarded every iota of Torah study as a major accomplishment.

There were some unique and extraordinary individuals who did manage somehow to learn Torah continuously in the camps. My uncle Naftali Abrahams, may Hashem avenge his blood, was one of them. He would learn alone, with his sons and with my brother Shmuel. I too merited occasionally to learn with him on some Sunday afternoons. My brother Elchanan, may Hashem avenge his blood, was another such individual — he devoted every spare moment he had to Torah study. In addition, I have already mentioned Rav Alexander Zimmer, may Hashem avenge his blood.

Father learned *Chumash* with Rashi's commentary during the

short half-hour afternoon breaks. He sometimes dozed off as he held the book in his hands, but only for a brief moment.

It is difficult to convey the value of Torah study in such appalling conditions.

In reference to the passage from the *Musaf* service of Rosh Hashanah, "To revive with the year's dew those whose decree [to die] is sealed," Rabbi Yechiel of Paris (as quoted in *Ma'aseh Oreg*) said, "When a person who is in the midst of learning Torah falls asleep over his book, the Holy One stores away the spittle that drips from his mouth and transforms it into the dew that will revive him in the end of days."

If Rabbi Yechiel said this in reference to any Jew who falls asleep in the midst of his learning, then surely it can be applied to one who fell asleep while learning Torah in Bergen-Belsen.

Rav Alexander Zimmer:
An Upright and Righteous Man   *(by Dr. Schweizer)*

The following is an excerpt from the sixth volume of Zachor, a publication containing recollections of various Holocaust survivors:

I met Rav Zimmer, *zt"l*, when we were still refugees in Holland. Even then I realized that before me stood a true Torah scholar and an extraordinarily righteous person. Here was a Jew who knew how to struggle and fight, both for his religious principles and for basic human values.

Even in the Bergen-Belsen concentration camp, amidst the most terrible and appalling conditions, the man did not stray even a hairsbreadth from the path that he had chosen for himself. He insisted on following in the path of the righteous at all costs.

Despite his being weak and infirm, he somehow managed to cling to life throughout the war years in the intolerably dreadful conditions that characterized our existence in Bergen-Belsen. To me, it seems a miracle that he survived so long.

In the summer of the year 5702 (1942), I saw him when he was showering himself in the bathhouse. Already then his body was unbelievably thin and gaunt — he looked exactly like those emaciated concentration-camp victims in the pictures. Only his powerful desire to live and his profound faith in the Creator of the universe enabled him to subsist for so long under such horrendous conditions. He returned his pure soul to his Creator in the month of Shevat 5705 (1945) in Bergen-Belsen.

Reb Alexander worked alongside us for an extended period of time. I kept track of his activities; I saw the great efforts he made to avoid performing one of the thirty-nine Torah-ordained prohibited types of work on Shabbat. I often saw him holding a wrench or screwdriver on Shabbat, pretending to be busy at work. I will never understand how he managed to pretend to be working for an entire day, without actually *doing* anything — only one who has attempted such behavior knows what a difficult and nerve-wracking feat he achieved.

I also witnessed Reb Alexander's awesome level of faith while standing through *Appel* (roll call) three times each day. According to the rules, the inmates had to stand ramrod straight and remain perfectly silent — we were not allowed to make the slightest movement or even to emit a whisper from our lips. Nevertheless, Reb Alexander made it his habit to hold a *Sefer Tehillim* in his hand and recite *tehillim* throughout the entire roll call. The S.S. guards frequently pummeled his frail body with potentially lethal blows for flouting the rules so brazenly, but he would not be deterred. He absorbed the blows as if they were the most natural thing in the world.

At work, he concealed a number of *sefarim* under his desk, including a *masechta* of *mishnayot*.

Reb Alexander stood so firmly by his principles that the possibility of swaying him to a different way of thinking was next to impossible. He and I used to have recurring arguments over the true intent of the Torah-ordained commandments, "Take very good care of yourselves" (Devarim 4:15) and "You shall live by them" (Vayikra 18:5). For a very long time, Rav Alexander categorically refused to eat any prohibited foods.

The first time I had the opportunity to eat a snail, I cringed inside at the very thought of ingesting this lowly creeping creature; but in time I became accustomed to eating them, and even began actively to search after them, for they are pure protein. In contrast, Reb Alexander would not touch snails; the thought of eating them never even crossed his mind. He would sometimes exchange his bread ration for other foods, but this practice did not offset his condition of severe malnutrition.

Reb Alexander adhered to his principles not merely for the sake of outward appearances. On the contrary, his refusal to sway from the path of Torah was rooted in a deep and sincere inner conviction that this was what God expected of him. He remained fully committed to his principles and made the strongest possible human effort to live in accordance with them throughout the years of his incarceration. He had come to terms with his fate, and in the depths of his soul he felt absolute peace and contentment with his lot.

I will never forget Reb Alexander's famous "protest" in Bergen-Belsen, a protest that was typical of him, although no one else in the camp would have had the courage. The Germans used to entertain themselves by subjecting both male and female inmates to cruel forms of torture. For committing the most minor infractions, they would force women to bend down until their fingers reached their toes, and remain in this position for hours at a time. Men were punished in similar fashion; they were ordered to cross their arms behind their heads and squat down close to the ground.

Upon seeing a group of inmates being subjected to this form of punishment, Reb Alexander reacted in his own characteristic way — as he could not stand to see his fellow Jews suffering in this manner, he decided to admonish the S.S. officer for treating the inmates so cruelly. We tried to stop him, but he was adamant.

He boldly strode up to the S.S. officer and pointed out to him that this form of punishment was cruel and inhumane, and that it must be stopped at once.

The repercussions were not long in coming. He sustained heavy blows and kicks, and then was forced to undergo the very punishment against which he had protested.

After enduring the long hours of physical torture, Reb Alexander apologized to his friends and explained, "I had my doubts as to whether my protest would produce any results, but I had no choice — my conscience would not let me stand idly by and watch my fellow Jews suffer. The least I could do was to voice my protest!"

During our last winter in Bergen-Belsen, in the year 5705 (1945), Reb Alexander's work group was assigned some excruciatingly difficult labor in the forest that bordered the camp. The work was much too difficult for a man in his frail condition — he simply could not keep up. In my capacity as a camp physician, I released him from work on grounds of "illness," and from that point on he remained inside the boundaries of the camp, confined to his bunk.

In Bergen-Belsen, it was no great luxury to stay in one's bunk all day long, for the Germans allotted no more than eighty centimeters of space to each inmate. People were crammed together like sardines; we could not move a limb in bed. However, the discomfort did not seem to bother Reb Alexander — whenever I visited him, I found him reading some *sefer* or another with a look of intense concentration.

To my great distress, I noted that Reb Alexander's removal from the work force came too late — his strength continued to ebb, to the point that he could hardly manage to lower himself from his bunk in order to drag himself to the kitchen to pick up his food.

His death was inevitable. When I visited him for the last time on January 23, 1945, he was extremely weak. Afterwards I myself contracted an extremely severe case of dysentery. By the time I recovered, Reb Alexander was gone. I would guess that he died sometime during the end of January 1945.

He had so much wanted to live. Unlike many of the prisoners, he never expressed a desire to die. He had always been optimistic about his chances of survival, and he fervently hoped that he would merit to remain alive and thereby continue serving Hashem with all his soul and with all his might.

Each year, as I recite the passage *"Eileh Ezkerah"* during the *Musaf* service on Yom Kippur, Rav Alexander Zimmer's image always comes to mind. In my opinion, his name should be eternally inscribed in the annals of our people.

May his soul be bound in eternal life; may his merit endure for him and for all the members of his family.

Words of Torah on Shabbat Eve   *(By Shmuel)*

In the process of writing this book, I paid a visit to Rebbetzin Erika Davids of blessed memory, the widow of the chief rabbi of Rotterdam, Rav Yissachar Davids, may Hashem avenge his blood. She told me the following:

After having been in Bergen-Belsen for a few weeks, I felt a strong desire to raise the spirits of the women in our barracks. I suggested that we get together every Shabbat eve, and I added that if anyone could, they should bring a white tablecloth with which to cover the table.

The women were overjoyed with the suggestion.

That Friday afternoon, I lit two small Shabbat candles in the middle of the barracks, and in the evening I said some words of Torah. During those Friday night get-togethers, I would simply open my *siddur* at random and expound upon the first words that I would come across.

Our Small Way of Sabotaging the German War Effort

In the end of the summer of the year 5704 (1944), our work group was assigned the task of constructing an anti-aircraft position. We dug a deep trench, erected a sand embankment and cut down so many trees that our hands began literally to drip with blood. An S.S. guard who did not seem to know much about the fine points of building anti-aircraft positions instructed us each step of the way and supervised our work.

When we finally completed the job, we were subjected to fierce beatings by an S.S. officer, who claimed that the bunker was completely worthless. Although I had never undergone any military training, even I could tell that far too much of the bunker was exposed for it to serve any purpose, but I had kept this awareness to myself throughout the construction process. I take great pride in the knowledge that I, in my small way, sabotaged the German war effort!

When we "completed" this task, the Germans assigned us a seemingly endless number of extremely difficult tasks. We began to feel then as though we would all collapse — the combination of arduous labor, starvation, illness, diarrhea, malnutrition, wounds and despair was just too difficult to bear!

The Shabbat Evening Trial

A collective punishment was issued against the entire population of inmates on Tishah B'Av of the year 5704 (1944) — food was to be withheld from all prisoners, including children, the elderly and the sick. What precipitated this harsh decree? The Germans had discovered that someone in the camp had burned a lice-infested mattress.

An unforgivable sin! All the Jews must suffer for this gross act of wanton destruction of the property of the Third Reich!

This was the first time that a collective punishment had been issued against all the inmates. How fitting that it was decreed on Tishah B'Av, of all days!

Bitya was only four years old at the time. Obviously, she could not have been expected to fast an entire day, especially in her already weakened condition, so my mother decided to prepare some gruel for her. This was no simple task, for we had no stove, nor even any fuel at our disposal; in fact, the camp's administration strictly forbade inmates to cook their own food. Nevertheless, Mother used a small bundle of hay and painstakingly cooked Bitya's portion of thin porridge.

As she was about to finish, two members of the *Judenrat* (Jewish Guard) discovered her. They assured her that she would be duly tried by a court of law for having committed such a blatant "infraction" of the hallowed camp rules.

Yes, in addition to enduring inhumane torture at the hands of the Germans, we also had to contend with the camp's Jewish administration, which was given jurisdiction to try and punish inmates who violated camp rules. It is difficult to believe, but this was an integral part of camp life. The Germans took great pleasure in seeing Jew punishing Jew — they always witnessed the scene with mirth and thoroughly enjoyed it.

Mother's trial was to be held on the following Friday night — *Shabbat Nachamu* of the year 5704 (1944). These trials were usually long and drawn-out affairs, which included all the elaborate ceremony of a civilian court: opening remarks by the prosecuting attorney and the defense counsel, the calling of several witnesses to the stand, the plea of the defendant, closing remarks by both the prosecution and the defense, and the final verdict of the judges. This entire legal apparatus was staffed exclusively by Jews — our fellow inmates!

However, in contrast to the norm, Mother's trial lasted a very short time. She waived her right to deny some of the wild accusations that the prosecution lodged against her. The verdict was handed down swiftly: no bread rations for two days. She even refused her attorney's suggestion that he try to abate the severity of the verdict by reminding the judges that she had committed this "infraction" only in order to alleviate the hunger of her four-year-old daughter.

When she returned to the barracks, I asked her why her trial had been so brief, and why she had waived her right to defend herself and refute at least some of the charges. She did not respond. Unable to contain myself, I repeated the question, and she finally answered me:

"The only people present were the judges, the prosecuting attorney, the defense counsel and the clerk who jotted down the minutes of the trial. Had I spoken in my defense, every single word would have been immediately written down by that Jewish clerk, even though it is now Shabbat. I therefore remained silent, for I'd prefer to starve a little more than to cause another Jew to desecrate Shabbat."

Without Yisrael to keep it, the Shabbat would have vanished entirely from mankind long ago. On the other hand, were it not for the Shabbat, the people of Yisrael would have succumbed long ago to the misery and affliction that have accompanied it upon its wanderings through history.

(Rav S. R. Hirsch: Commentary to Lecha Dodi)

Chapter Twelve
High Holidays of 5705 in Bergen-Belsen

As the High Holidays of the year 5705 (1944) approached, an undercurrent of anxiety stirred the camp. All the inmates were troubled by the same questions: Would we find the opportunity to pray? Would we hear the sound of the *shofar* this year? How would we observe Yom Kippur?

Father organized a *minyan* for *Selichot*, which assembled every weekday immediately after work, from the week of Rosh Hashanah until Yom Kippur. We would first recite *Minchah*, and then say the corresponding *Selichot* for that day. In order to avoid disturbing the exhausted inmates returning from work, Father decided to recite the prayers outdoors rather than inside the crowded barracks, in the area between one barrack and another. It was unclear to us at first whether we would have a quorum at all, but word of our *minyan* spread quickly throughout the camp, and in a matter of a few days, dozens of Jews had joined us. Many inmates shared a single volume of *Selichot* while Father led the prayer service.

I was absolutely amazed at how pertinent the words of *Selichot* were to our own situation. Phrases such as "Strengthen buckling knees," "Refrain from the wrath of Your anger," "Remember the pact of thirteen" and "Hear our pleas" resonated powerfully with our own hopes and feelings.

The availability of a wide range of religious literature in Bergen-Belsen was clearly a miracle in and of itself. One person had a Haggadah for Passover, another had a High Holiday *machzor*, yet another, a volume of *Selichot*. It seems that when Jews were being forced out of their homes to be sent to the camps, they often quickly grabbed a holy work pertaining to the approaching religious occasion — those arrested in the fall would bring along a *Chumash Bereishit*, while those arrested in mid-summer would stuff a *Chumash Bemidbar* into their packs. Our family alone brought several volumes of *mishnayot*, High Holiday *machzorim* and *Selichot*.

As Rosh Hashanah approached, we learned that there were several *shofar*s to be found in the camp, but the Germans forbade us to blow them. Thus, on Rosh Hashanah we hastily recited the prayer service and raced to roll call without hearing the blowing of the *shofar*.

At the time, I was working within the boundaries of the camp, fixing boards in the Bergen-Belsen equivalent of that place which civilized people call a "bathroom." Mr. Cohen, one of the leaders of the pioneer movement, was in charge of our group. Security within the perimeters of the camp was generally more lax than without, so we decided to take a chance and try to fulfill the mitzvah of hearing the sound of the *shofar*. We found someone who both possessed a *shofar* and knew how to blow it — the chazzan De Jong, may Hashem avenge his blood. He agreed to blow the *shofar* for us, but he was terrified by the prospect of getting caught. His fear was well founded, for if an S.S. guard who might happen to be walking among the barracks heard the *shofar*, all of us would pay a very high price.

I agreed to stand at the door of the barracks and be the group's lookout. The verse, "He looked all around, and he saw that there was no one there" (Shemot 2:12), reverberated in my mind. I thus became one of a handful of inmates who merited to fulfill the mitzvah of hearing the sound of the shofar on Rosh Hashanah of 5705 (1944).

Prior to Yom Kippur of that year, there was a heated debate among the inmates regarding whether we should request permission from the Germans to leave the soup pot inside the camp until the evening so that we would be able to break our fasts with the soup. Some argued that it would be dangerous to inform the Germans when Yom Kippur was to be, for often they deliberately carried out their most sadistic atrocities on the Jewish holidays. Finally however, the general consensus was that we should put forth our request.

Yom Kippur 5705 (1944)   *(By Shmuel)*

I began to "tithe" our food rations a few days before Yom Kippur. In this manner, I managed to set aside enough food to enable us to prepare a relatively satisfying *seudah hamafseket* (the last meal preceding the fast).

On the eve of Yom Kippur, hundreds of our fellow inmates gathered next to our barracks to hear *Kol Nidrei*, the introductory prayer that precedes the evening services of Yom Kippur. Many of those in attendance intended to fast until nightfall of the following day. Father, wearing his *kittel* and *tallit*, led the "congregation" in prayer. His melodious voice and heartfelt prayers captured the hearts of all those in attendance — the broken-hearted, miserable, desperate inmates of Bergen-Belsen, who had gathered to hear *Kol Nidrei*.

As Father intoned the words, "from this Yom Kippur until the next Yom Kippur, may it approach in benévolence," the sound of muffled cries emerged from the large assembly. The second time he recited these words, his voice increased in strength. The third time, his voice boomed out the words in a spellbinding chant that tore open the hearts of the inmates and elicited unabashed weeping and wailing. The same question haunted all who were assembled: "Would we still be alive by next Yom Kippur?" One fact, however, was clear to everyone — this would be our last Yom Kippur in

Bergen-Belsen. Either we would soon be liberated from this living hell, or . . .

When *Kol Nidrei* was finished, Rav Abraham Levisohn, may Hashem avenge his blood, delivered a sermon full of encouragement and hope. Then Father earnestly intoned the supplication,

> O God, grant us life for the sake of Your Name. Extricate our souls from distress with Your righteousness. Our God, do it for Your sake, not for ours. See our condition — we are destitute and empty. The soul is Yours, and the body is Your handiwork; show compassion towards Your toil. The soul is Yours, and the body is Yours; O God, do [our bidding] for the sake of Your Name!

Father uttered these words with all the strength of every fiber of his being. It was difficult for him to continue leading the prayer service after this, but somehow he found the inner resources and carried on. At the conclusion of the service Father was surrounded by a large number of those who participated (many of whom were not observant) who wished to congratulate him for leading the prayers so movingly. I waited my turn along with the others. When I finally got close enough to thank him and shake his hand, Father said to me, "You are the one who deserves to be thanked — were it not for the *seudah hamafseket* that you prepared for us, I would not have been able to pray so intensely."

The Germans Demand that We Shower on Yom Kippur

There was a chill in the air on Yom Kippur day. To our horror, at around noontime, the Germans ordered all the men to go to the showers. Father had up to this point obeyed the camp rules and suffered in silence, in the hope of eventually leaving this living hell, but this time, he felt that the Germans had gone too far, and he categorically refused to comply with their order.

In Bergen-Belsen, the Germans had managed to turn the innocent act of showering into a sadistic and often lethal instrument of torture. The "showering facilities" consisted of a narrow, cold and damp chamber that was completely unsuitable for bathing. We would be forced to run at high speed to the gates of this building, line up, remove all of our clothing and stand shivering outside as we waited for our turn to enter. Five inmates shared one tap of ice-cold water. We would wash ourselves quickly and, while still soaking wet, were ordered to run back out into the cold air and dress ourselves. A number of inmates contracted pneumonia as a result of these "showers."

Upon learning that Father had no intention of complying with this order, one of our Jewish supervisors tried to change his mind. He explained to Father that if he refused to go, others would surely follow his lead, and the entire camp would suffer the consequences of defying the Germans' order.

Nevertheless, Father was determined — he would not go to the showers under any circumstances. He explained to the Jewish supervisor that the Germans were deliberately attempting to demoralize us by taking away from us the few *mitzvot* that we were still able to observe (see *Shulchan Aruch, Orach Chaim* 611:1; although this torturous "shower" is not strictly prohibited by halachah, my father felt that the Germans' intention was to strip us of the last vestiges of our religion). As proof, he cited the fact that the Germans had categorically refused to allow us to shower throughout the warm summer months. Why did they suddenly deem it necessary for us to take showers precisely today, on Yom Kippur? Obviously their only intention was to force us to violate the sanctity of the holiday.

Father assured the supervisor that he would not urge the other inmates to defy the order, but he emphasized in no uncertain terms that he and his sons would not comply, come what may. Realizing that nothing in the world would change my father's mind, the supervisor turned and left.

We quickly scattered and went into hiding in various sectors of the camp. I wandered around aimlessly for a while and finally headed for the latrine. (I prefer not to go into a detailed description of this facility; suffice it to say that it was abhorrent beyond belief.) I decided to sit inside this repugnant place and wait until the other inmates returned from the showers.

When I stepped into the latrines, I found Rav Ya'akov Yekutiel Neubauer, may Hashem avenge his blood, sitting by the entrance. Before the war he had served as the dean of the Rabbinical College of Amsterdam. Despite his advanced age, he had been assigned the revolting job of cleaning the latrines for several hours each day. I did not explain to Rav Neubauer the purpose of my visit.

I sat inside this disgusting facility for several hours. The smell was dreadful; I believe that on that day I devised an original way of fulfilling the mitzvah, "The tenth of the month shall be the Day of Atonement. It is a sacred holiday when *you must afflict your souls...*" (Vayikra 23:27). However, our sacrifice was rewarded — after the rest of the inmates returned from the showers, we emerged and continued with our daily routine. It seems that our absence had gone unnoticed.

We had originally intended to begin reciting the Yom Kippur *Minchah* and *Ne'ilah* services approximately an hour and a half before nightfall, but the Germans ordered an additional roll call. It was held outdoors while gusty winds and a driving rain chilled us to the bones. We had no choice but to postpone the prayer service until the roll call ended.

Sukkot 5705 (1944)

Just two years earlier, in 5703 (1942), we had celebrated the Sukkot Festival at home. At that time we had even obtained a set of *arba minim* (the Four Species). We had preserved an *etrog* from the previous year in paraffin oil, and we had carefully wrapped a *lulav* in a large number of newspapers. *Aravot* were available every-where, and we had obtained *hadassim* in the city's subtropical bo-tanical garden. The following year, in 5704 (1943), we spent Sukkot in Westerbork, and we were able to eat all of our meals in-side the only *sukkah*.

Sukkot in Bergen-Belsen was completely different — there was no *sukkah*, no *arba minim*, and not even the faintest hint of the Festival.

At that time, Elchanan and Shlomo were working at unload-ing trucks bearing construction beams and prefabricated walls, for the Germans were preparing additional barracks in which to ac-commodate the thousands of new inmates who had been trans-ported to Bergen-Belsen. On the afternoon preceding Sukkot, El-chanan and Shlomo secretly took advantage of their access to con-struction materials and built a small *sukkah* from a few beams and prefabricated walls.

Unfortunately, they were not assigned work in the vicinity of their *sukkah* on the first night of the Festival. The following morn-ing, however, they took their breakfast (a couple of dry slices of bread) with them to work and eagerly anticipated eating it inside the *sukkah* and reciting the blessings, "Blessed are You . . . Who has sanctified us and commanded us to dwell in the *sukkah*," and "Blessed are You . . . Who has kept us alive, sustained us and brought us to this season."

But in the evening Elchanan and Shlomo returned to the bar-racks in low spirits. The Germans had caught them in their *sukkah* and had beaten them severely. I do not recall at what stage they were apprehended, nor whether they had managed to eat inside the *sukkah* before they were caught. Elchanan and Shlomo had re-alized that they were not obligated to risk their lives in order to ful-fill this mitzvah, but they still tried to celebrate the holiday any way they could. Their level of dedication to Hashem's Torah was truly awe-inspiring.

Sadly, we were not able to feel the festive spirit of that Sukkot. The prayers we uttered were our only reminder of the special nature of the day.

The Sukkot Minyan

From the day we arrived at Bergen-Belsen, we held public prayer services in our barracks (number 11 and, later, number 20). We *davened* every day — including Shabbat and Festivals — and read the corresponding Torah portions. I myself enjoyed the honor of being called to the Torah in Bergen-Belsen. It was truly a surreal experience. On the one hand we were forced to carry out exhausting labor seven days a week, to endure punishments, hunger, malnutrition and disease, while on the other hand, we would be called up to the Torah to recite the blessing, "Blessed are You . . . Who has chosen us from all other nations and given us His Torah" — such a paradoxical situation!

In the year 5705 (1944), praying one day during *Chol Hamo'ed Sukkot*, we lost track of the time, and the prayer service continued into *Appel* (roll call). The S.S. guards surrounded the camp and burst in on us while we were still reciting *Musaf*. Their shrill screams and curses echo in my ears to this very day: *"Nur mauscheln koennt Ihr!"* They cried, "All you know how to do is mumble!" The Germans struck the inmates indiscriminately, and even shattered some of the few tables that we had in our barracks. By some miracle, they did not notice the box containing the *sefer Torah*, which remained unscathed. Afterwards, the Germans summoned Mr. Groenman, the person in charge of our barracks, and pummeled him repeatedly with their fists.

Our *Minyan* had been convening for nine months, and this was the first time that it had endangered someone's life. At noontime Father was summoned to Mr. Groenman's quarters; he assumed that he would be sternly warned to never again assemble the *minyan* in our barracks. Even though it was my father alone who had been summoned, I accompanied him. This is what Mr. Groenman said to him:

"Mr. Emanuel, did you see the blows I received? It all happened as a consequence of your *minyan*! I hereby request of you to refrain from allowing the *minyan* to extend into *Appel*.

"But please, do not cancel the *minyan*! For the sake of your prayers, I am willing to endure another beating. I see how you pray, and what care you take to ensure that the *minyan* does not disturb anyone."

We were transferred to a different barracks in Cheshvan of 5705 (1944), and shortly thereafter we were transferred once again. At this point we all became ill, and the *minyan* was discontinued.

Simchat Torah 5705 (1944)

I have described some of the difficult experiences that we underwent during the High Holidays in Bergen-Belsen — the prohibition against blowing the *shofar* on Rosh Hashanah, the yearning in our hearts during *Kol Nidrei*, the German order to shower on Yom Kippur and the violent intrusion of the S.S. men during our *minyan* on *Chol Hamo'ed Sukkot*.

The one redeeming factor of all these experiences is that I retain at least some memory of those holy days. Sadly, I cannot say the same of Simchat Torah — regarding this holiday in Bergen-Belsen, my mind draws a complete blank. We must have completed the morning service extraordinarily quickly, raced out to *Appel* and then spent the rest of the day working.

I discovered, however, that some Bergen-Belsen inmates did have a meaningful Simchat Torah. The *minyan* in barrack 17, for example, had sufficient time to assign the honor of *chatan Torah* and *chatan Bereishit* to two of the participants. It seems that this *minyan* was comprised of a group of men who worked polishing diamonds for the Germans; unlike us, they were not required to rush out to *Appel*. When this work program was eventually discontinued, the diamond polishers were transferred from Bergen-Belsen on the eighteenth day of Kislev of the year 5705 (1944) to the Oranenburg Concentration Camp. Only a few of these unfortunate individuals survived the Holocaust.

In Tevet of 5746 (1986), *Keshev* newsletter (published by Bar Ilan University's Holocaust Research Department) featured a unique certificate that was issued in Bergen-Belsen on the day following Simchat Torah of the year 5705 (1944). The certificate bore the following words:

> We the undersigned hereby testify that Reb Eliezer son of Reb Uri De Pauw was chosen by the residents of barrack 17 as *chatan Torah* during this past Simchat Torah, when we were still incarcerated and afflicted in Bergen-Belsen. Reb Uri son of Aharon De Pauw was chosen as *Chatan Bereishit.*
>
> May Hashem guard them from all evil and lead them to their desired destination with life, peace and health, speedily and in our day. Amen!
>
> 24 Tishrei 5705, Bergen-Belsen
> Aharon Yaakov son of Naftali Halevy Duizend
> Meir son of Asher Lehman
> Shlomo son of Yaakov Halevy De Walde

Saved by Evil's Own Hand

Around this time, following the High Holidays of 5705 (1944), I became seriously ill with diarrhea and stomach typhus. The Jewish doctor to whom I turned for medical care explained to me that he could not help me. Only the chief medical officer — an S.S. doctor — had the authority to prescribe the medication I needed to cure my condition, but he would see only those patients who had obtained a referral slip from the Jewish doctor. The German gave the Jewish doctor only a small number of referral slips to hand out to the patients every day, and by the time I arrived on that particular day, the daily quota had been filled.

I was feeling so desperately ill that I decided to show up at the S.S. doctor's office, even without a referral slip. I waited there until all the patients who had obtained referral slips were treated. After seeing the last patient, the German yelled, "Anyone else out there?" I entered the reception room in a state of great apprehension and explained to the doctor that I had lost control of my diarrhea. As soon as he realized that I had had the audacity to show up at his office without a referral slip, he began screaming his loudest at me. He demanded to know my name, and when I responded he screamed, "*Arbeits-faehig*," which means "fit for work" — despite my grave condition, he intended to send me back to work. He had in effect signed my death warrant.

He wrote my full name on a slip of paper, added the initials "A.F.," which signified that I was *Arbeits-faehig* — "fit for work" — and signed the paper. Then he ordered me to deliver the handwritten slip of paper to the camp's Jewish work supervisor immediately.

I realized that this was the end. My strength and resolve melted away, and I broke down in tears. However, as I headed towards the work supervisor's barracks, a bold plan suddenly entered my mind. Could it work? I had nothing to lose by trying.

I approached the work supervisor and informed him that I had just been to the German doctor, and that due to my serious condition, he had prescribed in his own handwriting that I be "A.F." — *Appel-frei*, "exempt from roll call." This Obviously meant that I was exempt from work duties as well.

Miraculously, the supervisor actually believed my explanation. For a while I took full advantage of the doctor's "exemption," and stopped going to work altogether. Several of the S.S. guards were absolutely convinced that I had been issued a special exemption by the German doctor. Later, as my condition improved, I was gradually assigned light work.

There is no doubt in my mind that, with Hashem's assistance, this ruse enabled me to survive . . . and it all began with the German doctor *ordering* me back to work!

> Were our mouths as full of song as the sea, and our tongues filled with joyous song as the multitude of its waves, and our lips as full of praise as the breadth of the heavens, and our eyes as brilliant as the sun and the moon, and our hands outspread as eagles of the sky, and our feet as swift as hinds — we still could not thank You sufficiently, God our Lord and Lord of our forefathers, nor bless Your Name, for even one of the thousands . . . and myriad favors that You performed for our ancestors and for us.
>
> *(From the Nishmat passage of Shacharit of Shabbat)*

One day the S.S. guards herded together all of the inmates in the camp, and the evil German doctor began to inspect the exemption permits of all those of us who had not shown up for work that day. I was also under scrutiny in this dragnet.

As the German doctor checked document after document and drew nearer to me, it became clear to me that I could not show him my "exemption" permit. He himself had issued the document in order to obligate me to work, not to exempt me! Luckily, I had been released from the camp hospital just two days before this surprise inspection and had been given a temporary three-day exemption from work. I presented this temporary exemption when the doctor finally reached me, and I mentioned to him confidentially, "I am exempt from work today, but of course I will resume my duties in another two days, as indicated on the exemption." Two days later, when my recently issued permit expired, I again began presenting the old paper written in the German doctor's own handwriting.

My life hung in the balance.

Mother Sits in Mourning

Around this time we received a very brief letter from Aunt Irma (Mother's younger sister) in Switzerland via the International Red Cross. We received such brief letters very infrequently. Although these letters contained an average of no more than twenty words, their arrival greatly lifted our spirits, for they were our only link to our family members living in Switzerland.

Aunt Irma wanted to share her good news with us — she had given birth to a baby girl, whom she had named Esther. My mother was shocked when she read the baby's name, for Esther was her own mother's name. This could mean only one thing — my mother's mother must have passed away some time ago, and this baby, the first born in the family since her death, had been named in her memory.

It came as no surprise to us that we did not receive the letters that had likely been sent to us from Switzerland announcing Grandmother's death, for the Germans blithely disposed of the majority of the correspondence that arrived at the camp. On those rare occasions when the guards did distribute the mail, it was usually done only to give a Red Cross observer the impression that they were behaving like civilized human beings, for they wanted to be seen distributing mail to the "residents" of Bergen-Belsen.

Mother knew that Grandmother had not been well, but she hadn't anticipated her death. Apparently our relatives had written us a letter at some earlier date to inform us of Grandmother's death, and in this last letter, they were trying to comfort us with news of the baby's arrival and of her being named in Grandmother's memory.

Grandmother had been a gracious woman. She was a grand-daughter of Rav Shlomo Zev Klein, the chief rabbi of the city of Kolmar-Elzas, France. Rav Klein was an illustrious Torah scholar who fought fiercely against Jewish ideology being disseminated by the assimilated elements of French Jewry.

Mother loved her parents intensely, and she would often share with us her many rich memories of growing up in the Goldschmidt household, both in Paris and in Zurich. What a dreadful experience it must have been for her to learn of her mother's death while herself incarcerated in the living hell that was Bergen-Belsen.

My mother asked one of the rabbis in the camp whether she should regard this short letter announcing the birth of her sister's baby Esther as conclusive proof of her mother's death, and if so, what she should do. The rabbi answered that the letter did indeed prove that her mother had died, but that since it had been sent more than a month earlier, she was to sit *shivah* for only one hour.

I vividly recall seeing my mother sitting on the ground as she mourned the death of our beloved grandmother.

On Shmuel's Merit

My brother Shmuel helped all of us greatly by picking up our meals, standing in line at noontime to get our soup, and generally by caring for the needs of each and every one of us. He relieved Father of a great burden and gave him the opportunity occasionally to rest his tired body for a few precious minutes.

In the early days of our incarceration, Shmuel even managed to acquire whole loaves of bread for *lechem mishneh* on Shabbat. He used to join Mother at the women's camp and help her prepare the Friday night "meal." Shmuel would also separate a small portion of food from each of our weekday rations so that we would be able to sanctify the Shabbat with a larger meal than usual. In this manner we fulfilled the mitzvah of "Remember the Sabbath to keep it holy" (Shemot 20:8) throughout the week. Mother also contributed a sizable portion of her own rations, to add more volume to this communal family meal.

Father would recite *Kiddush* over the bread, and we would even sing a few *zemirot*. During the summer of 5704 (1944), our entire family ate the Friday night meals outdoors. Some of the inmates joined us and sang along with us, while others simply looked at us incredulously — they were utterly astounded to see Jews sanctifying the Shabbat, eating together and singing *zemirot* in the harsh and cruel environment of Bergen-Belsen.

Shmuel contributed a great deal of his time, energy and attention to creating these special occasions. He would frequently forgo his own food ration for the sake of others.

On Shabbat mornings, Father, Elchanan, Shlomo and I would head out to work holding only the required tools in our hands, but carrying absolutely nothing else. We used to empty our pockets before Shabbat, and would not even carry the ubiquitous spoon with which we had to eat all our meals.

Is Reb Yitzchak Levi of Lemberg Still Alive?

During the early part of the year 5705 (1944), Father worked at unloading beams and prefabricated walls that had been sent to the camp. The Germans intended to use these materials to build additional barracks to accommodate the thousands of new inmates that had poured into Bergen-Belsen over the preceding few months. By that time Father had grown extremely weak; he kept going by sheer strength of will.

One day Father returned from work bearing good news — while unloading a shipment of lumber, he had noticed an inscription on one of the beams: "I, Yitzchak Levi of Lemberg, am alive!" Evidently the beams had been loaded by the inmates of a different concentration camp, one of whom had conceived of an ingenious way to let the world know that he was still alive.

Strangely enough, Father actually knew a person by this name who used to live in Lemberg, an erudite chassid who worked as a fur trader. My Father had maintained a business relationship with him for quite some time. Reb Yitzchak Levi had often been our guest for Shabbat when his business affairs brought him to Rotterdam. It had been several years since Father had last heard from Reb Yitzchak, so he was overjoyed to receive this unexpected message from his dear friend. I pointed out to Father that Yitzchak Levi was quite a common name, so it was altogether likely that there were a few Yitzchak Levis of Lemberg who had been interned in the camps. Father dismissed my suggestion on the grounds that he recognized his friend's handwriting; he was absolutely convinced that the message had come from the Yitzchak Levi he knew.

Reb Yitzchak Levi had attended my bar mitzvah on the Shabbat of *Parashat Vayeishev*, on the eve of Chanukah of the year 5699 (1938). He had given me a very beautiful present — a set of *Mikra'ot Gedolot Chumashim* published by Schoken Publishers, Inc., in Berlin in 5697 (1937).

As has been mentioned, we managed to hide most of our *sefarim* under the floorboards of our apartment, and to retrieve them after the war. To this day I occasionally use these *Chumashim*, and each time I open them, I fondly remember Reb Yitzchak, the chassid from Lemberg.

Living in the Shadow of Death   *(By Shmuel)*

Throughout 5705 (1944–1945), the situation in Bergen-Belsen deteriorated from day to day: food rations grew sparser, our physical strength waned as a consequence of prolonged malnutrition and a steadily increasing number of victims succumbed to starvation.

Then a ray of hope shed a bit of light on the encroaching darkness — we learned that a shipment of care packages had arrived at the camp. Apparently the packages had been sent by the Dutch Red Cross, which was still operating from foreign offices in the free world. They were delivered by the Red Cross Organization of neutral Sweden.

Our family was among the recipients of these care packages. The sudden increase in calories and nutrients raised our spirits, but our joy was dampened when the distribution of the first shipment ended, and it became evident that there were not enough packages for everyone. It was difficult to enjoy the food while our hungry neighbors looked on with ravenous eyes.

A second shipment of care packages arrived about a week later, and our names again appeared on the list of recipients. Even before the arrival of this second shipment, Mother had prepared a list of friends and acquaintances who were in desperate need of additional rations. Mother began her *mishlo'ach manot* campaign on the very next morning after the distribution of this second shipment, even though she herself urgently needed these extra rations.

The care packages turned out to be nothing more than a temporary reprieve. A growing number of victims succumbed to starvation with each passing day. When a third shipment of packages arrived, our names did not appear on the list. This time others received the extra rations while we did not. Actually, there were quite a few individuals who received several such packages in a series of shipments.

Meanwhile, Father had become ill and was desperately in need of additional rations. Sadly, the women to whom Mother had distributed the contents of her second care package neglected to reciprocate the kindness in our hour of need. This distressed Mother to no end. Although she never uttered a word of reproach, she found it terribly difficult to deal with the callous ingratitude of these individuals.

Bella, Baruch's twin sister, helped Mother with absolute devotion throughout this difficult period. Nine-year-old Shalom and five-year-old Bitya had grown extremely weak. Mother and Bella spared no effort to provide them with the best possible care that could be offered in the harsh environment of Bergen-Belsen — they warmed water for them and gave them as much food as they were able to obtain. While caring for Shalom and Bitya, Mother and Bella also tended to the needs of others who had fallen ill.

At the time, Bella was only fifteen years of age. She herself was suffering from malnutrition and extreme physical weakness, yet she continued caring for her younger brother and sister until their very last days. Bella was with them when they breathed their last. It is impossible to imagine what Bella endured during this period

Spare us, O God, in the land of our captivity and pour not Your wrath upon us, because we are Your people, the sons of Your covenant.

(From the siddur)

Chapter Thirteen

Kislev–Nissan 5705

From Hope to Despair

We were all still alive on Chanukah of 5705 (1944), but the situation had deteriorated significantly. Almost all of us had fallen victim to disease, and at that point, we had precious little reason for optimism. We occasionally heard a few snippets of news regarding the Allies' successful offensives, but as far as we were concerned, the Allied forces in Western Europe were advancing much too slowly.

In the month of Tevet of 5705 (January 1945), several hundred Jews in Bergen-Belsen were told to prepare for a journey in a few days' time. This announcement sent a tremor of excitement throughout the camp — it seemed that the long-rumored prisoner exchange was finally in the making. The fact that the Germans were disqualifying the ill from this group supported this theory. We were relieved to see that the names of all of our family members appeared on the list — both of our parents and all eight children. This development filled us with new hope. Perhaps we would survive after all; perhaps we would be whisked away from the Valley of Death in the nick of time.

We knew that it would not be easy to get onto this transport. Father, Elchanan and Shlomo were bedridden with illness, and

Mother was running a high fever and suffering from diarrhea, dysentery and typhus. She was so weak that she was not even able to stand up. I myself had been sick and weak, and only recently had begun to feel a little better.

The inmates whose names appeared on the list were required to appear before a committee of German officers. This committee evaluated the condition of the inmates; those who were deemed too ill or weak to survive the trip were disqualified. Since my parents could hardly stand up, they requested that I represent the family before the committee. I knew that my chances of success were minimal, but I felt I had to make the effort.

The first question the Germans asked me was where my parents were. "Why aren't they here?" they demanded.

"They are not feeling very well," I replied, "but they are able to travel." I responded in the same manner when they asked me about the health of Elchanan and Shlomo.

Unfortunately, my presentation was unsuccessful. They casually crossed the names of all the members of our family off the list, dashing in an instant our hopes of winning our freedom. Did I ever really have any chance to begin with? Objectively speaking, I certainly did not. Nevertheless, I berated myself for my failure, and the memory of this experience tormented me for many years after the war.

We were by far not the only ones whose names were removed from this list — almost half of those originally selected were disqualified. Most of them were simply too weak to stand on their feet.

Eventually, three hundred joyful inmates were loaded on a train and borne away. After the war we learned that on their way to Switzerland, the Germans took some of the inmates off that train and transferred them to other camps such as Biberach, which were supervised by the Red Cross and provided a more humane environment. Inmates enjoyed far better living conditions in these camps than in S.S.-administered facilities such as Bergen-Belsen.

Those inmates who remained on the train arrived in Switzerland, and most of them survived; but a few died there — their release had come too late.

As for us, we were left behind in Bergen-Belsen. It is impossible to describe the conditions in which we lived. The Germans packed tens of thousands of new inmates into the camp and transferred us into older, more dilapidated barracks. A single bed was to be shared by two people. There was hardly any food or water, and we lacked even the most minimal sanitary standards. Mother once said to me, "If you ever leave this place, never fast again. You've fasted here for an entire lifetime!"

You will go insane from the vision that your eyes will see.
(Devarim 28:34)

The camp was transformed into a miserable place of confinement for thousands of hopeless, sick and despairing individuals. There was almost no one who was capable of performing any kind of work at all. Every day we learned that another friend or acquaintance had died, and that his or her body had been incinerated in the crematorium.

Starvation claimed countless victims. Many people became obsessed with food and spoke of nothing else — there were those who lost their minds from hunger. I clearly remember waking up one night from a loud dialogue between two inmates who slept on opposite sides of the barracks. They were having a conversation with each other across the expanse of the room about the delicacies they used to eat in various restaurants. The other inmates asked them to stop their midnight reverie, because the mention of food accomplished nothing other than to intensify everyone's hunger pangs. But these two inmates refused to stop — they claimed that their memories sated their hunger!

We were witness to the fulfillment of the verse, "The utterings of our lips shall take the place of bullocks" (Hoshea 14:3).

A good deal of theft also prevailed in the camp, especially of bread. Respectable people turned into thieves. It was extremely difficult for young people like us to come to terms with this harsh reality, which left us traumatized. There were those who did not literally "steal" bread, but rather only "borrowed" it. They would ask someone to lend them a piece of bread, promising to return it on the following morning. When the following morning arrived, they would renege on their promise. We saw the disheartening application of the verse, "You will descend lower and lower" (Devarim 28:43). "Woe to us for what has befallen us!" (*Tishah B'Av Kinot*).

We became orphans, fatherless.

(Eichah 5:3)

Throughout Chanukah of the year 5705 (1944), Father returned exhausted from work each day and lit a single candle for the entire family. On the first night of Chanukah, as Father lit the first candle, one of the inmates in our barracks screamed at him, "How *dare* you light Chanukah candles at a time like this!"

My father did not respond. We sang *"Ma'oz Tzur"* and recited the passage, "Bare Your Holy Arm and hasten the end for our salvation. Avenge Your servants' blood from the wicked nation, for the triumph is too long delayed for us, and there is no end to days of evil. . . ."

Father collapsed a few weeks later. My mother cared for him with indescribable devotion. She persuaded a Jewish doctor to treat Father in exchange for her bread ration. Mother gathered loose strands of hay and other combustible materials and heated water for Father, as well as for all the rest of us who were afflicted with digestive disorders. The warm water soothed our damaged intestines.

On Sunday evening, the twenty-first day of Shevat, Mother came to us in our barracks and asked us to come to the barracks where Father lay ill. She told us that Father wished to bless us. We had not realized that his condition was so serious. That night Father blessed us for the last time.

Mother informed us on the following morning that Father had passed away during the night. He was fifty-one years old when he died.

Today, as I remember my reaction to Father's death, I realize that I did not fully comprehend the magnitude of our loss. "He, the Merciful One, is forgiving of iniquity" (Tehillim 78:38) — we did not rend our clothes, sit *shivah* or assemble a *minyan*. None of us thought of it. Rav Levi Forst, *zt"l*, was one of the few people who remembered to come to comfort us.

I merited to learn many things from Father, may Hashem avenge his blood. He was a man "who cherished life and loved days to see good" (Tehillim 34:13). Father always tried to establish and maintain good relationships with everyone. He would greet people with a friendly demeanor and speak with them in a calm and amicable manner. At the same time, Father strictly observed every halachic requirement and devoted much of his time and energy to providing his children with a Torah education and Torah values.

Upon our arrival in the Netherlands, Father would buy no meat other than that prepared under the strictest rabbinical supervision, which had been established by Rav Ritter, *zt"l*, of Rotterdam. Even this meat Father would not buy from just any butcher — he always made it a point to buy it from Mr. Brodman's butcher shop, for he knew beyond any doubt that Mr. Brodman was a truly devout and God-fearing man. What was even more impressive is that our friends and acquaintances were not even aware of Father's personal stringencies.

This was how Father always conducted himself — in times of peace and in times of great challenge alike. Father demonstrated to all those with whom he came in contact that it is possible to continue fulfilling *mitzvot* under the most difficult circumstances and, at the same time, to be thoughtful and respectful of the feelings of others.

The large majority of Bergen-Belsen's inmates lived in a constant state of tension and anxiety. Father was one of the few exceptions — his complete trust and faith in God enabled him to remain calm and optimistic throughout this inhuman ordeal. Thus it is not surprising that many of the inmates flocked to seek his counsel and ask his advice — people saw evidence of Father's piety and righteousness, both in the way he served God and in the way he related to his fellow men. There were a number of illustrious communal and rabbinical leaders among the inmates of Bergen-Belsen who had never met my father before the war, yet they came to value his opinion greatly.

The harsh conditions of our incarceration in Bergen-Belsen shattered all facades and exposed the raw core of every inmate. This was a place of stark reality — here there were no pretenses or illusions behind which anyone might hide. Every negative character trait was stripped of all disguises and set out in the open for all to see. The fact that people flocked to Father for guidance in this "world of truth" says much about the spiritual level he had attained.

Father Merits to Be Buried with Earth from Eretz Yisrael

Rav Shimon Dasberg, may Hashem avenge his blood, had been the last chief rabbi of Amsterdam. In Bergen-Belsen, he worked for quite some time alongside my father in the Benedict Unit, which was assigned the excruciatingly difficult job of felling trees for twelve hours a day in a nearby forest, all the while enduring beatings and all manner of cruel punishment. Despite their different backgrounds, Father and Rav Dasberg forged a very close relationship. Both men were observant, but Rav Dasberg was a graduate of the Amsterdam Rabbinical College and supported the Mizrachi movement, while Father was a businessman and a member of Agudath Yisrael. They had not known each other before coming to Bergen-Belsen.

Father and Rav Dasberg had more in common with each other than their staunch adherence to halachah; they were two of the few individuals who cared not only for their own needs, but who also tried to alleviate the suffering of those around them. Both men assisted and encouraged others. Their words instilled hope in the souls of those who had given in to despair and restored basic human dignity to individuals who had temporarily lost control over themselves as a result of malnutrition and unrelenting hunger.

By the time Father passed away, in Shevat of 5705 (1945), Rav Dasberg himself had grown so weak that he could hardly stand on his feet. Upon hearing of Father's passing, Rav Dasberg came to the place from which the deceased were taken to the crematorium and proclaimed that he intended to ritually purify Father's body. I doubt whether this ceremony had ever before been performed in Bergen-Belsen.

After the purification, Rav Dasberg said to us with great emotion, "I brought with me from Amsterdam a few bags of earth from Eretz Yisrael. This is my last one. I was saving it for myself, but I will now scatter it upon your father's body before the Germans incinerate it."

His was a generous deed of unparalleled proportions.

Shmuel went to bring the *kittel*, the white garment that Father used to wear during the High Holiday prayer service (even the ones held in Bergen-Belsen); on his way, he was chased and beaten by a *kapo* wielding a stick with a nail protruding from one end. Upon his return, we accompanied Father's body to the camp gate and said *Kaddish*.

Only nine days later, our younger brother Shalom passed away. He was not even ten years old. Shalom had been suffering from starvation and typhus. The night before he died, Shalom made just one request of Mother — that she bring him the *siddur* that he had placed inside his pack. With it he fell into his eternal sleep. We recited *Kaddish* together beside the camp gate once again.

Little Bitya passed away just a week later, on the eighth day of Adar. After her body was brought to the crematorium, we saw a red cloud of smoke emerge from the smokestack. The very air we breathed contained smoke from the crematorium. "Woe unto us!"

O, accursed Germany! "Happy will be the one who unleashes upon you your just reward for all that you have done to us! Happy will be the one who will grasp your young ones and smash their skulls upon a rock!" (Tehillim 137:8–9).

Elchanan, our eldest brother, passed away a week later.

"Would we ever stop dying?" (Bemidbar 17:28).

Elchanan, May Hashem Avenge His Blood

It is a difficult undertaking for me to delve into my memories of the Holocaust years and write a detailed account of them, but it is especially difficult for me to discuss my eldest brother, Elchanan. I have already said much about him, but the sum total of my words falls far short of conveying what an extraordinary individual Elchanan was and all that he represented to us. At this point I will add a few details about him that have not yet been mentioned.

During our stay in Westerbork, Elchanan became an unofficial guardian of the camp's orphans. These children, whose parents had either been caught and transferred elsewhere or were still in hiding, lived in a separate barracks. The children were slated for the extermination camps. It was only due to the efforts of Westerbork's Jewish administrators that their imminent transfer was postponed. Sometimes, when new captives were brought to Westerbork, the children were reunited with their families. For some reason these "family reunions" always resulted in the entire family being sent east to the death camps.

Elchanan taught Torah to these children and even sang religious songs with them. He developed a very close relationship with them and cared for their every need at all hours of the day or night. One day, Elchanan informed my father that the children were scheduled soon to be transported to the east — that is, to the extermination camps in Poland. Elchanan told my father that he would like to accompany them, for he felt obliged to take care of the children during the trip and upon their arrival in the new camp. Father emphatically forbade Elchanan to carry out his plan. Elchanan wept bitterly when he bid them farewell.

In Bergen-Belsen, Elchanan was assigned physically grueling work, yet I never heard a word of complaint issue from his lips. He even found time for Torah study in that brutal environment. In one instance he helped a boy of bar mitzvah age learn the laws of donning *tefillin*. That boy survived the war and is now the head of a blessed household. In the camp, Elchanan took devoted care of his revered teacher and rabbi, Rav Meir Halevy Landau, may Hashem avenge his blood.

Wherever he was and whatever he endured, Elchanan always focused on the fulfillment of *mitzvot*. Throughout Passover of the year 5704 (1944) he did not eat *chametz*. On one occasion, he pointed out to me that if the soup served in the camp contained meat of an impure animal, then the prohibition of mixing milk and meat would not apply to it. Before Sukkot of 5705 (1944), he noted that if it were possible to lift and shake the beams that comprised the roof of our barracks, we would be fulfilling the Torah-ordained mitzvah to live in a *sukkah*. Once when I was sick in bed, Elchanan brought me a few pages of *mishnayot* from *masechet Zevachim* and told me, "Learn one *mishnah* every day and try to remember it by heart." These are the kinds of things that Elchanan thought about in the midst of our affliction.

Elchanan passed away on Shushan Purim (the fifteenth day of Adar, the date Purim is celebrated within walled cities), 5705 (1945), as my brother Shmuel was trying to feed him a small amount of food that he had prepared for him. On the fourteenth day of Adar — just one day before his death — he had heard the reading of *Megillat Esther* (the Scroll of Esther) from Reb Shimon Kol-tov, *zt"l*, who lay beside him. Reb Kol-tov continued reading the *Megillah* even when it seemed to him that Elchanan had fallen asleep. Immediately after the conclusion of the *Megillah* reading, Elchanan opened his eyes and pointed out to Reb Kol-tov that he had not paused to take a deep breath before the passage listing the names of Haman's ten sons, as required by halachah! This was what concerned Elchanan on the day before his death.

Elchanan passed away when he was but twenty-one years of age. "Righteous men shall surely praise Your Name; the upright shall dwell in Your presence" (Tehillim 140:14).

O Elchanan, my eldest brother, your parents' pride and joy, your teachers' delight, your brothers' and sisters' friend, your disciples' beloved! What vast amounts of Torah you learned, how many good deeds you performed, how many *shiurim* you delivered and how intense was your desire to continue learning and teaching.

May Hashem avenge your blood.

Justifying the Divine Decree   *(By Shmuel)*

My little sister Bitya returned her pure soul to her Creator on Wednesday morning, the eighth day of Adar 5705 (1945). The cause of death: prolonged lack of sufficient nutrition. We saw the verse fulfilled, "The tongue of the suckling clings to his palate out of thirst. Young children beg for bread, but there is no one to offer it to them" (Eichah 4:4).

Prior to our internment in the camps, Bitya used to melt the hearts of all those who saw her. Even the German female soldiers would pat her head when she walked past them in the city's streets. She was five years old when she passed away. I sat with my mother beside Bitya's bed and tried to find words of comfort. Our youngest brother Shalom had died only eight days earlier, just two weeks before his tenth birthday. He too died of starvation, but despite his hunger and the inhumane conditions in which we lived, I never heard a word of complaint leave his lips. Unlike most of the children in the camp, Shalom did not torture Mother by repeatedly asking her for food. He endured his pain and suffering in silence.

After sitting speechless beside my mother for a few minutes, I willed myself to say, "Mother, let us learn from and be strengthened by the Talmud's account of Beruriah, the wife of Rabbi Meir, when her two sons died on the same day."

My mother burst into tears and said, "You are right, my son. Beruriah did lose both her sons. But she still had her husband to comfort and support her."

Mother lost Elchanan just a week later.

Many years after the war, I heard from Rebbetzin Davids, *zt"l* (the widow of the chief rabbi of Rotterdam, Rav Aharon Yissachar Davids, may Hashem avenge his blood), that Mother had come to speak with her shortly after the deaths of Father, Shalom, Bitya and Elchanan. Mother sadly confessed to her that in the wake of the deaths of her husband and three of her children, she was finding it difficult to pray. Rebbetzin Davids responded by comforting my mother with words of encouragement and support. Mother came back to her about a week later and told her with great emotion, "Thank God, I am able to pray again!"

We learned many noble traits from Mother; in this instance, we learned to acknowledge the justness of divine judgment. It turned out to be the last lesson that we would be privileged to learn from her.

Despair and Guilt   *(By Shmuel)*

Our hope that our entire family might merit to leave Bergen-Belsen unscathed was brutally shattered with Father's death. The subsequent deaths of Shalom, Bitya and Elchanan — all within two weeks of each other — plunged us into a deep well of despair. I personally was overcome with feelings of guilt for having been spared hard-labor duty; I was assigned relatively easy maintenance work, including the job of picking up the rations of food allotted to my family and distributing them among all of us. I tried to give the sick and weaker members of the family slightly larger helpings. It is difficult for me to describe what I was going through, seeing one family member after another descend into critical condition. I constantly encountered impossible dilemmas and was forced to make extremely difficult decisions. Perhaps the following Talmudic passage will convey the problems that I faced on a daily basis:

Two people were traveling on the road together, and only one of them possessed a flask of water — if both would drink, they would both die, but if only one of them would drink, one of them would be saved. What should they do?

Ben Petorah taught: It is preferable that they both drink and that they both die, lest one of them witness the death of his fellow. But Rabbi Akiva came and taught, "'Let your brother live alongside you' (Vayikra 25:36) — your life takes precedence over your fellow's life" (*Bava Metzia* 62a).

The case described by the Talmud is unquestionably a difficult and tragic one, but I daresay that our situation was even more difficult. The question I faced was closer to, "What if *five* people were walking in the desert and there is not enough water for all of them? One is sick and in need of a large amount of water, and the second has been assigned the task of distributing the water. The second is willing to forgo his own ration of water and give it to the sick person, but is he permitted also to take from the water rations of the others for the sake of the sick person?"

Hallel on Rosh Chodesh Adar 5705 (1945)

After the war, Rebbetzin Davids shared with me the following account:

> My husband's condition deteriorated significantly in the end of Shevat of the year 5705 (1945). He grew so weak that he could no longer utter the words of the prayer service.
>
> One day as I sat by my husband's side he said to me, "Today is Rosh Chodesh, isn't it?"
>
> After I confirmed that it was indeed Rosh Chodesh, he asked me to read *Hallel* to him. I picked up the *siddur* that I always carried around with me and began to read *Hallel*. When I reached the words, "I shall not die, but I shall live and relate the deeds of God," I broke down and could not continue. . . .
>
> My husband passed away one week later, on the ninth day of Adar.

Seder Night 5705 (1945)

In the beginning of Nissan 5705 (1945), Mother could endure it no longer; she collapsed, and her condition steadily deteriorated. I spent the first night of Passover by her bedside. Shmuel stayed with Shlomo.

I held nothing in my hand but a Passover Haggadah; I had neither matzah nor bread, not a morsel of food or a drop of water. I quickly recited the entire Haggadah. I simply read through the words; I am not even sure whether Mother heard all of it.

Upon reaching the words, "so may You, O God, our Lord and the God of our fathers, bring us in peace to the other Festivals that approach us, rejoicing over the building of Your city and delighting in Your service," I began weeping uncontrollably and was unable to continue reading further.

Bergen-Belsen a few days after the camp was liberated by the British

Pour out Your wrath upon the nations that do not know You and upon the kingdoms that call not upon Your Name, for they have consumed Ya'akov and laid waste his dwelling. Pour Your fury upon them, and may Your rage overtake them. Pursue them with anger and obliterate them from under the heavens of God!

(Pesach Haggadah)

Chapter Fourteen
Leaving Bergen-Belsen

By the end of Nissan of 5705 (1945), the Allied liberation forces had penetrated deeper into German-controlled territory and were stationed near Bergen-Belsen. The Germans decided to transport by rail all the inmates in our section of the camp to points further east. By this time many of the inmates were so weak and ill that they could hardly walk. Some crawled on all fours; some just lay immobile on their beds.

We tried to evade the round-up to the trains, but eventually the Germans caught Mother, Baruch, Bella and myself and stuffed us into the cattle cars. Shlomo was allowed to remain in Bergen-Belsen because of his critical condition, and Shmuel somehow managed to remain behind in order to care for him.

The train made frequent stops throughout the journey, sometimes due to aerial bombardments by Allied aircraft. My brother Baruch would occasionally jump off the train during these stops and dig out potatoes from the fields alongside the railroad tracks. He learned quickly how to detect where something edible grew and how to dig it out as swiftly as possible. He would then roast the potatoes right there in the field beside the train. Once he even entered the home of a local farmer we passed and returned with food and drink.

We traveled for thirteen days in these incredibly cramped railroad cars which, needless to say, lacked even a semblance of sanitary facilities. Baruch and I were in a different compartment from that in which Mother and Bella made the trip. We sat near the car's entranceway, which gave us access to plenty of air, but this was also the place where everyone came to relieve themselves throughout the day and night — almost every inmate was suffering from a serious case of diarrhea and typhus.

Incredibly, a faint glimmer of hope glowed in our hearts despite the inhumane conditions to which we were subjected. At least we were no longer surrounded by barbed-wire fences and watchtowers. Just the sense of moving forward and seeing fields and rivers raised our spirits somewhat. The sight of German cities lying in ruins — including the capital city of Berlin, which had been reduced to rubble and resembled a ghost town — gave us particular pleasure.

Despite the illness and the fact that people were dying all around us, the overcrowded railroad car and the diarrhea, the severe hunger and the intense fear, there was still hope!

Baruch and I still had our *tefillin* and a *siddur*. Once, after we had finished reciting our Friday night prayers, a couple of Hungarian girls asked to borrow our *siddur*. I knew that most people had lost all track of time and were not even aware of what day it was, so as I passed the *siddur* to them, I informed them that it was Shabbat evening, the second day of Rosh Chodesh Iyar. They were amazed at learning that anyone still possessed such precise information about the Jewish calendar.

Mother's life ended on the train during Shabbat night, the first day of Iyar. She was then forty-three years of age.

Almost two years had elapsed since the Germans had come to arrest us in our apartment, in Tamuz of the year 5703 (1943). At that time, just before being taken away, my mother had managed to scribble the word "murderers!" on the back of a picture. She had entertained no illusions about the true nature of the Germans.

Mother's Last Days   *(By Bella Emanuel Shindler)*

The Germans — may their name and memory be erased forever — had issued an order obligating all of the camp's inmates to evacuate the area. In order to bait us to come to the trains, they told us that food was waiting for us at the train station. Rumor had it that the British were rapidly approaching Bergen-Belsen, and that they would liberate whoever remained alive within a matter of days.

Not wanting the world to discover the atrocities that they had perpetrated against us, the Germans decided to evacuate the entire camp and obliterate all the evidence. They went from barrack to barrack to make sure that every last inmate left the camp. Under no circumstances would they allow us to see the fulfillment of our fondest dream — the long-awaited day of liberation.

Mother was so weak that she could not even stand up, much less walk. Typhus and various other maladies had drained all of her strength. Not long before, Mother had helped to care for others who were afflicted; now, she herself had fallen victim to malnutrition and disease. On quite a few occasions in the past, Mother had given a portion of her own food ration to others; now, in her time of need, we lacked the means to help her. Mother's suffering towards the end was intense, but she remained fully conscious throughout her ailment.

We tried to evade the roundup to the trains, but to no avail — we left Bergen-Belsen aboard one of the last trucks that departed for the train station. Upon our arrival we saw numerous rail cars — including cattle and coal cars — lined up on the tracks waiting to transport us. I found space in one of the passenger cars for Mother and myself. By then she was so weak that she could not even sit on the seat; she lay on the floor. Yona and Baruch were placed in a cattle car.

After many delays, the train finally began to move forward. What was our destination? No one knew for certain. Some of the passengers said that we were headed east, in the direction of the

Elbe River. We saw very few other trains on the way, although we did pass a number of trains transporting inmates in the opposite direction, from *east* to *west*! It seems that it really made no difference where our camps were — inmates of eastern camps were being transported to the west, and inmates of camps in the west were being transported to the east. The Germans apparently had resolved to prevent our being liberated by the Allies at all costs. It is truly incredible — transportation had come to a near standstill throughout Germany, yet instead of using their last few trains for important things, such as mobilizing troops to the front, the accursed Germans wasted them on shuttling concentration camp inmates, who were in any case either on the verge of dying or of being liberated by the Allies.

The train stopped frequently, apparently because those in charge of the transport did not really know where they were meant to go. The British were advancing from the west, the Americans from the south and the Russians from the east. In addition, British and American aircraft were bombing railroad tracks and bridges throughout the countryside at a furious pace. No doubt this was another reason our train made so many stops.

We took advantage of these frequent stops to bury our dead alongside the tracks. Incredible as it may sound, people actually participated in this mitzvah, despite the severe weakness and hunger that plagued us all. Others used the time to scavenge for food in the adjacent fields. But many were simply too weak to move, and they could do nothing more than to lay in their compartments waiting to die.

We often wondered whether we would ever again live normal lives. I did my best to care for Mother, but she was extremely weak. Baruch came to our compartment from time to time, mainly to visit Mother. During one of the train's frequent stops — this one took place on a Friday — Baruch jumped down from the train, crossed a field and walked right into a German farmhouse. I grew concerned when Baruch did not immediately return to the train. I feared that he would be left behind and stranded (as though there were actually something to miss on the train!).

Baruch eventually returned and brought Mother a treasure — a fresh egg! It had been so long since we had seen a real fresh egg! As Mother ate it, I could see the pleasure she derived from this delicacy. I believe that this egg was the last thing Mother ate before her death.

As night descended, we attempted to sleep on the overcrowded floor. Mother asked me to help her find a comfortable position and apologized for "inconveniencing" me. When I awoke the next morning, I took one look at Mother and realized that I would never again have the opportunity to help her.

Mother did not receive a Jewish burial.

May the Almighty one day unleash upon the Germans — may their name and memory be erased forever — the punishment they truly deserve, and may all our Jewish brethren who were slaughtered rise to life in the Revival of the Dead!

Our Dear Mother, May Hashem Avenge Her Blood

Mother had a unique trait: she always found time for everyone. She was a devoted mother who cared for each of her children's every need, down to the last detail — she herself sewed most of her young children's clothing — yet at the same time, she was always involved in helping others, often through ingenious and creative ways. Her fertile mind always managed to devise a wide range of possibilities.

Many years after the war, I met an elderly woman who shared some of her memories with me. She told me that in her youth she had lived in Hamburg, and that at the time she had known very few people there. My parents took her under their wing and would often invite her to our Shabbat meals. She proved the veracity of her account by listing the names of all my brothers and sisters; this was no small feat for a woman in her eighties! The woman also told me that Mother would often invite her to accompany her when she shopped, in order to alleviate her loneliness and engage her in lively conversation. These occasions have remained engraved in her memory as the most pleasant experiences she had in this strange city.

I vividly remember Purim of 5696 (1936). We had arrived in Rotterdam, in the western sector of the Netherlands, two months earlier. Our home was brimming with joy, and all of the children were dressed in costumes. I was ten years old at the time. As Mother looked at us, she suddenly declared that she would give us a special treat — she would order a taxi (a highly unusual occurrence back in those days!), and we would go for a ride.

Inside the taxi Mother informed us that we would be paying a surprise visit to a certain young couple living in the same city, and that she expected us to be even more rambunctious than we had been at home. We did not disappoint her.

Later, we learned that this young couple had lost their first child in childbirth a short time before Purim.

Mother always fulfilled *mitzvot* with a touch of grace, always taking into consideration the feelings of others. On Purim, Mother prepared *mishlo'ach manot* (gifts of food) not only for her friends and acquaintances, but also for the indigent members of the community. She would prepare packages for the poor containing a bottle of wine (a very expensive item where we lived), a large sausage and a variety of other delicacies. By our standards each of these packages constituted a very generous gift — I can imagine the reaction that such a gift elicited from the recipients.

We had guests not only on Shabbat; throughout the week, people from all walks of life would join us for lunch and enjoy a warm, kosher meal. Mother frequently served our guests better food than she served us!

Mother ran our household with much devotion. She would stay up until the wee hours of the morning cooking, cleaning and sewing, even though she had hired help. Her greatest joy was to sit with the guests and the entire family gathered around the table on Shabbat evening and listen to the children speak about the weekly Torah portion and add their own commentary. On Shabbat morning Mother would go to pray in shul. She loved the melodious tunes of the *tefillot* of Shabbat and Festivals, and she derived much pleasure from the *zemirot* that we would sing during the Shabbat meals at home.

She had always hoped that one of her sons would learn to read *Megillat Esther*, so that if for some reason she would not be able to go to shul on Purim, he would be able to read it for her at home. Elchanan, her firstborn, consummately fulfilled this hope.

Mother told me that she had once been asked to join the *Chevrah Kaddisha* (Jewish Burial Society), but that she had felt obligated to refuse. "A woman taking care of young children must not occupy herself with corpses," she explained, "for she is liable to lose her maternal instincts towards her own young ones." Only many years later did I fully grasp the significance of her words.

My mother used to describe to us the hardships she had encountered trying to observe Shabbat while attending a non-Jewish school. It was certainly from these struggles early in her life that she drew the inner strength and resolve necessary to observe Shabbat in the camps.

Mother was a naturally lively and cheerful person, and this is the picture I retain in my memories of her from the years before the war. She enjoyed traveling and visiting friends and relatives. Mother was born in Paris, and she was especially fond of French, her mother tongue. She enjoyed meeting French speakers and conversing with them, and occasionally she would read French rhymes to us. As for Germans, she always hated them with a passion.

I have already described some of the kind deeds that my

mother performed for others during the war years. The following account, which was related to me by Rav Levi Vorst, *zt"l*, exemplifies the extent of Mother's concern for and generosity towards others.

During her last months in Bergen-Belsen, my mother was so weak from malnutrition that she was barely able to walk. Nevertheless, she would frequently shuffle around the barracks and sit next to a dying child. Once, when she heard the sound of a woman crying, Mother drew near and made out the form of Rebbetzin Dasberg, may Hashem avenge her blood, who was lying on her bunk in critical condition. When mother asked her what was the matter, the *rebbetzin* told her, "I finally obtained a little bit of milk, but I am unable to drink unboiled milk!"

Mother took the cup of milk and brought it outside. Some time later, she returned with red eyes and a fresh coat of soot on her face and handed a cup of warm milk to Rebbetzin Dasberg. Apparently, Mother had gone outside and searched for stray pieces of straw and paper, which she somehow managed to ignite, and with it heated Rebbetzin Dasberg's milk. Her determination to help a fellow Jew enabled her to overcome her weakness and to muster the courage to defy the strictly enforced prohibition against lighting fires within the confines of the camp.

Rav Vorst, *zt"l*, concluded his account with the words, "Your mother was one of the three righteous women whom I was privileged to know in Bergen-Belsen."

Mother instinctively sensed the needs of the sick, especially those of orphans and lone individuals who had been separated from their loved ones. She would immediately translate her feelings of concern into deeds, and she was not deterred by any obstacles or difficulties. Mother always refrained from asking favors of others, even during the last weeks of her life in Bergen-Belsen. Despite her own acute suffering she made every effort to help others, and at times she would even give them that most precious of commodities — a portion of her meager food ration.

I saw Mother for the last time in the truck that took us from Bergen-Belsen to the train station. Mother died beside Bella, in a different train compartment from the one in which we were traveling. She passed away on the night of Shabbat, the first day of Iyar 5705 (1945). When the train stopped in the morning, her body was carried out of the compartment. I tried to go to her to give her some sort of burial, but as I attempted to walk in her direction, I fell down from weakness and exhaustion. I attempted to crawl to her on all fours, but I collapsed before I could reach her.

Mother's body was not incinerated in the crematorium like all the others, but neither did she receive a proper Jewish burial.

Years later I heard from my rabbi and teacher, Rav Shlomo Zalman Auerbach, *zt"l*, that if faced with a choice between leaving a corpse without proper burial and desecrating the Shabbat, the observance of the laws of Shabbat takes precedence over the burial. I confessed to Rav Auerbach, *zt"l*, that I had not been aware of this law at the time, but that in the end, it had been observed.

I am convinced that Mother was spared from having caused me to desecrate the Shabbat in the merit of the self-sacrifice involved in her decision to remain silent during her trial in Bergen-Belsen, when she refused to defend herself so as not to cause the Jewish clerk to desecrate the Shabbat.

A letter written by Mrs. Irma Haas, from New York:

Tishrei 5750 (1989)

... I will attempt to describe some of the events that we experienced in Bergen-Belsen as best as my sister and I are able to remember them.

We lived in the same barracks as your mother, *zt"l*. She slept in the bottom bunk (it could hardly be called a bed), while we slept in the middle and upper tiers.

Your mother, *zt"l*, was always ready to lend a helping

hand whenever the need arose. One night, my sister (at the time her surname was Eiseman; today it is Mayer), who slept in the upper bunk, became ill — she was running a high fever (over 40° C) and was suffering excruciating pain in her urinary tract. She was feeling the urge to relieve herself every few minutes, but she was so weak that she could hardly stand up, much less walk; and so, every time she felt the urge to relieve herself, we would lift her up from her bed and help her climb down the bunk.

Your mother had a small bowl that she used for laundering clothes. When my sister no longer had the strength to make the short trip outside the barrack, we used your mother's bowl as a bedpan. I was worried that your mother would grow frightened [since according to camp rules, it was strictly prohibited for inmates to relieve themselves inside the barracks], but she was not the least bit afraid. On the contrary, her faith in God was so strong that nothing frightened her. She stressed that the most important issue at that moment was to help my sister.

The Jewish doctor arrived the following morning, and after examining my sister he ordered that she be transferred to the infirmary. She lay there for many days in critical condition, but eventually she recovered.

After her ordeal was over, the doctor mentioned that had we not helped her as we did on that last night before she was sent to the infirmary, my sister would never have recovered from this severe illness. I would certainly not have been capable of lifting her out of bed alone. My sister owes her life to your mother, *zt"l.*

Your mother was a very special woman. It is always a great source of pain to think that she, along with so many others — people like our husbands and your father — is no longer with us. Nevertheless, it is incumbent upon us to submit to the decrees of Hashem. You, along with your children and grandchildren have merited to continue along the ways in which your precious parents guided you. My sister and I send our warmest regards to your wife and to your sister, Bella.

Irma Haas

The Wayfarer's Supplication

Once, during one of the many instances when the train's progress was impeded, I saw my uncle, Naftali Abrahams. Like me, he had become so weak that he was practically incapable of walking. As soon as we met, his first question was whether I had recited the Wayfarer's Supplication (a prayer for a safe journey) on that day.

His question took me by surprise. I had managed to obtain water with which to wash my hands in the morning, and I was even praying and donning *tefillin*, but it had not crossed my mind to recite the Wayfarer's Supplication on every single day of our journey.

I replied, "We have been compelled to travel on this journey against our will, and we have no desire to continue it. Isn't it enough that I recited the Wayfarer's Supplication on the first day of the journey?"

My uncle pointed out to me that according to halachah, the Wayfarer's Supplication must be recited every day throughout the course of a journey, regardless of whether one has embarked on it against one's will. Of course he was right.

It may seem difficult to believe that my uncle Naftali, may Hashem avenge his blood, could have initiated such a conversation in this macabre setting, but it was typical of him. Officially he was a layman, but in fact he was an accomplished Torah scholar who fulfilled every aspect of *halachah* to its finest detail under all circumstances, including during the most difficult days of the war.

Torah study and strict observance of the *mitzvot* were the two pillars of my uncle's life. He had grown up in the home of an illustrious, Torah-oriented family in the Netherlands. As a young man he went to learn in the yeshivah in Frankfurt, where he developed a strong attitude of true devotion to Torah. He continued to dedicate much of his time to Torah study even after his marriage — while he did not shirk his responsibility to provide a livelihood for his family, Torah study remained his first priority. My father-in-law, Rav Shlomo Adler, *zt"l*, related to me that he once saw Uncle Naftali walking one evening in Frankfurt alongside his regular study partner. Suddenly Uncle Naftali stopped under a streetlight, opened a volume of Talmud and vociferously continued the discussion they had not managed to finish in the study hall.

My uncle consummately fulfilled the Sages' dictum, "One should not feel embarrassed before others who mock one for serving God" (*Shulchan Aruch, Orach Chaim* 1:1). At all times he took pride in being a Jew, even throughout the humiliating era of the Holocaust. He would wear the yellow patch without shame and silently endured the Nazis' degrading edicts. Uncle Naftali continued to fulfill God's will until the very last day of his life. Nothing would deter him from doing so.

Uncle Naftali, may Hashem avenge his blood, was forced to perform very difficult work in the camps, but he still somehow managed to find time to learn Torah. He learned with his sons on a regular basis, and he occasionally learned with his daughters and with my brother Shmuel as well.

During the early stage of our incarceration in Bergen-Belsen, we would be released from work earlier than usual on Sundays — at noon instead of in the evening. I remember Uncle Naftali suggesting to me that we take full advantage of this free time. First we would repair and oil our working shoes, and then we would learn together.

I have already mentioned that the *sefer Torah* that Uncle Naftali smuggled into camp enabled us to read the Torah on the appointed days. Even with the meager quantities of food we were provided in Bergen-Belsen, Uncle Naftali refrained from eating the nonkosher food that we were served until finally he became so weak that he contracted pneumonia. Only then did he begin eating most of his food rations.

In addition to taking care of her children and husband, Aunt Bea also devoted much attention to the children who were incarcerated in Bergen-Belsen without their parents.

I had known their eldest son Mishel before the war, and in the camps we sometimes worked together in the same unit. Once, as punishment for some "infraction" on my part, I was ordered to remain at our work station through the afternoon break, which meant that I would not be able to receive my food ration in camp. Mishel risked his life to smuggle my food out of the camp and carry it to the place where we were working.

Mishel learned much Torah from his father, as he had under the tutelage of Rav Jaffe, *zt"l*, in The Hague. He was only eighteen years old when he died. May Hashem avenge his blood and the blood of his parents.

Uncle Naftali passed away a few days after the train was liberated. His wife, Bea, and their firstborn son, Mishel, died shortly thereafter. They were laid to rest in Troebits with proper Jewish burial rites.

Their memory will remain a source of inspiration for their entire illustrious family. Indeed, those of their children who survived the Holocaust, and their grandchildren and great-grandchildren, carry on the unique legacy of the Abrahams family.

Chapter Fifteen
The Liberation

The mental images we had formed of the long-awaited day of liberation were much more dramatic than the reality.

The S.S. soldiers who had been guarding us on the train fled one night, leaving other guards in their place. The train continued moving forward until it reached the next obstacle, and then came to a full stop. We had imagined columns of tanks descending upon our oppressors, but instead, a ragged Siberian unit of Red Army troops mounted on horses and camels rode towards us.

The mere knowledge that we had been freed infused me with strength. I attempted to walk again, and this time I succeeded to a degree. I walked alongside the train and met my uncle Naftali Abrahams. He told me to recite the blessing, "Blessed are You . . . Who is good and Who does good."

It was a good thing that I did not think about my family at that point. The losses were too heavy to bear: Father, Mother, Elchanan, Shalom and Bitya had died; I had absolutely no idea whether Shlomo and Shmuel were still alive; Baruch, Bella and I were suffering from severe stomach typhus, with swelling and festering sores all over our bodies. We were completely filthy, stricken as we were with uncontrollable diarrhea. Hardly any prisoner was capable of standing on his own two feet. Meanwhile, we had received neither medication nor medical care of any kind.

Baruch, Bella and I found ourselves in a forsaken village southeast of Berlin, severely ill and sinking into despair. What would become of us? Where would we go? Would we survive? Hundreds of individuals who survived the awful train ride died in the aftermath of the war. They were simply left to die.

Fortunately, I did not think about these things at the time. In fact, I could no longer think at all.

Shlomo, May Hashem Avenge His Blood

As I have mentioned, Shmuel remained behind in Bergen-Belsen to care for Shlomo, who was in critical condition. Shmuel spared no effort to save Shlomo's life, but it was an impossible task — two days after the liberation of the camp, on the fourth of Iyar, Shlomo returned his soul to his Creator.

Shlomo had studied electrical engineering and also learned Torah on a regular basis. He was a quiet young man who thought a great deal and spoke very little; in this distinguishing characteristic, Shlomo was different from the rest of his brothers.

Once, on a Shabbat evening in the summer of 5704 (1944), Shlomo failed to return to the barracks in time to hear Father recite *Kiddush* and join us for the family meal. He showed up after dark, and I immediately noticed the fresh bruises and cuts on his face. A while later I asked him how he had come to be beaten. He was surprised that I was aware of the beating he had endured, for he thought that he had succeeded in concealing the evidence.

This is what he told me occurred:

His work unit had been unloading a shipment of kohlrabi. As soon as the group returned to the camp and entered the front gate, the S.S. guards caught the prisoners unawares, ordering them to line up for a surprise inspection. When the S.S. guards searched the inmates' clothing and found the kohlrabi that they had intended to smuggle into camp, they vented the full force of their

wrath on these poor individuals. Shlomo had refrained from trying to smuggle in any kohlrabi on that occasion, because he did not
wish to violate the prohibition of carrying on Shabbat.

Terrified by the fate that awaited him, one of those who had
smuggled the kohlrabi, who was standing in the row directly ahead
of Shlomo, surreptitiously dropped the vegetables behind him.
The kohlrabi landed next to Shlomo's feet. An S.S. guard approached Shlomo and demanded to know who had thrown the
contraband on the ground. Shlomo remained silent and suffered
the blows in place of the smuggler.

This was Shlomo. May Hashem avenge his blood.

Shlomo's only winter vest was stolen one night during the winter of 5705 (1944–1945). Although he knew the identity of the
thief, Shlomo refused to reveal it. "It seems that he needs a warm
vest more than I," Shlomo said by way of explanation.

I took issue with his attitude and did my best to persuade him
to reclaim his vest, but to no avail. Shlomo would not hear of turning in a fellow Jew, even though that person had stolen his only
winter vest.

Shlomo was buried in a large mass grave in Bergen-Belsen in
an unknown location.

> It is a good sign for a man if he is not eulogized or buried as
> he deserves.
>
> *(Tishah B'Av dirge by Rabbi Klonimus son of Yehudah)*

Between Life and Death

While it is difficult for me to describe my experiences throughout the Holocaust, it is even harder for me to discuss what we lived
through in the period immediately after the end of the war. Years of
oppression had transformed us into unfeeling automatons.

The Russians liberated us near the village of Troebits, in the
southeastern sector of Germany. Two days later, we mustered the

last ounce of strength in our emaciated bodies and somehow walked all the way from the stranded train to nearby Troebits. On the way I asked a bearded Russian soldier for some food, and he

Bergen-Belsen, some weeks after the liberation. On the right is Shoe Mountain.

gave me an entire loaf of bread! It had been a very long time since we had possessed such a large quantity of food.

When we reached the village we simply entered one of the buildings and settled there. Baruch, Bella and I joined the Abrahams family and shared an apartment with them. All of us were ill, and our energy was completely sapped. Many inmates in comparable condition died during this time.

As I have mentioned, it was at this time that Uncle Naftali passed away, just a few days after our liberation, on the thirteenth of Iyar 5705 (1945). Aunt Bea and the Abrahams' firstborn son, Mishel, soon followed. May Hashem avenge their blood.

Like many other concentration-camp victims, Baruch, Bella and I were all suffering from severe typhus and diarrhea. Although we managed to find food, our bodies were incapable of digesting it. At first I had sufficient strength to get up and empty the pail in which we relieved ourselves, but then my energy dwindled even more. The filth in which we lived is impossible to describe. It had been months since we had washed ourselves. My recollections of this period are unclear. All I can remember is the experience of lying in a dark corridor.

One day a Jewish doctor walked into the apartment. He had been assigned the task of determining which inmates were most urgently in need of medical treatment in the makeshift field hospital that the Red Army had set up nearby. As the doctor approached me, I realized that it was the same doctor whom Mother had hired to treat Father in exchange for her bread ration.

When I requested of him that he register me for hospitalization, he took a second look at me and asked me whether I was a member of the "religious Emanuel family." I answered in the affirmative.

Incredibly, he then responded, "If you are religious, then go ahead and pray. We cannot help you any more." Having said that, he turned around and left without adding my name to the list of patients slated for hospitalization.

I lay in this condition — seriously ill and despairing — for another week, until some female Russian soldiers walked into the apartment on a routine inspection, to see whether there were any more inmates in urgent need of medical care. They immediately slated me for hospitalization, but by this time I was convinced that I would not leave the apartment alive.

Meanwhile, Bella's condition had improved somewhat, and she was soon able to be of some assistance to me. I was obviously in no condition to pray or don *tefillin*, but Bella brought my *tefillin* to me nevertheless — they were all that I owned in the entire world — and she encouraged me by saying, "You will don *tefillin* again one day!" It was many weeks later that I realized the true value of Bella's support.

It was just at that point that the Russian female soldiers walked into the apartment and approved my hospitalization. Bella helped me to lie down on a horse-drawn wagon that transported me to the Russian field hospital.

The first service I received at the hospital was a shave at the hands of a German barber. The hospital attendants then undressed me and threw all my "clothing" to a corner, from where it would be taken to be deloused and laundered. I grasped my *tefillin* with all my strength, but the German tore them out of my hands and tossed them onto the dirty laundry pile in the corner. The loss of my *tefillin* distressed me greatly, but I was completely helpless. They took me to a different room and bathed me.

Then a most amazing thing happened. A Russian nurse clad in army fatigues walked into the room, and after making sure that no one was watching her, took out my *tefillin* and showed them to me with a silent gesture that said, "Are these yours?" When I nodded, she surreptitiously slipped them under my bedsheet.

I later discovered that she was Jewish, and that when she had spotted the *tefillin* lying on the pile of soiled clothing, she had taken them to look for their rightful owner.

This nurse continued to give me special attention throughout my term of hospitalization, but because she spoke only Russian, we were unable to communicate. This Jewish nurse remains for me a symbol of self-sacrifice. Even though she lived a completely secular life and was the only Jew in her unit, she put herself under considerable risk in order to return the discarded *tefillin* to their owner.

They placed me in the intensive care unit. Quite a few of the patients in this unit died during the time that I was hospitalized. We lay directly on the ground on straw mattresses. I was fed intravenously by means of four daily injections. The Jewish nurse brought me an extra blanket, which she folded into the shape of a balloon so as to alleviate the painful bedsores that had developed on my skin from my having remained in a prone position for an extended period of time. A Russian commander who walked in a few days later ordered the attendants to remove my extra blanket — such preferential treatment was inconsistent with the Communist ideal of equality for all. Later they transferred us to proper beds.

I began donning *tefillin* again about two weeks after I had been hospitalized. Two days later, a Hungarian youth came to pay me a visit. "I didn't realize that Western-European Jews were so ignorant," he began. He then informed me that two days earlier, the day I had begun donning *tefillin* again, had been Shabbat! I realized that I had lost track of the days of the week. I remember saying to him, "If today is Monday, then it must be the first day of the month of Tamuz 5705 (1945)." The date turned out to be correct. Until today, it remains a mystery to me how I could possibly have made such an accurate calculation in my state.

Baruch was also admitted to this field hospital, although he was placed in a different room. At first he was able to walk around a bit, but then his condition deteriorated sharply. At one point he weighed no more than twenty kilos (forty-four pounds) and lay in critical condition.

A vehicle belonging to the U.S. Army Medical Corps came to the hospital in the middle of Tamuz and transferred us to Leipzig, a relatively large city in the east of Germany. We lay there in a cavernous building that had served as the regional headquarters of the German Army during the war. We received only minimal medical care; in fact, there were not even any medicines available! In contrast, the Russian army had set up a field hospital immediately after the end of the war and had provided us with professional medical care and all kinds of medication.

We had no idea what had happened to Shlomo and Shmuel. We understood that Shlomo was already in very critical condition when we left Bergen-Belsen, but what had become of Shmuel?

Later we learned that Shmuel had been liberated in Bergen-Belsen and had endured terrible suffering. One day, the Jewish chaplain of the British army's Dutch Brigade, Rabbi S. A. Rodrigues Pereira, came to the camp and asked Shmuel whether he could do anything to help him. Shmuel made one request of him — to salvage Uncle Naftali's *sefer Torah*, which had remained in the camp all this time. Preparations were under way to burn all of the barracks along with their contents. True to his word, Rabbi Pereira intervened, and the *sefer Torah* was saved from destruction.

A diary of events preceding and following the liberation,
Nissan–Av 5705 (April–August 1945)   *(By Shmuel)*

Sunday, 25 Nissan (April 8)
Most of the camp's inmates have been evacuated to an unknown destination. Very few remain in our camp. The majority of those who stayed were too ill to travel, as was Shlomo. I was permitted to stay behind in order to care for him.

Tuesday, 27 Nissan (April 10)
Gentile Dutch prisoners have been assigned to our section and have assumed responsibility for guarding and administrating what has come to be known as the "Camp of Stars."

The dispensing of water has been discontinued in the camp. Our general situation is deteriorating by the hour. Thousands are dying. Nightmarish scenes fill the main road that crosses the camp from end to end. Someone shot at me from one of the watchtowers as I walked between barracks.

Friday, 30 Nissan (April 13)
Rumors are spreading that the Allied forces have reached the vicinity of the camp.

Shabbat, 1 Iyar (April 14)

We clearly heard the sounds of motorcars and tanks. The camp's chief *kapo* has died.

Sunday, 2 Iyar (April 15)

British Army troops entered the camp in the afternoon. There is a unit of Dutch soldiers among the British troops. A soldier named Monasch from Rotterdam brought bread and other food to the residents of our section.

Monday, 3 Iyar (April 16)

The inmates are raiding the kitchen and storehouses.

In accordance with the terms of surrender, the German officers continue to carry their guns. They shoot at the inmates at random. Today, a number of bullets pierced the walls of our barracks. Miraculously, no one was injured. One inmate was wounded in a shooting incident outside the barracks; he was brought into our barracks and is receiving medical treatment.

Shlomo's condition continues to worsen. Today I went for a walk around the camp, and when I returned a short while later, Shlomo was in a state of great agitation. I have decided to remain at his side at all times.

The British have ordered the S.S. guards to carry the corpses strewn throughout the camp to a mass grave. One of the Germans who has been assigned to this task is the infamous S.S. officer whom we called "Red Miller."

Tuesday, 4 Iyar (April 17)

Shlomo, of blessed memory, has passed away. I have neither the strength nor the opportunity to oversee his burial.

Exact date of entry unknown (rough approximation: 7 Iyar)
The chief Jewish chaplain of the Free Dutch Army, Rav S. A. Rodrigues Pereira, has come to Bergen-Belsen. I have requested of him that he take back Uncle Naftali Abrahams' *Sefer Torah*, which was entrusted to my care. I hope that our evacua-

The commandant Joseph Kramer the "Butcher," first of Auschwitz, and then in Bergen-Belsen, was arrested by British soldiers and hanged later in 1947 at the Nuremberg trials.

tion from the camp will be hastened in the wake of his visit.

Meanwhile, my own condition is deteriorating. Most of the inmates have been evacuated; many have died. I am lying on a third-level bunk, suffering from a severe case of diarrhea and painful coughing attacks, yet I have received no medical treatment whatsoever. I am no longer capable of leaving my bunk.

The evacuation of surviving inmates is being carried out by British soldiers. The inmates are transported in Medical Corps vehicles.

My fear that I will not merit to leave this living hell alive increases with each passing day. Occasionally I call out to the British soldiers, begging them to come and take me, but to no avail. No one answers my pleas for help.

Exact date of entry unknown (rough approximation: 23 Iyar)

Two hellish weeks elapsed, fourteen awful days and nights, before my turn to be evacuated finally came — "God does not reject forever" (Eichah 3:31). I was instructed to leave behind all my personal belongings — the British were attempting to control the spread of typhus by prohibiting the removal of any item from within the boundaries of Bergen-Belsen. Nevertheless I managed to conceal my *tefillin* and Shlomo's *siddur* under my blanket.

I was taken in an ambulance to a large German army camp, which was located not far from Bergen-Belsen. (Later, thousands of refugees awaiting the opportunity to emigrate to Eretz Yisrael stayed in that very same camp.) Upon my arrival, I was immediately given a thorough washing, and then they "disinfected" me. It took the attendants more than half an hour to remove the filth that had become encrusted on my skin from the period when I lacked the strength to rise and relieve myself in the latrines. They then transferred me to a different building and, as evening descended, assigned me a "bed" — a large sack filled with straw, which was placed directly on the floor. I was sure that this was just a temporary station, but when I asked an attendant when I would be assigned a real bed, he did not respond. As dawn broke following a restless night, I realized that, for the time being, this was to be my "permanent residence." I received extremely meager food rations — two slices of bread per day and a small measure of diluted beet soup.

Exact date unknown
(rough approximation: Rosh Chodesh Sivan)

I have been transferred to a different room in which there are real beds. At first I was completely naked; I had nothing more than a sheet and a blanket with which to cover my body. It was another week before I received a hospital robe, at which point I was able to begin donning *tefillin* again.

The worst part of this entire ordeal was the persistent, gnawing hunger. When I complained to a major in the British Medical Corps that I was starving, he replied, "The whole world is starving!"

Eventually, the responsibility of administering medical treatment to the patients was delegated to a group of captive German soldiers and officers who had formerly served in the Medical Corps. In general they treated the patients well. They took a special liking to me due to my command of the German language, so whenever a shipment of rare goods (such as units of blood or a few fresh eggs) would arrive at the infirmary, I was usually the first beneficiary.

One of the German medics cared for me as though I were his own son. His name was Mattius Borkhart, from a hamlet called Baknang, located in the vicinity of Stuttgart. Our friendly relationship blossomed the moment I asked him to borrow his Bible. He used to try to give me his bread ration without my noticing. On one occasion, he confessed to me that he was being so helpful to me for two reasons: he could sense how important it was to me to recuperate, and he knew that my strong determination to live obviously emanated from my faith in God. (Our relationship continues to this day. In 5749 [1989], almost forty-five years after the liberation of the camps, Mattius and his daughter came to visit me at Kibbutz Sha'albim. Both he and his daughter are devout Christians.)

For a few weeks I also enjoyed the assistance of a friendly Russian youth who lay recuperating in a bed adjacent to mine. He was in better shape than I, for he was capable of rising from his bed and walking about.

Throughout this convalescence period, two urgent questions were constantly on my mind: Did any other member of my family survive? And would my digestive system ever function normally again?

8 Sivan (May 20)

I had my first opportunity to send a postcard to Switzerland. I also asked a British soldier from Manchester to notify our relatives that I am alive.

End of Sivan

My health improved to the point that I was deemed fit to be transferred back to the Netherlands. Dutch volunteers carried us on stretchers to large trucks commonly used for moving furniture.

During an overnight stay in a hostel near Hanover, a group of local residents came to visit us. When they asked us whether we needed anything, I pointed out to them that I did not possess any clothes — I was still wearing the same robe that I had been given in the British hospital. The residents returned a few hours later and presented me with a complete wardrobe for . . . a girl! There were plenty of dresses and long socks, but no pants or shirts.

Rosh Chodesh Tamuz (June 12)

We arrived safely at Nymegen, where we were admitted to a makeshift clinic established in a Catholic monastery.

Children gathered around the trucks as they were being unloaded and gawked at us in wide-eyed amazement. One child pointed at me and said to his friend, "Look at his arms! Have you ever seen such thin arms?" Hearing this comment, I realized that I was still far from completely recuperated.

A few days later, I heard that one of our fellow patients — the young secretary general of the Jewish Community Council of Amsterdam, Mr. Van Der Horst — had passed away. The thought suddenly hit me that his physical condition was no worse than mine. His death greatly disturbed me and plunged me into dark despair. Would we ever stop dying? After a few days I ran a high fever and was diagnosed as suffering from a very severe ear infection.

Weeks later I was notified that Yona, Baruch and Bella had returned from Germany and were convalescing in a hospital in Maastricht, a city in the southern region of the Netherlands. Their hospital, like mine, had been established in a Catholic monastery. Because "their" monastery happened to be affiliated with "our" monastery, we were able to correspond quite frequently.

My health continued to improve. I experienced the fulfillment of the verse, "God has punished me severely but did not hand me over to death" (Tehillim 118:18).

Rosh Chodesh Elul 5705

I was sufficiently recuperated to be released from the hospital, and I headed straight for the home of the Sekbach family in Utrecht. There, on Rosh Chodesh Elul, I merited to eat kosher food for the first time in two years.

In Bergen-Belsen, fifty years after the war, in the spring 5755 (1995) Shmuel davens next to the mass grave where our brother Shlomo is most probably buried. Behind Shmuel stands his son, Shlomo, who is named after his uncle.

A letter written by Shmuel to our relatives in Zurich:

Nymegen, 8 Tamuz 5705 (June 16, 1945)

To my dear ones:

I hope that you are all in good health, and that you have received my letter from Bergen-Belsen.

I returned to the Netherlands — specifically, to Nymegen — on the twelfth of June. It would not have been possible to travel directly from Bergen-Belsen to Switzerland.

On Sunday I was unexpectedly removed from Bergen-Belsen on a stretcher and transported to the Netherlands in a truck meant for moving furniture. My condition did not deteriorate as a result of the journey, and we arrived safe and sound.

I am now convalescing in a wing of a Catholic monastery. It has been set aside for the treatment of Dutch citizens returning from the camps who are not well enough to return directly to their homes. Most of them stay here no more than a few days, but I will have to remain until I find suitable living quarters. I have a bed in the sick ward, which at the moment contains no more than four patients.

I feel very good as far as my health is concerned, but I weigh only forty kilos (I am 1.65 meters tall). Yesterday my lungs were examined and were found to be perfectly in order, unlike the lungs of many concentration-camp victims.

. . . I heard news from Frankfurt regarding a group of twelve hundred Dutch Jews who are being treated in an area near the Oder River. This is very likely where Yona, Baruch, Bella and the Abrahams family are being treated.

Is there anything you can do for them? Would it be possible to transfer them from there to Switzerland? I would also like to come to you at the earliest possible opportunity; however, I am in better condition than Yona, Baruch and Bella. The food and the medical treatment here are excellent. I have absolutely no clothing, but I expect to receive some over the course of the next few days. All that I own in this world are my *tefillin* and my faith.

Night and day, I think about the precious ones who are lost to us. May our God remember them for good, together with the other righteous people of the world, amen!

I hope to hear from you soon. There is no more news from here.

Regards to the entire family. From now on, may we hear only good tidings. I wish you an easy fast.

Shalom,
Shmuel

A letter written by Shmuel to our relatives in Zurich:

Friday, June 22

To my dear ones:

Someone had offered to take this letter to Switzerland for me, but in the end he was not able to get there himself. In the meantime, I have moved to a different monastery, which was recently refurbished and outfitted with new furniture from England in preparation for the ninety or so concentration-camp survivors who are due to arrive here soon. Right now there are just four patients here, including myself.

A list of nine hundred Dutch Jews from Bergen-Belsen arrived at the monastery today. They are in Troebits, a town near Leipzig. The names of Baruch and Bella appear on the list, but Yona's name does not, so I am very concerned about him.

The newspaper reports that a Red Cross vehicle has left for Leipzig. I have no idea whether its mission has anything to do with the Jewish refugees being treated there.

I may require an entry visa into Switzerland. Could you kindly take care of this for me? Please address your next correspondence to me to the following address. . . .

Regards to everyone.

Sincerely yours,
Shmuel

A letter written by attorney-at-law Aaron De Haas to Uncle Felix:

> Utrecht, June 31, 1945
> Mr. F. Goldschmidt
> Limoges, France

Dear Mr. Goldschmidt,

Your letter of the seventeenth of July, addressed to this city's chairman of the board of the Jewish Council, has been forwarded to me along with a request that I respond to your query.

As I believe you know, Mordechai Emanuel and Naftali Abrahams were very good friends of mine; it is therefore even more painful for me to pass on to you some very sad tidings.

Yona, Shmuel, Bella and Baruch Emanuel, as well as Helene, Shlomo, Irma, Ruth, Renee and Lilly Abrahams — all of whom are now in the Netherlands — have informed me that their parents and some of their siblings passed away. It is incumbent upon me to give you the awful news that Mordechai and his wife, Chana, along with their children Elchanan, Shlomo, Shalom and Bitya, as well as Naftali and his wife, Bea, and their son Mishel, were summoned to a better life [in the World to Come], either in Bergen-Belsen or in Troebits.

Although the sea of catastrophe that has been poured over Israel knows no limits, I must express my profound sorrow over the loss of these particularly precious souls. God alone knows why He has gathered them to Himself, for as far as our limited human minds can see, these wonderful Jews were destined to fulfill extremely important positions in our community. Words cannot serve to express my feelings as I think of my students, Elchanan and Shlomo; these two brothers were truly extraordinary personalities in the eyes of today's Jewish youth.

May Hashem comfort your grieving father. May He grant you the strength to find comfort in the fact that all of these precious souls sanctified God's Name until their last breath of life, as many eyewitnesses have reported.

The children who survived, with God's help, arrived in the Netherlands approximately six weeks ago. Yona, Shmuel and Baruch are still hospitalized, even though they have basically recovered. The others are either in Jewish children's institutions or in Amsterdam under the care of Rav and Rebbetzin Tal. I am in constant communication with all of the children — we correspond frequently. I am trying to have them transferred to Switzerland, either for a vacation or to take up permanent residence.

I am also in contact with Mordechai's brothers in Johannesburg and Manchester.

With friendly blessings,
Aaron De Haas

Chapter Sixteen
The Monastery in Maastricht

"He Hears the Sound of Israel's [Shofar] Blast."

Baruch and I left Leipzig, Germany, aboard an American Medical Corps train bound for Maastricht, the southernmost city of the Netherlands. Upon our arrival we were separated again, for the authorities placed us in different temporary hospitals. I managed to find out that Baruch was in critical condition, and after approximately a month, I succeeded in having myself transferred to his hospital. At the time Baruch weighed less than twenty kilos — he was literally a living skeleton, seemingly devoid of flesh.

The hospital was staffed by a dedicated team of doctors and nurses; Baruch was placed in a separate wing run by a Jesuit monastery. Although the hospital was not affiliated with the monastery, unofficially the institution's administration had assigned three monks the task of disseminating Catholicism among the patients, most of whom were Dutch gentiles returning from forced-labor duty in Germany. The monks took a special interest in the Jewish patients; they graciously assisted them with all their needs, while at the same time attempting to persuade them to convert to Christianity.

"You've suffered enough," they would tell us over and over again. "Now you deserve to live in peace. You have seen with your own eyes that the Jewish people are destined to suffer until the day when they will finally acknowledge the truth. Here we offer you everything you could possibly desire — a good education, a secure future. . . ." These were the kinds of things they would say to persuade us, day after day.

After approximately two months in this place, I felt strong enough to get out of bed for short periods at a time. The monks helped me take my first tentative steps. Our conversations invariably centered around one topic — Christian belief. They often invited me to visit the chapel which was housed in the same building, but I politely declined.

Five months had elapsed since the liberation. By then we had succeeded in reestablishing contact with the rest of our family abroad, and with my former teacher, Mr. Aaron De Haas, who had settled back in Utrecht. Mr. De Haas sent us packages containing various necessities, including *Chumashim*. Throughout this time we did not see a single Jew from the outside — we were under the impression that very few of our brethren had survived the Holocaust.

A few days before Rosh Hashanah, an elderly Jew named Rabbi De Liever came to the hospital. He informed us that he was the *chazzan* (cantor) and *ba'al korei* (the person who reads the Torah portion) of the congregation of Jews who had returned to Maastricht. Just seeing a fellow Jew made us feel elated. He asked us if there was anything he could do to help us. I surmised that he would not have been able to arrange for us to be served kosher food, so I asked him to try to arrange some way for us to hear the blowing of the *shofar* on Rosh Hashanah. He assured me that he would do his best, but he added that it would be very difficult for him to blow the *shofar* in every room. I volunteered to have all the patients who showed an interest in hearing the *shofar* convene in a single room, at whatever hour of the day he chose. He agreed, and as soon as he left, I began to notify the other Jewish patients that the *shofar* would be blown in the monastery on Rosh Hashanah.

Indeed, during the afternoon hours of the second day of Rosh

Hashanah (the first day fell on Shabbat, when the *shofar* is not blown), Jewish patients from every corner of the hospital were carried on stretchers to a specially designated room. True to his word, the *chazzan* arrived on time. He was exhausted after leading all the prayer services in the Maastricht shul, but he mustered the strength to blow the *shofar* for the Holocaust survivors recuperating in the hospital.

Thus did we merit to hear the sound of the *shofar* within the walls of a Jesuit monastery! By that time, approximately six months had elapsed since the dreadful scourge of the Holocaust had ended.

I had merited to hear the blowing of the *shofar* in Westerbork, in Bergen-Belsen and again in the Jesuit monastery in Maastricht.

A New Test: The "True" Belief

A very disturbing event occurred on the second night of Rosh Hashanah. I had often requested of the monk who would regularly come to visit us that if he wished to discuss religion, he should do so only with me, and not with the younger patients — Baruch and another Jewish youngster who lay near us. On this particular night, I got out of bed to spread the word among the Jewish patients that the *chazzan* would be arriving on the following day to blow the *shofar.* Upon my return, I was appalled to see the monk sitting beside Baruch's bed and telling him about the founder of Christianity. This infuriated me! In a loud voice I accused the monk of attempting to complete the task which Hitler — may his name be erased forever — had undertaken, and of trying to eradicate the scant remains of the Jewish people. I even yelled the word *"moordenaar!"* (murderer) at him.

In response to my screaming, the director of the hospital, Dr. Casteman, came rushing into my room. After hearing my complaints, he instructed that I be injected with a tranquilizer, but more importantly, he explicitly forbade the monk to speak to us.

The director explained that since he was responsible for our health, he could not allow visits by someone who was upsetting his patients to the point that they required tranquilization.

Dr. Casteman treated all of us very well, but he made an extraordinary effort to save Baruch, who was in very critical condition. He forbade Baruch to fast on Yom Kippur; as for me, while he allowed me to fast, it was only on condition that I remain in bed the entire day.

One of the monks used to help me descend to the ground floor to take short strolls around the garden of the monastery. After a few such outings, he invited me to follow him into a small cloister in which the monks would pray. "You needn't worry. It is not a church," he told me. I refused his offer, but he insisted. It was a difficult test, for I knew that if I would yield this one time, Heaven forbid, he would torment me ceaselessly with his "kindness" in the wake of this victory. In the end I told him bluntly that I could not enter the cloister because it is forbidden for me to enter a room used for the purposes of idolatry. The monk was visibly insulted by my insensitive statement and disappointed by my refusal to enter the cloister.

Is this what I get for all my efforts? he probably thought.

I tried to appease him by explaining to him that although the cloister may be an appropriate place to pray for most of humanity, Jews are forbidden to enter it, for it represents a religion that does not meet the Jewish definition of monotheism.

Every morning, monks came to each patient and offered to help him recite the Catholic prayer service. Baruch and I categorically refused to participate. We finally decided to don *tefillin* during the hour when the monks usually approached us, in order to avoid having to ward off their overtures day after day. It turned out to be a wise strategy — when the monks saw that we were immersed in prayer wrapped in our *tefillin*, they left us alone and did not even come near us. We saw the fulfillment of the Talmudic dictum, "Rabbi Eliezer the Great said: 'All the nations of the world will realize that God's Name is upon you, and they will be in awe of you' (Devarim 28:10) — this refers to the *tefillin* worn on the head" (*Menachot* 35b).

Our stay in the hospital was especially frustrating, because although we were still within the first year of mourning over the deaths of Father, Mother, Elchanan, Shlomo, Shalom and Bitya, we could not even recite *Kaddish* for them. However, we took pride in defying the monks by letting them see us don *tefillin* every morning in full view of their idol. We regarded this act of defiance as a kind of a *Kaddish* in honor of the departed souls of our loved ones, may Hashem avenge their blood.

Still, our inability to recite the words of *Kaddish* tormented me. I wrote a letter from the hospital to Grandfather in Zurich in which I informed him that we were not able to say *Kaddish*. His response in his next correspondence comforted me — he said that if we would observe the laws of the Torah devotedly, then our very lives would become a living *Kaddish* in memory of our loved ones. Grandfather added a personal request — that we not let a single day pass without learning Torah.

> *All this has come upon us, yet we have neither forgotten You nor been false to Your covenant. Our hearts have not turned back; our feet have not strayed from Your ways. When You humbled us in the place of jackals and covered us with Death's shadow, did we forget the name of our God or spread forth our hands to a strange God?*
>
> *(Tehillim 44:18–21)*

A letter that Baruch wrote to Grandfather from the Maastricht hospital:

21 Tishrei 5706 (September 28, 1945)

Dear Grandfather,

This week, on the first day of Chol Hamo'ed, we received the letter you wrote us on the day before Yom Kippur. Dear Grandfather, in your letter you mention our parents, *zt"l*, but it seems that you forgot to write the words "Gan Eden" in one of the sentences. Those words are inscribed in a handwriting different from your own; also, the ink is a different color. It seems that a Jewish employee of the Dutch censor edited your letter and added the missing words.

Bella stayed with Shmuel [in Utrecht] during the first days of Sukkot, even though there was a *sukkah* in the orphanage in Laaren, where many Jewish children who have lost their parents are staying. Yona is well enough by now to be able to travel to Utrecht, but he chose to stay with me. He wants us to go to Utrecht as soon as possible, for there we will be able to obtain kosher food. We will soon be transferred to the Jewish hospital in Amsterdam, where the surviving members of the Abrahams family are being treated.

On the first days of Sukkot we ate the food that Uncle Theo sent us with a healthy appetite. I showed my doctor the anti-diarrhea pills that were in the package. The doctor was very impressed — he said that such medication is not currently available in the Netherlands. I am taking the medicine on a daily basis, and it is helping me significantly.

Chag same'ach.

Kisses,

Baruch

A letter that I sent to the family in Zurich from Maastricht:

Hoshana Rabbah 5706 (September 28, 1945)

My dear ones,

I should be writing to you with a *shinui* [writing in the standard way is forbidden under certain circumstances during *Chol Hamo'ed*; one may write by forming the letters in a noticeably different way — in Hebrew, this alteration is called a *shinui*] but I fear that if I do, the censor may not let the letter through. Furthermore, since I am also fulfilling the mitzvah of honoring my parents by writing this letter, I am permitting myself to write during *Chol Hamo'ed* in the normal manner.

Dear Grandfather, thank you for your warm letter. You wrote to us on the day before Yom Kippur, and we received it just a few days later, on the first day of *Chol Hamo'ed*. I forwarded it to Bella and Shmuel, and they showed it to Shlomo [Abrahams] and everyone else. This is how we share every letter we receive from the family, whether it be from Switzerland, England or Eretz Yisrael. I hope that in the meantime you have received the letter we sent you on the day before Sukkot.

Baruch's condition is improving, thank God, and he already looks much better. His weight has doubled in the course of the last three months. I have regained my health, but I am not leaving Baruch, for there are monks circulating around us every single day. Although they are very nice and friendly, their real intention is quite obvious.

When they began trying to offer us "contentment," I told them that apparently they had nothing better to do with themselves than to attempt to destroy the remnants of the Jewish people that survived the Holocaust. I made myself very clear — I told them that as far as I could see, they were taking advantage of this difficult period in our lives in their efforts to complete the job that Hitler had set out to do. They have not spoken to us about their "truth" since.

Do you know, dear Grandfather, that the sack containing your letters about the weekly Torah portion is now in our possession?

The medicine that Uncle Theo sent us is helping Baruch tremendously. He would certainly appreciate it if you would send him some more pills.

Many blessings. A good month to all of you.

Shalom,
Yona

Arguments in the Monastery

The Jesuit monks did not relent in their efforts to convert us. From their perspective, they had a holy obligation to try to persuade us to "see the light."

Sometimes our arguments grew very heated. The monks claimed that "the Messiah" had already come, and that we must all believe in him; when they spoke to us about these kinds of things, their tone seemed to indicate that they were imparting to us unquestionable truths.

I countered that it was very difficult for me to believe such claims, for in reference to the Messiah, Scripture teaches that the wolf and the lamb will reside peacefully side by side. Our experiences in the camps proved beyond any doubt that we were still far from this idyllic state; millions of innocent men, women and children had been murdered in cold blood. How, then, could they possibly claim that "the Messiah" had already come? All evidence pointed to the contrary! Furthermore, who were the perpetrators of these vicious murders? They were none other than devout Christians who believe in "the Messiah"! We witnessed with our own eyes that their faith had not prevented them from turning into bloodthirsty beasts of prey.

One day, a more learned monk stopped by to visit us. He was a Vatican graduate and a professor of Scripture who knew a little Hebrew. We conversed in a friendly manner, showing mutual respect for one another. He mentioned to me that he was teaching the first chapter of Genesis to his students in the monastery. Keeping in mind Rashi's two interpretations, I asked the professor how he translated the word *"bereishit."* As I had expected he would, he answered, "in the beginning." I then asked him what he made of the construct state of the word *"bereishit,"* as opposed to the seemingly more correct, simpler form of the word *"barishonah,"* which is not used there. He had no clue.

On another occasion, the professor mentioned that he saw a correlation between the six days of Creation and the six days of the week. "Every Jewish child knows that the six days of Creation correspond to the six days of the week!" I said. "However, you Christians moved the Sabbath from Saturday to Sunday, and as a result, you begin the week on your Sabbath and end it on a workday. Your weekly cycle is clearly out of sync with the process of Creation!"

The professor came once or twice more, after which he did not appear again. It seems that he despaired of ever converting us. With the passage of time I forgot his name, but forty-seven years later he and I reestablished contact, as is related below.

On another occasion a monk paid us a visit and began to outline many common points that our two religions shared; one example was our mutual goal of eradicating idolatry. He mentioned that he vaguely remembered a verse in Scripture that spoke derisively of a certain idol worshipper who would fell a tree, offer half of it to his idol and then use the other half for his own needs; the monk asked me if I knew to which verse he was referring.

I said that I did not own an edition of Prophets and Writings, and that it had been more than two and a half years since I had been able to look into one of those holy books, but that I would nevertheless try to remember the verse by the following day. When he was gone, I searched through my *Chumash*, which included the weekly *haftarot* from the Prophets, and located the verse, "He burns half of it on the fire, with half he prepares meat to eat, roasting it and sating himself; he will even warm himself and say, 'Ah, I have warmed myself; I enjoy the fire' " (Yeshayahu 44:16, *haftarah* of *Parashat Vayikra*).

The next morning, I casually told the monk to open to Yeshayahu 44. He checked the source and was stunned — he thought that I knew all of Scripture by heart! After that incident, he never returned. That was the last we saw of him.

Arguments such as these did not weaken us. On the contrary, they served to raise our spirits and strengthen our faith.

After having committed to writing this section of my narrative describing our hospitalization in the monastery during the postwar period, I began to have doubts regarding the accuracy of my account, for in this case I had relied entirely on my memory. Perhaps I had unwittingly distorted the facts as a result of the poor state of my health and my low spirits at that time? I could not rule out that possibility. I therefore decided to try to corroborate my recollections of this difficult period by contacting the monks with whom I had spoken and argued so often. I realized, however, that this would be next to impossible — I did not remember even a single one of their names, and our conversations had taken place nearly half a century before.

In the spring of 5752 (1992), I wrote a letter to the Jesuit monastery in Maastricht and requested the names of the monks who had been assigned the task of assisting Jewish Holocaust survivors towards the end of 1945. The monastery's address was still engraved in my memory; I wrote it on the envelope and wondered whether anyone would take my unusual request seriously.

A few weeks later I received a response from Father Teo Van Eik, director of the National Archive Center of the Jesuit Order in Nymegen. He had written to inform me that the monastery had long since been relocated, and that the building in which we had stayed was transferred to the University of Maastricht. In reference to my request, he informed me that he could not help me, for the archive department under his directorship did not contain documents from the period that I had specified. He did assure me, though, that he would try to find additional information to assist me with my research. Two weeks later I received another letter from him, this one containing the names of all the monks who had treated Jewish Holocaust survivors during the post-war period. A postscript noted that none of these men were alive.

I wrote another letter to the director of the archives department thanking him for all his efforts on my behalf. I also asked him whether he happened to know of a monk who had studied Scripture in the Vatican, and who had taught this subject to the monks in the old Jesuit Maastricht monastery during the post-war period. It was a shot in the dark; I did not even expect a response to my query.

To my great surprise, a few months later I received a long letter signed by Professor Han Raankens. He was eighty-four years old at the time, and he had taught Scripture in the Amsterdam Catholic School of Theology. He began his letter in a very emotional and affectionate tone, describing what a moving experience it had been to receive the letter from his former student, the director of the archives department.

Professor Raankens confirmed that he had visited the Maastricht monastery on a number of occasions in the post-war period. He recounted in great detail the discussions and arguments that we had had during the summer of 1945. He wrote that he remembered our talks so vividly because of the profound influence they had wielded upon him — his knowledge of Scripture had increased significantly as a result of our discussions, and my opinions had influenced his entire approach to teaching. He added some details of which I myself had been unaware: on one occasion, he had searched the entire monastery for a *Sefer Tehillim* written in Hebrew, and brought it to us for our use. He also found and brought us *siddurim* (prayer books) from the Maastricht shul.

I am very grateful to him for all the kind deeds that he performed for us.

His letter confirms the accuracy of my memories of that period. Now I can rest assured that I have written a true account of our experiences in the Jesuit monastery.

A letter that I wrote to the family in Zurich:

Marcheshvan 5706 (October 12, 1945)

My dear ones,

Thank you very much for the small package. We received it three days ago. As you can imagine, Baruch was overjoyed [to receive more anti-diarrhea pills]. Thank God, he no longer needs to take them quite so frequently; his intestines are almost cured as a result of the previous shipment of pills that you sent.

This week we received another encouraging letter from Helen and Shlomo [Abrahams] — Shlomo is almost completely recovered. Bella received a letter from Uncle Felix this week. He writes that he hopes to visit us soon. We are very anxious to see him.

We have also received letters from Eretz Yisrael and England. Mr. Wagschall [Father's former partner] will try to obtain shoes for us from the leather merchants. We certainly hope he succeeds!

This week the Hebrew teacher gave us an edition of *mishnayot Seder Mo'ed* with the commentary of *Tiferet Yisrael*. Obviously, it made me very happy. I hope that tomorrow morning, on Shabbat, they will permit me to walk to shul, for I very much want to recite *Kaddish*.

Helen informs me that you do not have an accurate list

of the dates of death. The exact dates are:

Father	22 Shevat 5705 (February 5, 1945)	Bergen-Belsen
Shalom	1 Adar 5705 (February 14, 1945)	Bergen-Belsen
Bitya	8 Adar 5705 (February 21, 1945)	Bergen- Belsen
Elchanan	15 Adar 5705 (February 28, 1945)	Bergen-Belsen
Mother	1 Iyar 5705 (April 14, 1945)	On the train, near Lunenburg
Shlomo	4 Iyar 5705 (April 17, 1945)	Bergen-Belsen
Uncle Naftali	13 Iyar 5705 (April 26, 1945)	Troebits
Mishel	29 Iyar 5705 (May 13, 1945)	Troebits
Aunt Bea	9 Sivan 5705 (May 22, 1945)	Troebits

It is such a sad list.

What are our chances of obtaining entry visas to Switzerland? Have you received any response to the application form you sent in?

Regards to everyone.

Yours,

Yona

A letter written by Baruch in the Maastricht hospital to Uncle Felix and Aunt Grete in France:

8 Marcheshvan 5706 (October 16, 1945)

Dear Aunt and Uncle,

Please excuse me for writing in pencil. I am lying in bed, and I find it impossible to write in pen without staining myself with ink.

Yesterday we received your letter and were overjoyed at the news. I am looking forward to seeing you again, Uncle Felix. I also hope to see Aunt Grete in Zurich, but I have a feeling it will be a long time before that happens.

Thank God, we are both feeling much better. Yona, who at the moment is lying in the next bed, is feeling so well that he is allowed to get out of bed. He is still suffering from backaches, but they are due only to weakness. He has permission to travel "home" — that is, to Utrecht, to some close acquaintances of ours (for as you know, we do not have any relatives in the Netherlands other than the Abrahams family). However, he has decided to stay with me until I am transferred to the Jewish hospital in Amsterdam. I am anxiously awaiting the day when we will leave this place and will finally have the opportunity to eat kosher food again. It has been two and a half years!

I will be living with Shlomo Abrahams and the others staying in the Jewish hospital. Part of the building serves as a hospital, while a separate wing serves as an orphanage. Shlomo has almost completely recovered, but he is still not quite well enough to be transferred to the orphanage. We communicate frequently with him.

I conclude this letter with warm regards.

Shabbat shalom.

Yours,

Baruch

My letter to Uncle Felix and Aunt Grete in France:

. . . It is true that the situation in Eretz Yisrael is tense, but we have decided to make aliyah nonetheless. Many relatives living there from Father's side of the family have expressed a strong desire to help us.

Our relatives in Zurich have applied for entry visas to Switzerland on our behalf, but the bureaucratic process is extremely slow. We learned to wait in the camps; I guess we will have to exercise those skills again!

. . . To our great sorrow, Jewish community life in the Netherlands is practically nonexistent. It will not be very difficult emotionally for us to leave this country.

Shmuel has found all the *sefarim* that we hid under the floorboards of our apartment during the war. He found among them all the *sefarim* that each one of us received for his bar mitzvah, as well as three sets of Talmud and three Scrolls of Esther.

. . . I assume that you've heard about our experiences and about all the terrible things that have happened to us through the family in Zurich. It is too difficult for me to write all the details to you. Dear Uncle Felix, if you can get a permit to visit us, I will tell you everything in person.

We receive letters from Shmuel and Bella regularly, as well as from Helen and Shlomo. We also receive mail weekly from our relatives in England. Uncle Baruch Kunstadt in Jerusalem has already written to us a number of times.

During her last days, Mother, may she rest in peace, begged us to go to Eretz Yisrael to live, and to visit Grandfather on the way. With God's help, we will fulfill her last request.

Warm regards.

Yours,
Yona

Chapter Seventeen
Veenendaal

In the Home of the Van Essen Family

Baruch was finally transferred to the Jewish hospital in Amsterdam at the end of Cheshvan 5706 (November 1945). When he was moved there, I went to stay with the Van Essen family in the village of Veenendaal. Later, Baruch and Bella also joined me there. We lived with this wonderful family for five years before we finally made aliyah.

Before the war I had studied under Mrs. Van Essen's father, Rav Mordechai Cohen, *zt"l*, the *dayan* of Rotterdam. In his youth Rav Cohen had learned in Galanta, Hungary, and was a senior disciple of Rav Yosef Tzvi Dushinski, *zt"l*.

The Van Essen household could be accurately described as a most beautiful and noble Jewish home, in the purest sense. In addition to earning a livelihood as a food merchant, Mr. Van Essen contributed a considerable amount of his time and financial resources towards rebuilding Dutch Jewry, solving the many *kashrut* problems that plagued the Netherlands in the post-war period, establishing Torah institutions and founding a yeshivah in the city of Leiden. He also spearheaded a project called "Five Hundred Children," which resulted in the transfer of five hundred Jewish orphans from Romania to the Netherlands.

Mr. and Mrs. Van Essen made aliyah in the early 1970s and settled down in Jerusalem, near Beit HaKerem Yeshivah. We were overjoyed by their arrival.

Mr. David Van Essen passed away on 21 Shevat 5752 (1992); five years later, on *erev Rosh Chodesh Shevat* 5757 (1997), Mrs. Femi Van Essen passed away. They were both buried on the Mount of Olives. May their memory be blessed.

Back to Reality

We found it most difficult to resume a normal lifestyle. To think once again like anyone else, to view mundane events from a reasonable perspective — these were daunting challenges! We felt literally as though we had been reborn. On the one hand we preferred to avoid speaking of the past, but on the other hand, the present seemed so bizarre. We harbored a subconscious fear that if we would embark on a new life, the events of the Holocaust would be forgotten. How could we abandon our memories, so dominated by our loved ones and look forward to the future? It felt like betrayal.

The first time Shmuel saw a funeral procession in Utrecht after the end of the war, he could not fathom what all the fuss was about. We had become so desensitized to death in the camps that he merely looked on in disbelief as the procession accompanied the deceased and eulogized him on his last journey to the grave. What a shock to see such intense reactions to death!

At that moment, Shmuel realized that he still had not recovered emotionally from the trauma of seeing thousands of corpses strewn all over the grounds of Bergen-Belsen.

In these years we received letters, food packages and clothing from every corner of the world. We had written countless letters to relatives and friends of our parents who showed an interest in our welfare. Uncle Yona and Aunt Gutty in South Africa sent us huge food packages on a weekly basis and even invited us to join them there, but we informed them that we had already made up our minds to make aliyah. Our relatives sent us not only food packages and clothing, but also many letters expressing their anguish and filled with words of comfort and encouragement.

However, the most essential and practical source of encouragement for us turned out to be the warm and loving household of Mr. and Mrs. Van Essen. They saw to our every need, both physical and spiritual. It was largely due to their support and assistance that we managed to reconstruct our lives and regain a sense of normalcy.

A letter from Uncle Yakov Emanuel:

Haifa, September 14, 1945

Dearest children,

You cannot imagine our grief and shock upon receiving the appalling news of what has happened to all of you. We received the message on Friday, 22 Elul, the anniversary of Grandmother Emanuel's death, *zt"l.*

We, together with you, are obligated to accept God's decree — "It is a decree before Me." It is clear that those who died were very special individuals. On the fifteenth day of Sivan we received a telegram from England informing us that the entire family had survived, but then weeks went by without any news. We then became very concerned. How unfortunate that our worst fears have been substantiated! Many others must have learned of your fate some time ago, but they neglected to tell us, apparently because they themselves could not come to terms with the awful news.

I guarantee you one thing — you are not alone! The entire family stands by your side, ready to assist you and to try to alleviate the pain of your bitter losses. Please make every effort to arrive here as soon as possible. For now, that is the most important priority.

Let us know how you are feeling at this point. I hope you will soon regain your strength. Do not give in to despair, despite the heavy blow that fate has dealt you. The Holy One, blessed is He, will surely not abandon you.

Regards and kisses.

Love,
Uncle Yakov

A letter from Uncle Yona and Aunt Gutty in South Africa:

Johannesburg, September 9, 1945

Dearest children,

After having received Aunt Gitta's letter from Manchester, we now know something of what you have gone through, our dear children. We have been very concerned about you these past few weeks, but we had hoped that our fears would be proven incorrect. What a pity! What a dreadful shame that things have not turned out as we would have liked to imagine! What a terrible loss you have suffered! To have lost your precious parents — sincere Jews who sacrificed so much for the sake of others — and your wonderful brothers; I cannot imagine how you must feel.

It is unnecessary for me to dwell on your loss, for you are already more painfully aware of it than anyone else can ever be. You also know more than anyone what a rich spiritual legacy your parents imparted to you.

As far as we are concerned, we would like to do everything we possibly can to help. We cannot replace your parents — no one can — but we intend to help you in any way we can, to support you in every way, by material means as well as by offering you sound counsel. We want to be of genuine assistance to you, now and at all times.

Write us about everything; open your hearts to us. We want to know everything that you have gone through. Write to tell us what to send you as well. We have already sent clothing and other necessities for Bella. We have been sending everything to Mr. De Haas' address, but if you have a new address, please notify us immediately. Do not be shy — let us know what you need, for we have the desire and the ability to help you with all your material needs. We sent money in the past to Uncle Baruch [Kunstadt]. We sent money for the certificates, in the hope that your entire family would be able to go to Switzerland. . . . To our great sorrow, everything has changed.

Your precious mother, *zt"l* once sent us a full family portrait. We will make a copy of it and send it to you by registered mail; if it arrives safely, we will send additional copies. We have also sent you other photographs and some *Chumashim*.

Write to us openly about all your thoughts. We would like to offer you counsel and assist you as though you were our own children. Dear children, please write us a long letter, today.

If you decide to move to Eretz Yisrael, we will be able to send you far larger packages than those we have sent you so far to the Netherlands, which has a weight limit of only five kilos.

We are with you in spirit always.

Your uncle Yona

In addition to these letters, we received many letters from Uncle Baruch (Rav Baruch Kunstadt) and Aunt Tziporah in Jerusa-

Bella visits Baruch in De Joodse Invalide, "the Jewish Hospital," in Amsterdam, Kislev 5706 (November 1945), eight months after the liberation.

lem. They were very enthusiastic about our decision to make aliyah and gave us much encouragement. Later, they agreed with us that it would be more prudent for us to learn a trade before immigrating.

We never wrote to our relatives about our Holocaust experiences, nor did we describe to them the suffering that our parents and siblings underwent, may Hashem avenge their blood. Eventually our relatives stopped asking us for more detailed descriptions of our saga, and we ourselves tried our best to suppress those difficult memories. Many Holocaust survivors resolved never to discuss their experiences with anyone. It soon became an accepted code of behavior among Holocaust survivors to avoid speaking about the war.

My letter to Shmuel after a visit with Baruch in hospital:

December 12, 1945

Dear Shmuel,

This time, a brief summary of the news:

1. On Monday Baruch received a package from Denmark [from the Samson family] containing the following items: twenty eggs, hard cheese, a salami and two kilos of smoked meat.

2. The doctor is satisfied with Baruch's condition. He thinks that Baruch will be completely recovered in approximately three months.

3. Mrs. Wolff has purchased a quarter of a kilo of butter for Baruch, as per the instructions that Uncle Yona sent from South Africa.

4. Baruch and I received two very warm letters from Copenhagen [from the Samson family].

5. Baruch is as mischievous as ever. He looks great.

6. I have registered our names in the office of Jewish emigration to Eretz Yisrael. I filled out a long questionnaire for each of us.

7. I urgently need two pictures for our passports — one of you and one of Bella.

8. On both Monday night and Tuesday morning I led the congregation in prayer in the Jewish hospital of Amsterdam.

Some more news:

I left the eggs and salami with Baruch, and I requested that he give a large portion to the Abrahams family. He does not like cheese. This coming Sunday, Leo [Katz] will bring smoked meat for you and Bella.

The people at the Jewish Agency were very impressed with the fact that before we even registered our names with them, a request for entry visas for all of us had already arrived from Eretz Yisrael.

. . . Baruch's weight is forty-six kilos; mine is seventy-two kilos. We have each doubled our weight.

I recently spoke with Rav Tal. He has not changed in the least.

Nothing else is new.

Regards to the Seckbach family.

Yona

A letter from Uncle Theo in Zurich:

20 Shevat 5706

Dear Shmuel and Bella,

Shmuel, I read the few lines that you appended to Yona's postcard. It's a pity that I do not have Bella's address; I would have liked to write her separately and ask her to send regards to Mr. Van Gelder.

While reviewing the *haftarah* to *Parashat Yitro* this week, I noticed the verse ". . . until cities become desolate without inhabitants, and houses without man, and the land becomes utterly desolate" (Yeshayahu 6:11). The Hebrew words for "and the land becomes utterly desolate" are numerically equivalent to 706, which is the same number as the last three digits of this Hebrew year. We have indeed witnessed the fulfillment of this prophecy!

Upon receiving this postcard, know that all of our thoughts are with you. We feel the absence of those to whom you would turn in your hour of need, as in the verse,

"They would bring the difficult cases to Moses" (Shemot 18:26). All we have left is the absolute certainty that our loved ones were indeed "able people, God-fearing men, men of truth who hate injustice" (ibid., 21).

I do not know whether Grandfather will manage to write to you, but if he does so before 22 Shevat [the anniversary of Father's death], he will surely pour out his heart to you and weep for many hours without interruption over the death of our loved ones, *zt"l*.

May the final redemption come speedily and in our day!

Yours,
Uncle Theo

Indeed, Grandfather did not neglect the first anniversary of Father's death. He sent us a letter in which he requested that we follow in the ways of our parents. One of Grandfather's hands was paralyzed at the time; he typed the entire letter with his only healthy hand.

Grandfather's letter on the first anniversary of Father's death:

22 Shevat 5706

Dear children,

Today I write to you with a heavy heart and mourn the death of your beloved father, *zt"l*. I mark especially the day of his death because he was the first of the martyrs in my family to have died.

Kaddish is not a prayer in honor of the dead, but rather a means of sanctifying God and accepting upon ourselves the yoke of His kingdom. Each *Kaddish* you recite is a new affirmation that you will emulate your father and will never forget the lessons that he taught you. In the future, when you will merit to build your own households, remember and emulate the wonderful example that he was to you. If you will do this, Hashem's angels will dwell in your midst, and peace and success will reside within the walls of your homes.

May peace always reign among you, as it did among our loved ones, *zt"l*, who are no longer with us.

At every opportunity, ask yourselves, "What would Father have said in this case? What would Mother have done now?" Know that your parents' souls are looking down on you from Heaven, and that they are praying to Hashem on your behalf.

Dry your tears and serve Hashem with joy, for this is the attitude that your parents always embraced. If you follow in their example, then, with the help of God, you will be blessed with success. When you will finally reside in the Land of the Patriarchs, pray to Hashem, and He will safeguard you and bless you with success.

I pray to Hashem that He grant me the merit of giving you my blessings when you pass through Switzerland on your way to Eretz Yisrael, in fulfillment of your mother's last request.

Be healthy and courageous, as those who have passed away so prematurely would have desired. Always remain faithful Jews — this is the most beautiful memorial that you can ever hope to build in your parents' memory.

A warm kiss,
Grandfather

The First Yahrzeit

On the evening of 22 Shevat 5706 — the first anniversary of Father's death, may he rest in peace — a special memorial service was held in the Utrecht shul. Father was posthumously awarded the title of "*chaver*."

The eulogy delivered by Rav Joseph Van Gelder:

I would like to say just a few words and deliver a brief eulogy, for a long speech would be superfluous for all those who knew the deceased, and to those who did not have the merit of knowing him, no amount of mere words can possibly describe the man's greatness.

The duty of a Jewish educator is defined by Moshe Rabbeinu in this week's *parashah*: "Clarify the decrees and laws for [the people]. Show them the path they must take and the deeds they must do" (Shemot 18:20). The Sages explained in reference to this verse, "'The path' — this refers to Torah study; 'the deeds they must do' — this refers to good deeds" (*Mechilta*).

The deceased not only clearly understood and internalized Moshe's words, he also made great efforts to implement them in his daily life. Moshe's words define the theoretical approach that an educator must embrace. The deceased, however, believed that it is not sufficient for an educator merely to teach — he must also do. He believed that a Jewish educator must lead by personal example. As the Sages say in reference to the verse, "Moses took Joseph's remains with him" (Shemot 13:19):

Two arks went before the people throughout the forty years [in the desert] — the contents of one were dead [the

casket containing Joseph's remains], and the contents of
the other were alive [the Ark containing the Two Tablets of
the Law].

In response to the nations, the Jewish people said,
"The one lying in this ark fulfilled that which is written
upon the contents of that Ark!" (*Yalkut Beshalach* 227).

Likewise, the deceased did not view *halachah* and practical deeds as two separate elements of religion, but rather
as intertwined units of a single continuum.

He was the head of a very special family in our congregation, a large family founded upon Torah study and the
fulfillment of *mitzvot*.

Tonight is the first anniversary of his death. His soul
departed exactly one year ago, after having lived a full and
rich life. Regarding him the Holy One, blessed is He, fulfilled the promise, "I will make you live out full lives" (Shemot 23:26). There is another reason to cite this verse in reference to the deceased, for as the Talmud states, " 'I will
make you live out full lives' teaches that the Holy One,
blessed is He, fills the years of the righteous, day by day and
month by month" (*Kiddushin* 38a; *Rosh Hashanah* 11a). So it
was with Moshe Rabbeinu, who was born and died on the
same date, and so it was with the deceased — 21 Shevat was
the first full day of his life [he was born on 20 Shevat], and
21 Shevat was the last full day of his life.

His grown children represent the bountiful fruit of his
life's efforts. They are righteous Jews who have remained
faithful to the lessons imparted to them by their father, *zt"l*.
In reference to him we may cite the Sages' praise, "He gives
forth nothing from his hand that is still in need of rectification" — he brought up, educated and instilled the fear of

God into the children that he "gave forth" to this world.

The Sages prefaced the above statement with the phrase, "One can assume that a *chaver* does not give forth anything from his hand that is still in need of rectification" (*Pesachim* 9a).

Therefore, tonight I have the honor and the merit of announcing that the regional rabbinate has decided to amend the name of the deceased. From this day on he shall be known as:

Chaver Rabbi Mordechai, son of Moreinu V'rabbeinu Harav Elchanan Moshe, son of Beila (Bella).

This name shall be used when saying *Yizkor* in memory of the deceased and when calling his sons to the Torah.

I would like to add that, were it not for his wife's constant support, the deceased could not have succeeded in such great achievements. As the Sages said, "The wife of a *chaver* is regarded as a *chaver*" (*Avodah Zarah* 39a). The wife of the deceased — the mother of his children — certainly deserves this honor.

May the memory of the deceased bring blessing upon his children, his family, his friends, his congregation and upon all of Israel. As King Solomon said, "The memory of the righteous is blessed" (Mishlei 10:7).

The Posthumous Certificate Awarding Father the Title of "Chaver"

"Awake and sing, you who dwell in the dust!" (Yeshayahu 26:19).

There was a man in the land of Ashkenaz — Rav Mordechai son of *Moreinu Verabbeinu* Harav Elchanan Moshe was his name. That man was blameless and upright; he feared God and shunned evil.

He married a noble woman, Chana daughter of Harav Joshua. She was a modest and worthy woman, God-fearing and dedicated to the performance of *mitzvot*.

Their actions were pleasing to the wise, to the populace at large and to the Almighty. They commanded their sons and daughters to walk in the ways of Hashem, to act righteously and justly.

But that man fled, he and his entire household, from the unsheathed sword wielded by that evil nation which the Holy One regrets having created. They then arrived here, in the Netherlands. We ourselves witnessed the righteous deeds that he performed every single day. . . . Great was his desire to learn Hashem's Torah; indeed, he learned and taught, sharing his knowledge with others in his home and with anyone who expressed a desire to study the Torah.

And behold — it is difficult to believe that such a thing can be told! — that accursed nation which caused the earth to tremble and kingdoms to shudder, transformed the face of the earth into wasteland and destroyed the righteous man's city. It seized captives, including himself, his wife and his sons and daughters. The evil nation placed them in camps of death and torture. And there Mordechai was summoned before the King — before the King of kings, in the *Yeshivah shel Malah*. . . .

We shall always recount the goodness of this *chaver* of ours, in whom one cannot find fault. Therefore, we have decided to publicize his righteousness and uprightness and declare his name to be:

Chaver Rabbi Mordechai son of Moreinu V'rabbeinu Harav Elchanan Moshe.

A photocopy of the posthumous certificate awarded to Father

May his name become great in Yisrael; may he be a source of pride to the children that he left behind, who survived the cruelty and who follow in his good and righteous paths — the ways of pleasantness and the paths of peace.

Signed by the *av beit din* of the Province of Utrecht, on the occasion of the first anniversary of his death, on the twenty-second day of Shevat 5706.

The letter that Baruch sent me on the day following the first anniversary of Father's death:

Dear Yona, Shmuel and Bella,

I just received your letter. I asked the doctor to grant me permission to go downstairs, and he agreed. There was a *minyan* at night, and I led the prayers then, as well as on the following morning. I thank God that I managed to pray as required.

A small envelope arrived yesterday from Uncle Felix in France. It contained a fountain pen (which does not work), envelopes, a writing pad and the paper upon which I am now writing to you.

Yona, you'll be glad to know that I gained one hundred grams this week. Definite progress!

To you, Shmuel, I send a warm *"Shabbat shalom."* Please

Rav Tzadok Tal, zt"l

send my regards to the holy congregation of Utrecht.

When they called me to the Torah last Thursday, I requested that they use the name "Baruch son of *Hechaver* Rabbi Mordechai."

Bella's letter to Grandfather in Zurich:

April 29, 1946

Dear Grandfather,

How are you? I hope your Passover Seder was as nice as the one we had here in Veenendaal. It was really very enjoyable and beautiful, and there were many guests. Mrs. Van Essen's brother [Mr. Nissan Cohen] and his family were also here. In all, there were seventeen of us. We even had a *minyan*!

This coming Thursday, on Rosh Chodesh, will be the first anniversary of Mother's passing. Yona and Shmuel will be in Utrecht; they will pray there. One year ago today (according to the Hebrew date), we were still together with Mother on the train. Over Pesach this year, we reminisced for a long time about the Pesach Seder we had two years ago, when we had all still been together in Bergen-Belsen; we observed the Yom Tov as best we could under the circumstances.

I learn *Chumash Devarim* with Yona every day after he returns from work. We are now studying *Parashat Nitzavim*. I hope to finish *Sefer Devarim* by *Shavuot*. I am also reading your letters on the weekly *parashah* on *Sefer Devarim*. Now I am able to understand them perfectly.

I will close here. Warm regards and kisses from your granddaughter, who thinks of you always.

Bella

Grandfather's letter on the occasion of the first anniversary of Mother's passing:

Zurich, April 29, 1946

Dear grandchildren,

On Rosh Chodesh Iyar, one year will have passed since your beloved mother closed her eyes for the last time. Ever since the news of her death reached me, not a single day has passed that I have not cried over our loss. Even now I am crying over the death of my beloved children.

Today I cite to you the verse, "Until the advent of the Redeemer!" You too must dry your tears and prove by means of your lives, which you must infuse with the fear of Hashem, that you are worthy descendants of such parents. They walked in the ways of Hashem throughout their short lives and served as shining examples for so many people, both in the Netherlands and in other regions.

Although you are unable to place a stone upon your mother's grave, know that every good deed that you perform during your lifetime will serve as a living headstone. God shall inscribe it as such in Heaven, for all your good deeds are the result of the righteous education that your parents granted to you. Know that the good name that you bear — of which you can be very proud — is the result of your parents' efforts. May Hashem be at your side and protect you when, with the help of God, you shall build a new future for yourselves in Eretz Yisrael.

Dear Bella, your relatives there will surely help you with wise counsel. Yona, Shmuel and Baruch, let Uncle Kunstadt be your example. He can be relied upon always. Both Uncle and Aunt Kunstadt knew your parents, held

JOSUÉ GOLDSCHMIDT
ZURICH
Waffenplatzstrasse 14/ 47
Téléphone 20.312
Compte de chèques postaux VIII/16670

Zürich 9.April 1946

Meine geliebten Enkel,

Rausch Chaudesch Ijer ist es ein Jahr her,dass Eure geliebte Mutter
ihre Augen geschlossen.Seit der Zeit,dass ich ihren Heimgang erfahren,ist
kein Tag vergangen,an dem ich nicht heisse Trähnen um sie vergossen hatte
& noch heute weine ich ob des Verlustes meiner Kinder. .Und heute rufe ich
Euch zu:al bine hagauel.Trocknet Eure Trähnen auch Ihr & zeiget durch Euer
gttefürchtiges Leben,dass Ihr würdig seid auf solche Eltern Euch stützen zu
könnenjie während ihres leider so kurzen Lebens stets in Ottes Wegen gegangen
sind,als Vorbild für gar manche Menschen.In Holland & im Ausland.
Wenn Ihr auch nicht am Jahrzeitstage an das Grag der Mutter, intreten könnt
'. ein Steinchen an den Grabstei Nederzu legen,so ist jede gute Tat,die Ihr
während Eures Lebens übet, eine lebende mazeywo,die Euch Oben gutgeschrieben
wird & die Ihr nur Dank der guten Erziehung ausführen könnt Seid versichert,
dass der gute Namen,der ,den Ihr geniesset,das Werk der Eltern, ist &
auf den Ihr stotz sein könnt.Wenn Ihr e.G.w. Euch in Erez Jisroel für Euch
eine neue Existenz aufbauen werdet,dann wird Euch der dahin begleiten,der
Euerer Bisher beschützt hatte.Dir,liebe Bella werden Deine dortigen
Verwandten stets mit guten Ratschlägen beiseite stehen,& Euch,liebe Jene,
Sam & Bernd,wird Onkel Kunstadt ein leuchtendes Beispiel sein,dem Ihr blind-
lings nach-gehen könnt.Onkel & Tante Kunstadt,kannten Eure Eltern ,die in
Hochachtung standen bei ihnen seit vielen Jahren & die wissen was sie den
Kindern der Heimgegangenen schulden.den Kindern meiner Mechutenestety,sie
as Allen vor dem himmlichen Throhn ein Fürsprech bleibt.
Mögen bald Eure Papiere zur Reise nach Palestina (über Zürich)ausgestellt
sein damit Ihr im Lande der Väter als würdige Kinder Eurer Heimgegangenen
ein glückliches Leben fortführen könnt ad meyo w'esarim schomo in Glück &
Freude.
Dieses Brief schicke ich an den ältesten von Euch,mit der Bitte,ihn an alle
Geschwister weiterzugeben.

Grandfather's letter

them in very high regard and know how much they owe to
you, the children of your wonderful parents.

May the deceased speak in our favor before the
Throne of Glory.

Your immigration certificates will soon be ready, and
you will finally arrive in the land of our forefathers. May

you lead joyous lives and remain loyal to the memory of the deceased, and live to the age of 120 with much joy.

I send this letter to the eldest among you; please forward it to everyone.

Warm regards and kisses.

Shalom,
Grandfather

 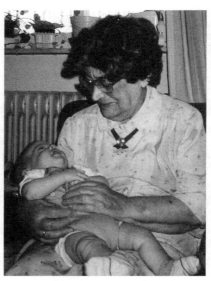

On the right, Mr. Van Essen, zt"l, and Mr. De Haas, zt"l, at a bar mitzvah in our Jerusalem home, 28 Adar, 5733 (1973)

Mrs. Van Essen, zt"l, with one of our grandsons, Jerusalem 5795 (1995)

Chapter Eighteen

The Road Home

As we waited in the Netherlands for our entry visas to Eretz Yisrael, we made great efforts to regain a semblance of normalcy in our lives.

We had decided to prepare ourselves for life in Eretz Yisrael by rounding out our schooling and learning marketable trades: Shmuel chose watchmaking, I studied optometry, Baruch became an electrician and Bella graduated from high school and took a course in early childhood education. We all gained practical experience in our chosen trades by working as apprentices, and accumulated theoretical knowledge by taking various correspondence courses, which included written examinations.

At the same time, we began to study Torah again. Baruch and I learned the fourth chapter of *masechet Pesachim*, and then we went on to *masechet Beitzah*; I also learned *Chumash* with Bella. Each *motza'ei Shabbat* we participated in a *shiur* that Mr. Aaron De Haas delivered on *masechet Ketubot* in his home in Utrecht. I also managed to review the weekly *parashah* with Rashi's commentary during the one-and-a-quarter-hour bus ride to work and back.

We became active members of the Netherlands Poa'lei Agudath Yisrael organization, which had been established soon after the war ended. Shmuel also devoted a considerable amount of his time and talents to establish the Shalshelet (Hasjalsjelet) youth group, in which we were also active; he spearheaded the publication of the organization's monthly newsletter, which was shipped to young Jews in every part of the Netherlands. Shmuel used to edit, proofread and transport the newsletters on his bicycle from the print shop to the post office, often working well into the wee hours of the morning.

Hashalshelet youth group made a significant contribution towards the preservation of the culture and heritage of the young Dutch Jews who had survived the Holocaust. For all intents and purposes, Shmuel was the group's national director — it was he who coordinated activities in the local branches and managed the summer camps. Hashalshelet's various activities exposed many participants to traditional Judaism for the first time: before they came to Hashalshelet, quite a few children had never heard a Friday night *Kiddush*. We were all thrilled with the inroads Hashalshelet made. Baruch and Bella worked as counselors in this group, and I helped edit the newsletter and ran the organization's Rotterdam branch.

In honor of Hashalshelet's tenth anniversary, Rav Kalman Kahana, *zt"l*, wrote the following statement in the newsletter:

> Hashalshelet youth group and its newsletter have made great contributions towards strengthening Dutch Jewry's devotion to Torah, drawing nearer to Hashem

those who have strayed, reinforcing the bonds between Jews residing in the Diaspora and those living in Eretz Yisrael, and, last but not least, encouraging Jewish youth to make aliyah.

Hashalshelet camp, 5709 (1949)

Although we devoted much energy to Hashalshelet, in retrospect, I think that we gained more from the organization than it benefited from us. Our responsibilities helped us to develop self-confidence, and perhaps more important, the work distracted us from the painful memories of the past. In addition, we merited to disseminate Torah among the young Jews of the Netherlands, to reach out to those who had gone astray and to encourage Dutch youth to make aliyah. All this was ample reward for our efforts!

Epilogue

Bella made aliyah at the end of 5710 (1950). She went to live in Haifa with Uncle Yaakov and Aunt Mina Emanuel, who treated her like their own daughter. Shmuel, Baruch and I arrived in Israel at the beginning of Adar 5711 (1951) and went directly to Jerusalem. Uncle Baruch and Aunt Tziporah Kunstadt (Father's sister) took us in and related to us as if we were their own sons. Our cousins greeted us warmly and were very kind to us; they helped us acclimatize to life in Israel. We always found sound counsel and a listening ear in the Kunstadt home.

Uncle Baruch explained to me that although Jews of the *Yishuv Hayashan* in Jerusalem did not dress like us, their simple lifestyle and general outlook on life was very similar to our own. Once, I asked him what I should do if a Jerusalem *minhag* (religious custom) differed from mine — should I follow the local custom, or do as we were taught by our parents? Uncle Baruch answered that in such cases, I must carefully review the sources of the particular custom in question. If I found that the Jerusalem custom was based on firmer halachic ground, then I should adopt the local custom; if on the other hand I found that our custom was more in tune with *halachah*, then I should adhere to my own family's custom.

When we arrived in Israel, Baruch learned for approximately a year in the Kol Torah Yeshivah. Shmuel and I began working in our areas of specialization.

Approximately a year after our arrival, Shmuel and Baruch moved to Kibbutz Sha'albim, in the Ayalon Valley. Baruch eventually moved back to Jerusalem, but Shmuel remained in Kibbutz Sha'albim and still lives there today. Bella joined me in Jerusalem, and that is where we stayed.

I married Chana Adler, and we have also merited to establish our home in Jerusalem. In addition to my work as an optician, I was asked to edit the quarterly newsletter *Hama'ayan*, published by the Yitzchak Breuer Institute. I have had the honor of supervising the regular publication of this newsletter since Tishrei 5724 (1963).

Shmuel married Ruth Levi, and they established their home on Kibbutz Sha'albim. For years his responsibilities on the kibbutz involved hard physical labor, and at the same time he occupied himself with various educational and communal projects beyond the boundaries of the kibbutz. He is considered to be one of the founders of Kibbutz Sha'albim, and it is largely due to his influence that the community has developed into an important Torah center.

Baruch married Shifra, Mr. Aaron De Haas' oldest daughter. While living on the kibbutz, Baruch was assigned the task of supervising the agricultural work in the fields. He participated in the "War of the Tractors," a vicious battle between Jordanian soldiers and Jewish farmers, which erupted in the Ayalon Valley shortly before the Six-Day War. The Jordanians attempted to capture a large section of no-man's land adjacent to the kibbutz's fields, but they were driven back by the Jews. It is difficult to believe that Baruch, who not many years earlier had emerged from the Holocaust an emaciated skeleton whose leg almost had to be amputated, became the fierce "Jewish warrior" whose picture appeared on the front page of newspapers all over the world, as well as on the cover of *Time* magazine.

Bella married Reb Yitzchak Shindler. They still live in Jerusalem.

We have all established families and raised a new generation. Some of our children were named after their grandparents and uncles who perished in the Holocaust. Most have already established homes of their own, and they too have remained faithful to

the ways of our forefathers. Together with our sons and daughters, sons-in-law and daughters-in-law, grandsons and granddaughters, our family today consists of over a hundred souls! May it continue to be fruitful and multiply! All of us live in Eretz Yisrael

Blessed with children in Jerusalem

and follow in our family's traditions. In the darkest days of 5703–5705, who would have dreamed that it could have turned out so? "It is incumbent upon us to praise the Master of all!" (from the *Aleinu* prayer)

I have delved into the painful memories of the past and compiled this memoir primarily for the benefit of our children and grandchildren, who have continually expressed a desire to know more details about our family's experiences during the Holocaust. However, the ultimate purpose of this book is to convey to future generations the efforts that our family made, each in his own way, to continue living as a Jew despite the dark terror and the hunger and suffering that enveloped us; to continue observing *mitzvot*, learning Torah and helping others in conditions much worse than anyone who has not experienced them can possibly imagine.

Throughout the Holocaust, our parents strove to carry on their righteous Jewish lifestyle in their characteristically unassuming way. Despite the horrors that they encountered on a daily basis,

Kibbutz Sha'albim, 5732 (1972). From right to left: Baruch and Shifra, Yona and Chana, Shmuel and Ruth, Yitzchak and Bella

they tried to the best of their ability to help others. Father, Mother, Elchanan and Shlomo looked upon the Holocaust as a difficult spiritual challenge that must be met and overcome at all costs. This is how they viewed that entire period. It was this attitude that enabled them to cling to the traditions passed down to them by their forefathers, in situations so horrible that they defy description. With their suffering and their tears, they made a modest but eternal impression, sanctifying Hashem's Name in the world.

This is my humble tribute to Father, Mother, Elchanan, Shlomo, Shalom and Bitya, may Hashem avenge their blood. They lived relatively short lives from a human perspective, but when viewed against the backdrop of the Jewish people's timeless existence, their lives were very long indeed. Not only did they die sanctifying Hashem's Name, they also lived solely for that purpose.

> *I raise You high, O God,*
> *for You lift me up and do not let my enemies rejoice over me.*
> *O God, my Lord, I pray to You and You heal me.*
> *You preserve me from descending into the pit.*

Sing to God, His pious ones, and praise His holy Name.

His anger endures but a moment, [and] granting life is His desire.

In the evening he lays down weeping, in the morning — a song of joy.

(Tehillim 30:2–6)

אלה מול אלה

אלה וגם אלה עלו על הדרך ירושלימה
אלה לכוון ירושלים, ואלה לכוון ג'רוזלם.
אלה נסעו בדרך הישנה ואלה בדרך החדשה.

גם אלה וגם אלה היו מוכנים לקרב
מול אלה עמדו ערבים, ומול אלה — יהודים.
לאלה היה יום שבת קודש, ולאלה יום ז'.

אלה קדשו אדמת קודש ואלה חללוה.
אלה באו לגאול אדמת ישראל ואלה באו להפקירה
אלה היו מקדשי שבת ואלה מחלליה.

פני אלה למקום המקדש ופני אלה למוזיאון
אלה באו בשם ברית בין הבתרים, ואלה בשם ליגת הכנענים.
אלה חרשו נירים ואלה חרשו מזמות.

אלה מפריחים שממות ואלה מפריחים סיסמאות.
אלה אנשי עמל ואלה אנשי מלל
אלה שוכנים באהלי שם ואלה — באהלי קדר.
אלה וגם אלה עלו על הדרך ירושלימה.

* * *

מתי אלה וגם אלה יעלו יחד ירושלימה
וישירו יחד שיר העבר והעתיד
שיר העולים בדרך ירושלימה:
"שמחתי באומרים לי בית ה' נלך".

שמואל עמנואל

A poem by Shmuel in the Sha'albim weekly paper

Harav Shlomo Zalman Auerbach, zt"l, attending various family celebrations

Afterword

More than fifty years after the Holocaust, on the tenth of Elul 5755 (1995), I received a long-distance phone call from someone who identified himself as Binyamin Zev Vorst. He told me that he had been born in Amsterdam, survived the Holocaust, was currently living in London, England, and was calling me from Johannesburg, South Africa. A complicated introduction, to be sure!

At first I could not place the identity of the caller, nor understand what exactly he wanted from me. Reb Binyamin Vorst informed me that he had been searching for me for over fifty years. He had been sent to Johannesburg by a British *kashrut* organization to supervise the ritual slaughter of animals there, and somehow he had landed in the home of my cousin, Mr. Aaron Emanuel, where he happened to notice a copy of the original Hebrew edition of this work. With mounting excitement, he asked my cousin how he could reach me and immediately dialed my telephone number.

The first question he asked me was whether I remembered the Yom Kippur of 5705, when the Germans forced the Jewish inmates of Bergen-Belsen to take showers.

"Yes, of course I do," I answered.

Reb Binyamin told me that he had been barely ten years old at the time. This came as a surprise to me, for I had not realized that the Germans had forced such young children to undergo this ordeal. Despite his young age, Binyamin knew that it is prohibited to wash one's body on Yom Kippur.

Reb Binyamin recalled that he was marched off to the showers along with a large group of inmates that departed through the gate next to barracks 17. On their way to the showers, they passed another a group of inmates returning from the showers and marching back to camp. Instinctively, little Binyamin ran from his group to the other without anyone noticing.

"That is how I avoided showering on Yom Kippur," he said to me. "I remember every detail of that episode to this very day. It seems as though it happened yesterday, not more than fifty years ago," he concluded.

Although I was moved by his account, I was still wondering why Reb Vorst had called me from the other side of the world, until he told me the following story:

"As we were being marched off to the showers, I saw a pair of German guards tormenting one of the Emanuel brothers. They ordered him to unload two heavy metal posts from a two-wheel wagon, but the weak and emaciated Emanuel boy could not even move the heavy objects, let alone unload them. The Germans began beating him viciously. All this happened on that same Yom Kippur.

"This scene has remained etched in my mind all these years. Tell me, who was that boy? Was it you?"

Reb Vorst was somewhat disappointed when I told him that I had been totally unaware of this incident. As for me, I was shocked to learn fifty years after the war that one of my brothers — either Elchanan or Shlomo — had been subjected to a brutal beating on that Yom Kippur. At the same time, however, Reb Vorst's account heightened my admiration for my brothers, for no more than four days after this incident, they risked their lives to build a *sukkah*.

The Germans tried to break our spirit on that Yom Kippur, but as my brother's determination proves, they failed miserably. "Who is like Your people, Israel!"

Appendix I

God remembered Chanah on Rosh Hashanah.

My parents were married in 5681 (1921). More than a year later, on the first day of Rosh Hashanah 5683 (1922), Father was given the honor of reading the *haftarah* in the shul that he used to attend when he lived in Hamburg. That portion recounts Chanah's emotional responses to her barrenness and her prayers to Hashem (see Shmuel I, ch. 1). Mother was sitting in the women's section of shul at the time. When Father read the verse "[Chanah] was of embittered soul and she prayed to God and wept continuously," my mother burst into bitter tears.

When an elderly woman approached Mother and asked her why she was crying, Mother replied, "My name is also Chana, and I am also praying for the Heavenly gift of a child."

The woman was very moved by Mother's response. She said to her, "Please stop crying. I will pray for you, and, God willing, by next Rosh Hashanah you will be embracing a son."

My parents did indeed give birth to a son ten months later, in the end of Tamuz of 5683 (1923), whom they named Elchanan. The elderly woman who had comforted Mother in shul the previous year would occasionally come to visit her and the child for whom she had prayed. Mother always felt very grateful to her for her generosity and for having prayed on her behalf. Seven more children were born to our family over the years, but Mother never forgot this elderly woman. She would occasionally retell to us the entire story of how Father read the *haftarah*, how she was reduced to tears and what that woman said to comfort her.

Elchanan grew to be a wise and diligent boy. He studied and taught Torah with exceptional diligence. Even today, I envision him leaning over a Gemara, studying a book of Scripture with commentators, or even a grammar book of Biblical Hebrew. He would study, review, think and occasionally jot down notes. Elchanan's brief but full life ended on Shushan Purim (the fifteenth of Adar) of the year 5705 (1945) in Bergen-Belsen. May his soul be bound up in the bundle of life, with the souls of our parents, brothers and sisters, and the souls of all those who sanctified God's holy Name in the course of their lives and by means of their deaths.

Appendix II

Father's Torah Thoughts

Regretfully, I remember only very few of the thoughts on the weekly Torah portions that Father shared with us during our Shabbat meals. Following are some of these:

Bereishit 37:5–10: Yosef dreamt two dreams. In the first dream, his brother's sheaves bowed down to his sheaf. In the second dream, the sun, moon and eleven stars bowed down to him.

We see that Yosef's brothers responded to his first dream by saying, "Would you then reign over us? Would you then dominate us?" When he told them of his second dream, however, they remained silent. Why?

After having interpreted Yosef's first dream, the brothers realized that Yosef was relating another dream to them in the hope of prompting them to interpret it favorably. (The Sages say in *masechet Berachot* that a dream is fulfilled according to its interpretation.) Therefore, when he told them of his second dream, they pretended not to comprehend its true meaning.

Yosef, however, would not be deterred — in an effort to evoke a favorable interpretation of this second dream, Yosef told it to his brothers again, but this time he related it in the presence of Yaakov, as it is written, "He related it to his father and to his brothers. His father scolded him, saying, 'What is this dream that you have dreamt? Are we to come — I and your mother and your brothers — to bow down to the ground before you?'" (Bereishit 37:10). Yaakov's final words were precisely what Yosef had been seeking — a positive interpretation of his second dream.

This is the intent of the next verse (11), "His brothers were jealous of him" — the brothers were angered not only by the content of Yosef's dreams, but also by his wise stratagem of retelling the dream in his father's presence in order to elicit from him a favorable interpretation.

Bereishit 40:17: The Torah recounts the dreams of Pharaoh's butler and baker. After Yosef had favorably interpreted the butler's dream, the baker related his own dream to Yosef:

"In the top basket, there were all kinds of baked goods for Pharaoh; but the birds were eating them from the basket on my head."

In contrast to his favorable interpretation of the butler's dream, Yosef understood that the baker's dream foretold bad tidings. What was it that led Yosef to this conclusion?

The baker told Yosef that he had dreamt that three baskets of food were piled on his head, and that the top basket contained Pharaoh's food. The birds, however, ate "from the basket on my head" — i.e., from the lowest basket that lay directly upon the baker's head, and not from the top basket that contained Pharaoh's food. From this Yosef inferred that the food in the top basket must have been unfit for consumption, for otherwise why would the bird not have eaten from it? If it was not fit to be eaten by a bird, it surely was not fit to be eaten by Pharaoh.

This was a bad omen for the baker, for let us remember that he had been imprisoned as a consequence of his having served Pharaoh unsuitable food. Hence the unfit food that the baker saw in the dream symbolized punishment. The dream foretold that he would once again be punished, but this time more seriously, as Yosef told him, "Birds will eat your flesh."

Shemot 32:17–8: After having remained on Mount Sinai for forty days and forty nights, Moshe descended to the Jewish people with the Two Tablets of the Law, only to find them worshipping a golden calf.

As he descended from Mount Sinai, Moshe encountered Yehoshua and informed him of the sin that the Jewish people had committed.

Yehoshua's response to the noise coming from the foot of the mountain was "There is a noise of war in the camp." In essence Yehoshua was saying to Moshe, "Not *all* the Jews are serving the Golden Calf. There are two warring factions in the camp — it is true that some support the worship of the Golden Calf, but there are also those who oppose it and are struggling against those who are worshipping it!"

Moshe, however, correctly assessed the situation. He said, "It is neither the song of victory nor the dirge of the defeated. What I hear is just the noise of those who sing." In essence he said, "I do not hear either battle cries or lamentations of the vanquished. Rather, I hear only a unified voice in support of the Golden Calf."

This is the true intent of Rashi's commentary to the verse: "This is not the sound of victors crying, 'Victory!' nor is it the sound of the vanquished crying, 'Let me flee!'"

Devarim 28:68: The Torah's admonishment of the Jewish people ends with the words, "You will try to sell yourselves as slaves and maids, but no one will want to buy you."

This teaches us that the Jewish people will pound on the gates of different nations, "but no one will want to buy!" No one will be prepared to "purchase" them.

This is the final admonishment. After we have experienced this punishment, we will merit the Redemption.

דברי תורה שכתב אלחנן הי"ד

A Torah treatise written by Elchanan.

Indeed, such is our current situation — we Jews want to flee Germany, yet all the developed countries in the world have denied us entry. We have reached the level of "no one will want to buy!" This is a sign that we have reached the final stage of the Torah's admonishment. Now the Redemption is before us. May it come speedily and in our days.

Esther 8:17: The verse begins with a description of the joy that overtook the Jewish people when Haman's evil decree was overturned and ends with the words, "moreover, many from among the people of the land professed themselves Jews, for the fear of the Jews had fallen upon them."

Notice that the verse does not say that the gentiles "among the people of the land" actually *converted* to Judaism — indeed, conversion is no simple matter for a gentile. Rather, the verse teaches that they "*professed themselves* Jews." In other words, these gentiles merely pretended to have converted to Judaism. Why?

With the issuing of the king's decree permitting the Jews to defend themselves against their enemies, the Jewish people's esteem in the eyes of the non-Jewish populace rose dramatically. Many non-Jews falsely "professed themselves Jews" in order to take advantage of the new situation and reap the benefits.

Passover Haggadah: "Blessed is the Omnipresent, blessed is He; blessed is He Who gave the Torah to His people Israel, blessed is He."

The Torah addresses itself to four sons — one is wise, one is wicked, one is simple and one is unable to ask.

These two statements are interrelated — each of the first four praises corresponds to one of the four sons.

The wise son says "Blessed is the Omnipresent," because he knows that Hashem is the foundation of the entire universe.

The wicked son speaks of Hashem in the detached third person, "Blessed is He" — he does not say "Blessed are You," but "Blessed is He."

The simpleton lacks a profound understanding of Hashem's presence. All he knows is that He "gave the Torah to His people, Israel."

Finally, the one who does not know how to ask has already been influenced by the wicked son. Thus he too uses the third person: "Blessed is He."

General Directives

While in Bergen-Belsen, we received clear instructions from Father regarding consumption of nonkosher food: Since Jewish law permits the consumption of nonkosher food in life-threatening situations, there is an *obligation* to eat such food in order to stay alive. Since it is a mitzvah to eat this nonkosher food, there is absolutely no justification for limiting one's intake of it.

Appendix III

Grandfather's first letter on the weekly portion:

Tishrei 5696 (1935)

My precious grandchildren, may you live many good years,

You are already mature young men, and with each passing day you are becoming more mature, more serious and more understanding. I will therefore attempt to communicate with you through correspondence — by writing to you my thoughts on the weekly Torah portion. Even if I fail to convey any novel ideas to you, my words will surely do no harm. They will refresh in your minds the ideas that you have already learned and will raise new questions and fresh challenges for you.

You are still too young to read *The Nineteen Letters* by Rav S. R. Hirsch, *zt"l*, and so I will begin my Torah words with one of his thoughts.

When we begin to read the Torah [from *Parashat Bereishit*] again this coming Shabbat, let us remember that we strive — as is our obligation — not to read it as an ordinary book that we can subjectively evaluate and criticize. The Torah is a book that Moshe wrote as it was dictated to him by Hashem. We received this Torah at Mount Sinai and swore eternal allegiance to it, that we would forever regard it as containing the unquestionable truth.

It is the "Book of Truth" that may not be modified by any man, regardless of the era in which he may live or the particular circumstances of his life. Although you will surely find in the Torah concepts that you will find difficult to understand, you must remember that we are not permitted to regard such concepts as requiring amendment or as outright mistakes, God forbid.

"We must read the Torah as Jews," said Rav Hirsch, *zt"l*. The Torah teaches us what we lack in order that we may become true and sincere Jews. There are no mistakes in the Torah; rather, the shortcomings are our own.

Remember that a great number of outstanding Jews have studied Torah from their earliest years until their old age. They based their entire lives on Torah, and the more they toiled in Torah study, they more they understood its truth.

How could we, with our limited intellects, dare to criticize that which is written in the Torah? Compared to the vast Torah knowledge of these luminaries, who learned day and night for decades on end, we are complete ignoramuses. They were absolutely convinced that our physical existence is only an antechamber to our eternal existence in the World to Come. They sacrificed their lives at the stake and so demonstrated to their descendants that no human being, nor any amount of suffering or torture, could possibly sway them from their recognition that Hashem is One and that His Torah is truth.

Let us now begin our discussion of the weekly Torah portion. Today we shall analyze the first letter of the Torah: the letter *bet*.

This letter has a special shape — three adjacent walls formed by two horizontal lines joined at their right ends by a vertical line. These walls "block" anything that precedes the letter [since Hebrew is written from right to left], and anything that is above or below it. The fact that the Torah begins with this letter teaches us the limitations of what we may investigate regarding the creation of the universe.

When we wonder what existed before the Creation, we bump into the vertical line that forms the back of the *bet*. The letter *bet* in essence tells us, "You shall never fathom the secret of what preceded Creation." Similarly, when we wonder what exists in outer space or in the depths of the Earth, we bump into the upper and lower walls of the *bet*.

All we are allowed to ponder is the meaning of that which lies opposite the open side of the *bet* — that is, the rest of the Torah. For the Creator has endowed us with intellectual and physical capacity in order to enable us to investigate the world as we know it, after Creation, not to investigate that which preceded Creation, nor that which exists above or below us.

Hashem has granted particular talents to each one of us, and at the same time, He has deprived us of many talents that other people possess. Why? This is the Will of the Creator. Consider the sharp eyesight of the bird — the swallow, for example, which in an instant can clearly discern thousands of mosquitoes. Consider the highly developed sense of smell of certain animals, the diligence of the ant, and the craftsmanship of the bee and the spider.

Our purpose is to sanctify Hashem's Name with our every step, with our every word, and with our every action. Hashem has endowed us with freedom of choice. Our ability to choose evil is our advantage over the angels, who cannot deviate from their assigned paths. We who are capable of sinning will nevertheless choose the path of good, and as a consequence, our merits will greatly increase.

This week's Torah portion recounts the creation of man, as he was fashioned by the hand of Hashem. Consider how parents toil to sweeten the lives of their children. How much suffering must a father endure in order to earn a livelihood to support his children, how many hours must a mother devote to clothing and feeding her children!

And yet, what do parents request in return for all of their efforts? Only that their children continue to follow in the path that Hashem has revealed to us. When children behave in a brotherly manner, loving their parents and constantly remembering to gladden them, then Hashem dispatches His angels to bestow goodness and joy upon them.

Gut Shabbos, my beloved grandchildren.

Kissing you always,
Grandfather

Appendix IV

Rabbi Alexander Dinkel, zt"l

The Dinkel family was deported by the Nazis from Amsterdam to Westerbork Transit Camp late in 5703 (1943). I met Alexander in Westerbork, and together we learned with Rabbi Yisrael Goldschmidt, *zt"l*. Alexander's family was transferred to Bergen-Belsen in the winter of 5704 (1944). The extremely taxing physical labor, the starvation, typhus and a host of other diseases left Alexander's father, mother and older brother very ill. They lingered another year before they finally succumbed. May Hashem avenge their blood.

Alexander persevered, and despite starvation and various severe diseases, he withstood all the afflictions of the Holocaust. He had been exempted from labor due to his young age. I would see him studying Torah with Rabbi Yaakov Yekutiel Neubauer, may Hashem avenge his blood. Many sorrowful memories of that era are engraved in my mind, but the memory of Reb Alexander Dinkel studying Torah in Bergen-Belsen is ever a source of inspiration to me.

Indeed, this was also part of the scene in Bergen-Belsen: a starving and oppressed young man studying Torah in a death camp! I must admit that I was jealous of him at the time, for although I was only a year older, they assigned me difficult work such as paving roads, digging trenches and transporting materials, while he merited to devote his time to learning Torah. My brother Shmuel also merited to learn Gemara with Rabbi Neubauer in Bergen-Belsen. Happy are you, O Israel!

Alexander was the grandson of Rav Tuvia Lewenstein, *zt"l*, of Zurich. After the Holocaust, he joined his relatives in Switzerland, where he learned a trade and became very active in his chosen task of inspiring Jewish youth and planning activities for them. He edited and distributed a monthly journal *The Voice of Youth*. He amazed us: Swiss Jewry had not suffered during the Holocaust, and yet here was a camp survivor — a Holocaust orphan, no less — strengthening the Jewish youth of Switzerland!

In his editing of the monthly journal and his other educational activities, Alexander benefited from articles that appeared in the monthly journal for Dutch Jewish youth, *Hashalshelet*, edited by someone bearing the name Ben Chana — who was actually my brother Shmuel, son of Chana Emanuel. This is how we reestablished contact with Alexander.

Alexander Dinkel eventually left for Israel to learn Torah in the Ponevezh Yeshivah, where he developed a very close relationship with the *rosh yeshivah*, Rabbi Yosef Kahanneman, *zt"l*. Rav Dinkel excelled in his piety and Torah scholarship. He went on to establish a wonderful household and teach hundreds of students in the Kol Torah Yeshivah in Jerusalem.

Rav Dinkel passed away on the sixth day of Cheshvan, 5744 (1983), at the young age of fifty-seven. His sons and daughters, sons-in-law and daughters-in-law, grandsons and granddaughters, all follow in the holy path which was established by the illustrious head of their household, Reb Alexander.

Appendix V

<u>Educational Problems after the Holocaust</u>

If there were a passage in Scripture describing the condition of European Jewry during the post-war period, it would surely have begun with the words, "And it came to pass after the Holocaust . . . ," for as the Sages say, "the words 'and it came to pass' foretell distress" (*Megillah* 10b).

During the post-Holocaust period, Amsterdam once again became the center of Jewish activity for the scant community of Dutch survivors. Although a Jewish elementary and high school were reestablished, religious parents did little to improve the religious environment in these schools.

Only a few hours were devoted to Jewish studies in the schools, and of these, classical Torah subjects were given little attention. Instead, Hebrew grammar, Jewish history and other such subjects were taught. Religious Jews invested much effort into electing Orthodox rabbis to the city's rabbinical council, but they did little to improve the quality of Jewish education in the city. Most parents were content with providing their children private lessons taught by God-fearing teachers.

Although I did not live in Amsterdam, I traveled there almost every month to attend one-day Torah seminars which were offered in the Po'alei Agudath Yisrael building. On one of my visits, a group of girls from Hashalshelet — a religious youth group established after the Holocaust by envoys of Po'alei Agudath Yisrael who had been sent to Holland — complained to me about the limited time devoted to Jewish studies offered in their Jewish high school. Jewish subjects were studied for only a few hours a week. The curriculum consisted of an hour of Hebrew grammar, an hour of Prophets and Sacred Writings, and an hour of Jewish history. With tears in her eyes, one of the girls recounted how in one of their Jewish history classes, their "religious" teacher had required the students to memorize the names of the disciples of the founder of Christianity!

I had known that the Torah education offered in the Jewish school was substandard, but I would never have imagined that it had sunken to such an appalling level. I discussed this scandalous matter with several individuals, even providing them with the name of the teacher and the details of the incident, but nothing was done to rectify the situation.

The girls who had lodged this complaint came from the most religious homes in Amsterdam, including rabbinical and illustrious communal figures.

Early in the winter of 5710 (1949), a proposal was raised to establish a "Shabbat Committee" among Jewish youth groups in Holland. Even the generally secular-minded youth group of the Zionist organization Habonim agreed to join in. The objective of the Shabbat Committee was to disseminate the idea of the importance of Shabbat among the Jewish youth of the Netherlands.

At the first meeting, my request that the committee be comprised only of Shabbat observers evoked conflicting responses. I emphasized that I had no intention of investigating the private activities of committee members, but rather as a matter of principle, it would be impossible to establish a committee for promoting observance of the Shabbat with committee members who themselves did not observe the sanctity of the Shabbat.

Interestingly, the Habonim group supported this suggestion and agreed to send a Shabbat-observant representative to the committee. However, the other groups refused to accept my request, among them the rabbinical representative! They argued that in Holland it was customary to include Shabbat violators among administrators of communal projects.

In the name of the Hashalshelet youth group, I announced that we would refuse to join the committee if Shabbat violators would be allowed to participate. In the end, nothing ever came of the program. The Hasalshelet representative — that is, myself — was blamed for "Frankfurt-style radicalism."

After the Holocaust, herculean efforts were made to rehabilitate Dutch Jewry. This fascinating chapter has not been adequately researched, but I believe that it would have been an opportune time for improving the depressed state of Jewish education in the country. This was the claim that Shalshelet leaders made on the basis of their experience with urban and rural Dutch youth. Sadly, while the religious Jews busied themselves with matters related to communal administration and politics, Jewish education remained neglected.

Rav Mordechai Katz arrived in Amsterdam in the mid-1950s and organized many Torah *shiurim* there. By that time I was already living in Israel, but Dutch boys who came to Israel to study in yeshivah spoke reverently about Rav Katz's Talmud classes. The following story, which was told to me by these boys, is typical of many incidents I heard.

The boys asked Rav Katz to study Talmud with them during their lunch break in the Jewish high school. All went well until the religious-studies principal found them and prohibited conducting the class inside the school building, claiming that the building — which was owned by the city of Amsterdam — had not been given to the school with the understanding that Talmud classes be conducted inside it.

With the passing of years, the Jewish community of Holland dwindled even further. Many religious youths moved to Israel and established religious homes there. Jewish education in Amsterdam continued on a downward trend, until the few religious Jews who remained there finally attempted to turn the tide. Several years ago, a *kollel* and religious elementary school were founded, a very welcome development.

Rabbi Tarfon said: The day is short, the task is great, and the Employer is insistent. He used to say: It is not up to you to complete the work, yet you are not free to desist from it.

Avot II 20–21

Appendix VI

<u>Important Dates (1933–1945)</u>

January 30,1933	Hitler is appointed chancellor of Germany.
March 9, 1933	A wave of riots against German Jewry begins; Dachau, the first concentration camp, is established.
April 21, 1933	Ritual slaughter is outlawed in Germany.
April 26, 1933	The infamous Gestapo (secret police) is established.
June 1935	A wave of anti-Semitic riots takes place in Poland.
September 15, 1935	The anti-Semitic Nuremberg Laws are enacted in Germany.
March 13, 1938	Germany annexes Austria.
April 26, 1938	According to government order, Jewish property is confiscated in Germany.
July 5, 1938	The international conference at Evian, France, fails to solve the problem of

German-Jewish refugees. Only Holland and Denmark are prepared to accept Jewish refugees on a temporary basis; other European nations refuse.

October 1, 1938   The Munich Conference results in British and French approval of German annexation of the Sudetenland from Czechoslovakia, as an attempt to appease Hitler and prevent another European war.

November 9 –10, 1938   *Kristallnacht* riots against German and Austrian Jewry. Hundreds of synagogues are burned and destroyed, some 7,500 Jewish stores are pillaged and approximately 30,000 Jews are imprisoned in concentration camps.

January 30, 1939   In a speech in the *Reichstag* (German Parliament), Hitler threatens to annihilate European Jewry.

March 15, 1939   Germany invades Czechoslovakia.

August 23, 1939   The Ribbentrop-Molotov Non-Aggression Treaty between Germany and Russia is signed; Poland's fate is sealed.

September 1, 1939   World War II breaks out when Germany attacks Poland.

September 3, 1939   England and France declare war against Germany as part of their mutual-defense treaty with Poland.

September 17, 1939   Russia establishes control of eastern Poland.

September 21, 1939	Germany orders the establishment of ghettos in Poland, which was conquered in less than a week.
April 9, 1940	The German army conquers Denmark and southern Norway.
April 27, 1940	The order is issued for the establishment of Auschwitz concentration camp.
May 10, 1940	The German army invades Belgium, Holland and France.
May 15, 1940	Holland surrenders to Germany.
May 28, 1940	Belgium surrenders to Germany.
June 9–10, 1940	Norway surrenders to Germany; Italy enters the war as Germany's ally.
June 22, 1940	The French army surrenders; the French government signs a cease-fire agreement with Germany.
June 1940	Russia annexes the Baltic states, Bessarabia and northern Bukovina.
July 1940	A wave of bloody riots against Rumanian Jewry begins.
October 1940	Anti-Semitic laws are legislated in Belgium and France.
February 22–23, 1941	Amsterdam Jews are arrested and sent to concentration camps.
June 22, 1941	Germany invades Russia and conquers the Baltic States, western Ukraine and Belorussia in only a few days.

June–December 1941	Special German killing squads perform organized mass murders of Eastern European Jews. Local sympathizers join the Germans in carrying out similar atrocities against the Jews.
January 20, 1942	The Vanse Conference details plans for the extermination of European Jewry.
March 1, 1942	Jews are killed in mass exterminations in the crematorium of Sobibor extermination camp. By October of 1943, approximately 250,000 Jews, including Dutch and other Western European Jews, are murdered there.
June 1, 1942	Dutch and French Jews are required to wear an identifying patch known as the "the Yellow Star."
July 17, 1942	Transportation of Dutch Jews to Auschwitz begins.
May–September 1943	Thirteen thousand Amsterdam Jews are sent to Auschwitz and Sobibor.
July 15, 1943	Russian counterattack.
September 3, 1943	The Allies invade Italy.
June 6, 1944	The Allied forces land in Normandy, France.
January 1945	Auschwitz and other concentration camps are evacuated; inmates are transported in open boxcars, or taken on death marches in the direction of concentration camps in Germany proper, primarily Bergen-Belsen.

March 1945	The American army crosses the Rhine river into Germany.
April 6 –21, 1945	Approximately 3,000 "exchange Jews" from Bergen-Belsen are evacuated in trains.
April 15, 1945	The British army liberates Bergen-Belsen concentration camp.
April 25, 1945	The American and Russian armies meet at the Elbe River in Eastern Europe.
May 8, 1945	Germany surrenders to Allied forces. It is the end of the Third Reich.

Glossary

Agudat Yisrael: An organization created in the beginning of the twentieth century for the purpose of uniting all segments of Torah-observant Jews.

Aravot: Willow branches, one of the four species incorporated as part of the halachic observance of the festival of Sukkot.

Ba'al tefillah: The leader of the prayer services in the synagogue.

Beit din: A rabbinical court of law, consisting of at least three judges.

Beit Hamikdash: The Holy Temple in Jerusalem.

Beit midrash: A Torah study hall.

Bemidbar: Numbers, the fourth of the Five Books of Moses.

Bereishit: Genesis, the first of the Five Books of Moses.

Birkat Hamazon: The Grace after Meals.

Chatan Bereishit: The person honored with the reading of the Torah portion of Genesis on Simchat Torah, which begins anew the annual cycle of the Torah reading.

Chatan Torah: The person honored on Simchat Torah with the reading of the final portion of the Five Books of Moses, thus completing the annual cycle of the Torah reading.

Chayei Adam: A halachic work, written by Rabbi Abraham Danzig (1748–1820), which condenses a large portion of the *Shulchan Aruch* (Code of Jewish Law).

Chazzan: The leader of the prayer services in the synagogue, synonymous with *ba'al tefillah.**

Chazzanut: The professional melodious chanting of Jewish prayers.

Cheshvan: The Hebrew month which usually corresponds to October and/or November.

Chol Hamo'ed: The intermediate days of the holidays of Sukkot and Pesach, during which most weekday activities are permitted.

Chumash: A bound volume containing one or more of the Five Books of Moses.

Dayan\im: Rabbinical judge(s).

Derashah: A lecture or sermon expounding topics of Jewish law and/or ethics.

Devarim: Deuteronomy, the fifth of the Five Books of Moses.

Eiruv [chatzerot]: A halachic device used to make it permissible to carry objects from one place to another on Shabbat by symbolically uniting those places.

Elul: The Hebrew month which usually corresponds to September and/or October.

Eretz Yisrael: The Land of Israel.

Etrog: A citron, one of the four species incorporated as part of the halachic observance of the festival of Sukkot.

Gabbai: One whose job it is to accord the various honors to the congregants during the prayer services in the synagogue.

Gemara: The Talmud, the embodiment of the Oral Law, as taught by the great Jewish masters between 200 C.E. and 400 C.E. Next to the Bible itself, it is the most important text for the Jew, serving as the basis for all Jewish theology and law. Formally printed individual volumes of the Talmud were published in Soncino as early as 1482; the entire Talmud was first printed as a set by Daniel Bomberg in Venice, in 1523.

Hachsharah: A learning experience to prepare youth for kibbutz life in Israel.

Hadassim: Myrtle branches, one of the four species incorporated as part of the halachic observance of the festival of Sukkot.

Haftarah: A portion from the Prophets read following the Torah reading on Shabbat and holiday mornings. There is generally a relationship between the Torah portion and its corresponding *haftarah* portion. The practice of reading the *haftarah* was originally instituted as a substitute for the Torah reading, at a period in history when reading the Torah in public had been prohibited.

Haggadah: The text used as the basis for the Passover seder.

Halachah: The body of Jewish law which dictates religious practice.

Havdalah: The prayer which marks the end of the Sabbath and of the holidays, recited over a cup of wine.

Hashem: The name of God.

Hirsch, Rabbi Samson Raphael (1808–1959): Monumental commentary on the Torah, first published in German in five volumes, Frankfurt am Main 1867–1878. The author was one of the greatest thinkers and Hebrew philologists of his time. He served as rabbi of the Orthodox community in Frankfurt am Main.

Hoshana Rabbah: The seventh day of Sukkot (21 Tishrei), distinguished by lengthy readings and prayers for the coming year's produce.

Hoshanot: The special prayers recited on each day of the festival of Sukkot.

Iyar: The Hebrew month which usually corresponds to April and/or May.

Kaddish: A prayer recited responsively, at several points in each prayer service, also recited in the merit of one (usually a relative) who has died.

Kedushah: Praises of God recited during the *chazzan*'s repetition of the prayer of silent devotion.

Keriyat Shema: The recitation of specific Torah portions which affirm one's faith in God and allegiance to his Torah.

Ketav Sofer: Rabbi Avraham Shmuel Binyamin Sofer (1815–1871), who followed his father (Rabbi Moshe Sofer, the "Chatam Sofer") as the chief rabbi of Pressburg.

Kiddush: A blessing proclaiming the sanctity of the Sabbath or holiday, recited over a cup of wine.

Kitzur Shulchan Aruch: A work by Rabbi Shlomo Ganzfried (1804–1886), which condenses most of the Code of Jewish Law.

Lag Ba'omer: The thirty-third day of the *omer** (18 Iyar), a day without the practices of mourning.

Lechem mishneh: The two loaves of bread upon which the blessing of *hamotzi* is recited in Sabbath and holiday meals.

Lulav: A young palm frond, one of the four species incorporated as part of the halachic observance of the festival of Sukkot.

Ma'ariv: The evening prayers.

Masechet: A tractate of the Mishnah or Talmud.

Masechet Berachot: The first tractate of the Talmud which deals with the recitation of the *Shema*, prayers, and blessings.

Masechet Eiruvin: Tractate of the Talmud which deals with the prohibition of carrying objects from place to place on the Sabbath, and the various halachic devices used to make it permissible to carry under certain circumstances.

Masechet Pesachim: Tractate of the Talmud dealing with the holiday of Passover and its sacrifices.

Masechet Sanhedrin: Tractate of the Talmud which deals with the Jewish judiciary system.

Masechet Shekalim: Tractate of the Talmud which deals with the half-*shekel* fee paid annually for the sacrificial requirements of the Temple.

Matzah: Unleavened bread, eaten especially on the holiday of Passover.

Mayim shelanu: Water which is drawn from a natural source and left in a container overnight, to be used for making matzah dough.

Midrash: A halachic or aggadic exposition of the underlying significance of the text of the Bible.

Midrash Tanchuma: Midrash on the Torah, ascribed to Rabbi Tanchuma (fourth century C.E.).

Minchah: The afternoon prayers.

Mishnah: Primarily halachic literature, edited c. 200 C.E., which forms the basis of the Talmud. It divides all of Jewish law into six main categories. Also, any single paragraph of that work.

Mishneh Torah: The monumental code of the Rambam (1135–1204). This was the first systematic codification of Jewish law and remains the only one that encompasses every aspect of the Torah. It is considered one of the greatest classics of Torah literature. First printed in Rome in 1475.

Mitzvah*mitzvot*: Commandment(s) of the Torah. Also used to refer to any good deed.

Mizrachi: An organization of religious members of the World Zionist Organization.

Mo'ed: The second of six major divisions of the Mishnah.

Motza'ei Shabbat: Saturday night, after Shabbat has ended.

Musaf: An additional prayer service which follows the morning service on Shabbat, Rosh Chodesh, and holidays.

Nashim: The third of six major divisions of the Mishnah.

Nevi'im: The books containing the prophecies and life events of the prophets, from Joshua until the destruction of the first commonwealth; the second section of the Scriptures.

Nezikin: The fourth of six major divisions of the Mishnah.

Omer: An offering of barley meal brought on the second day of Passover. Also, the period of time between the festivals of Pesach and Shavuot, distinguished by certain practices of mourning because of several national calamities which occurred during that time of year.

Oneg Shabbat: The mitzvah of eating delicacies and enjoying other pleasures on the Sabbath. Also, a party or gathering held on Shabbat.

Orach Chaim: The first section of the *Arba Turim*, written by Rabbi Yaakov ben Asher in the early fourteenth century. Also, the first section of the *Shulchan Aruch*, which is based on the *Arba Turim*.

Parashat hashavu'a: The weekly Torah portion.

Parochet: The drape in front of the ark which holds the Torah scrolls in synagogue.

Pesukei D'zimrah: The portion of the morning prayers which follows the morning blessings and precedes the *Keriyat Shema*.*

Radak: Acronym for Rabbi David Kimchi (1160–1235): Author of one of the most important commentaries on the Bible, first printed in Venice, in 1517. The author, who lived in

Narbonne, Provence, sought to ascertain the precise meaning of the Scripture, striving for clarity.

Rambam: Acronym for Rabbi Moshe ben Maimon (1135–1204), also known as Maimonides. He is considered one of Judaism's leading Torah authorities and philosophers. Born in Cordova, Spain, his family fled the country to escape Moslem persecution.

Ramban: Acronym for Rabbi Moshe ben Nachman (1194–1270). He was the leading spiritual leader of his time and wrote over fifty works on Bible, Talmud, Jewish law, philosophy, Kabbalah, and medicine. He lived in Gerona, Spain.

Rashi: Acronym for Rabbeinu Shlomo Yitzchaki (1040–1105). He composed the most important commentaries on the Bible and Talmud, known for their clarity and conciseness, published in virtually all editions. His commentary on the Torah was the first known Hebrew book to be printed (Rome, c. 1470). He headed yeshivot in his native Troyes and in Worms in France.

Rav Ovadiah MiBartenura (1450–1516): The major commentator of the Mishnah. He lived in Italy and later in Israel.

Rebbetzin: A rabbi's wife.

Sefer\sefarim: Holy book(s).

Sefer Hayashar: A history of the Jewish people, written in story form, first printed in Venice, in 1525. Some believe that the work was written in Talmudic times or earlier, while others consider it a medieval work.

Sefer Igrot Tzafon: The Hebrew title of *The Nineteen Letters*, authored by Rabbi Samson Raphael Hirsch (1808–1888).

Sefer Mitzvot Gadol: Also known as the *S'MAG*. A halachic work on the 613 commandments by Rabbi Moshe ben Yaakov of Coucy (1198–1274), one of the Tosafists. The work was first printed in Rome, in 1474. The author preached in France and Spain and played a major role in stemming the tide of assimilation there.

Sefer Or Zaru'a: A halachic commentary on the Talmud authored by Rabbi Yitzchak of Vienna.

Sefer Torah: A holy Torah scroll.

Selichot: Prayers and supplications specifically for the forgiveness of sins, recited on fast days and during the High Holy Day season.

Seudah shelishit: The third meal of Shabbat, eaten on Saturday afternoon.

Shacharit: The morning prayers.

Shamash: The synagogue attendant, who performs minor duties related to the synagogue services.

Shavuot: The festival of Pentecost, on 6 Sivan, which celebrates the Revelation of the Torah at Sinai.

Shemot: Exodus, the second of the Five Books of Moses.

Shiur\im: Class(es) of religious Jewish interest.

Shivah: The seven days of mourning, observed by relatives of the deceased.

Shlomo Ibn Gabirol (1020–1070): A major Jewish poet and philosopher in Spain.

Shofar: A ram's horn, blown in the synagogue before and during Rosh Hashanah and at the end of Yom Kippur.

Siddur: A book of Jewish prayers.

Simchat Beit Hasho'evah: A celebration held on *Chol Hamo'ed** of Sukkot, commemorating the festivities associated with the water libation in the Temple.

Simchat Torah: The holiday which immediately follows Sukkot, celebrating the completion and the start of the annual cycle of the reading of the Torah.

Siyum: A celebration of the completion of a volume of Jewish study.

Sofer stam: A specially trained scribe of *sifrei Torah*, *mezuzot*, and *tefillin*.

Sugyah: A topic in the Talmud.

Sukkah: The temporary hut erected for the holiday of Sukkot, in which Jewish men are required to eat and dwell for the duration of the holiday.

Sukkot: A Jewish festival of seven days, beginning on 15 Tishrei, which commemorates the temporary shelters used by the Jews in the wilderness and which celebrates the ingathering of the harvest.

Tachanun: Supplicant prayer recited after the *amidah* prayer of silent devotion in *Shacharit** and *Minchah*.*

Tallit: The prayer shawl with fringed corners, worn by men during certain prayers.

Talmid chacham: A Torah scholar.

Tamuz: The Hebrew month which usually corresponds to June and/or July.

Tanach: An acronym for the Torah, Prophets, and Holy Writings, comprising the Jewish Holy Scriptures.

Tehillim: The Book of Psalms.

Ushpizin: An Aramaic word meaning "guests," used specifically to refer to the seven spiritual "visitors" who are believed to come to each *sukkah** during the festival of Sukkot.

Vayikra: Leviticus, the third of the Five Books of Moses.

Vilna Shas: The Talmud in the form that was published in Vilna in 1886, which has become the standard format for all subsequent editions.

Yeshayahu: The Book of Isaiah.

Yeshivah: A school of intense Biblical and Talmudic study.

Zemirot: Songs composed in honor of God and the Torah, usually sung during Shabbat meals and other religious celebrations.

Zt"l: An acronym for *"zecher tzaddik livrachah,"* literally, "may the memory of this righteous person be blessed," equivalent to the commonly used English term, "of blessed memory."